PRAISE FOR *THE POWER OF CUSTOMER EXPERIENCE*

As we try to make sense of how to grow our businesses in a disrupted world, Martin Newman has done the thinking for us. Here is a well-researched and practical guide on how to build a sustainable and commercially successful business based around customer-centricity. It takes us on a journey of how customer-centricity has evolved since the internet changed the balance of power. The 10 building blocks provide a road map for how to embed customer-centricity into your organization, using case studies to help bring the theories to life. This book is an essential read for anyone, at any level, involved in selling products and services to customers.
Andy Rubin, Deputy Chair, Pentland Group

Customer-centricity is one of those topics that is easy to talk about but hard to do. Martin Newman does a brilliant job of breaking it down in this thoughtful and eminently practical toolkit.
Doug Gurr, Director, Natural History Museum, London; formerly CEO, Amazon UK and President, Amazon China

A superb read for customer-centric leaders on a mission to embrace the best ways of leveraging and driving the new paradigm of how and why consumers buy and build your brand equity. *The Power of Customer Experience* is packed with insightful and comprehensive reference points – Martin Newman has provided an excellent combination of a thought-provoking read and a pragmatic framework to implement.
Vince Gunn, former CEO, Sofa.com

A masterclass for anyone who has a genuine interest in improving the experience of their customers. It is full of real-life examples of brands that have lost their way, as well as those that have found a whole new way to excel. An insightful and practical read that is an enjoyable journey. So many powerful lessons from so many different sectors, delivered with authority.
Debbie Hewitt MBE, Chairman, White Stuff

Another excellent book by Martin Newman – packed with helpful case studies and examples, providing easy-to-understand frameworks that can be applied in any business. The world is continuously changing, and Martin picks up on the shifts in consumer behaviour driven by global questions such as diversity and inclusion, climate change and the broader ethical questions of consumerism.
Eve Henrikson, Online Director, Tesco

If you are serious about transforming your business to become customer-centric, which only a few very successful companies truly managed to achieve, then this is your must-read book. Martin Newman, in his typical authentic style, shows us the way with clarity and conviction, providing valuable, actionable insights and useful frameworks supported with numerous up-to-date case studies. For me, this is a handbook for retailers to thrive not just survive.
Koray Gul, former COO, Missguided

Imagine working for an organization that creates value for customers, value for those in the organization who create it, value for stakeholders and value for the planet. Martin Newman is one of the few people I know who really understands the meaning of the word 'value'. This is a fantastic book that will show you how to create it.
Professor Malcolm McDonald MA(Oxon) MSc PhD DLitt DSc, Emeritus Professor, Cranfield University School of Management

The Power of Customer Experience

How to use customer-centricity to drive sales and profitability

Martin Newman

Publisher's note
Every possible effort has been made to ensure that the information contained in this book is accurate at the time of going to press, and the publisher and author cannot accept responsibility for any errors or omissions, however caused. No responsibility for loss or damage occasioned to any person acting, or refraining from action, as a result of the material in this publication can be accepted by the editor, the publisher or the author.

First published in Great Britain and the United States in 2021 by Kogan Page Limited

Apart from any fair dealing for the purposes of research or private study, or criticism or review, as permitted under the Copyright, Designs and Patents Act 1988, this publication may only be reproduced, stored or transmitted, in any form or by any means, with the prior permission in writing of the publishers, or in the case of reprographic reproduction in accordance with the terms and licences issued by the CLA. Enquiries concerning reproduction outside these terms should be sent to the publishers at the undermentioned addresses:

2nd Floor, 45 Gee Street	122 W 27th St, 10th Floor	4737/23 Ansari Road
London	New York, NY 10001	Daryaganj
EC1V 3RS	USA	New Delhi 110002
United Kingdom		India
www.koganpage.com		

Kogan Page books are printed on paper from sustainable forests.

© Martin Newman, 2021

The right of Martin Newman to be identified as the author of this work has been asserted by him in accordance with the Copyright, Designs and Patents Act 1988.

ISBNs
Hardback   978 1 78966 789 9
Paperback 978 1 78966 787 5
eBook   978 1 78966 788 2

British Library Cataloguing-in-Publication Data

A CIP record for this book is available from the British Library.

Library of Congress Cataloging-in-Publication Data

Names: Newman, Martin (Business consultant), author.
Title: The power of customer experience : how to use customer-centricity to drive sales and profitability / Martin Newman.
Description: London ; New York, NY : Kogan Page, 2021. | Includes bibliographical references and index. |
Identifiers: LCCN 2021007259 (print) | LCCN 2021007260 (ebook) | ISBN 9781789667875 (paperback) | ISBN 9781789667899 (hardback) | ISBN 9781789667882 (ebook)
Subjects: LCSH: Customer relations. | Customer services. | Brand name products. | Marketing. | BISAC: BUSINESS & ECONOMICS / Marketing / General | BUSINESS & ECONOMICS / Strategic Planning
Classification: LCC HF5415.5 .N4953 2021 (print) | LCC HF5415.5 (ebook) | DDC 658.8/12–dc23

Typeset by Integra Software Services, Pondicherry
Print production managed by Jellyfish
Printed and bound by CPI Group (UK) Ltd, Croydon CR0 4YY

CONTENTS

About the author x
Preface xii
Acknowledgements xiv

Introduction 1

01 The fundamental building blocks for sustainable commercial success 8

Commercially successful brands over a sustained period are those that are customer-centric 8
Social responsibility is top of mind 10
Show them the way and surely, they will follow? 11
What it takes to deliver customer-centricity 13
Conclusion 21
References 22

02 Buy less, eat better, experience more 25

The shift in consumption from buying material possessions to having experiences 25
The rise of the conscious consumer – why mindsets are changing 26
The impact this will have on all consumer sectors moving forward 26
Brick-and-mortar stores are here to stay, but the experience needs to step up 30
Case studies of successful brands that deliver great experiences and the effect on sales performance 32
Conclusion 37
References 38

03 The fallen: The brands that have sadly bitten the dust and why 41

Why do businesses not work in the first place? 41
Examples of a number of failed consumer brands from a range of sectors 43

What was wrong with their model? 44
Were they too slow to adapt? 44
What were the death knells? 51
Conclusion 53
References 54

04 The resurrected 56

Brands that have bounced back 56
Conclusion 63
References 65

05 Brands that have stood the test of time and why 67

Heritage counts – brands with history and why they're still successful today 68
Reinvention is the mother of necessity – brands that have reinvented themselves to stay relevant 74
Top five traits of continually successful brands 75
Conclusion 76
References 78

06 Customer-centricity – it all adds up 81

The direct correlation between how customers view and perceive a consumer-facing brand and their commercial performance 81
Measuring the impact of great customer service and experience 85
The cause and effect of different aspects of customer experience on profit and loss 87
Conclusion 93
References 94

07 Employee-first: The first building block in driving customer-centric transformation 96

The different types of organizational culture 96
People-centric businesses that are commercially successful 101
What it means to put your employees first 104
Conclusion 107
References 109

08 Purpose before profit: The shift from value to values 112

Purpose is a key driver of profitability 112
The cultural drivers for sustainable success 114
What constitutes a values-led business 118
The commercial impact of businesses who put purpose before profit 121
How and why to avoid purpose greenwashing 123
Conclusion 125
References 126

09 Diversity and inclusion: On the outside and the inside 130

The broad range of requirements that fall within diversity 130
The benefits of being a diverse organization 133
Brands that have embraced diversity and inclusion 135
Conclusion 138
References 140

10 Commercially successful disruptive business models in consumer sectors 142

Women entrepreneurs lead the way in disruptive businesses 144
Disruption in the travel sector 144
Changing the eyewear, hygiene and fashion space 145
How gyms are being disrupted 147
Automotive is electrifying 148
Delivery and logistics in the restaurant space 149
Telecoms sector – the next to be disrupted? 149
Conclusion 151
References 152

11 If you were starting a retail business today, what would it look like? 153

To be relevant to consumers, retailers need a very different operating model 153
The rise of independent retail and what makes independent retailers successful 156
The future of the high street 156
The last mile is the most important touchpoint on the customer's journey 161

It's not what you sell, it's how you sell it that counts 163
How you can tap into the move to conscious consumption 164
Conclusion 165
References 167

12 To infinity and beyond: What makes a successful bank, airline and car dealer in the 2020s? 169

How banks can engage more effectively with their customers 170
Fintech leads the way – new payment solutions that work for younger consumers 172
Airlines – even when you have a monopoly or operate in an oligopoly, you need to be customer-centric 173
The need for car dealers to dramatically transform focus from sales to service 176
Conclusion 179
References 181

13 We all gravitate towards social people: The same can be said of brands 183

Generating brand awareness and engagement 184
Commercial performance and social engagement have a direct correlation 187
Social media as a service 188
Guidelines and checklist for social media 191
Conclusion 195
References 197

14 Generation Z will show us the way 201

Who are Generation Z? 201
If you want to know the future, look to the past 202
Gen Z will tell you where you're going wrong 204
How to engage with Gen Z 205
How Gen Z will reshape all consumer sectors for the next 50 years 208
The marketing mix for Gen Z 211
Conclusion 212
References 214

15 The road map to customer-centricity 217

The 10 building blocks for customer-centricity 218
Doing the right thing doesn't have to be rocket science! 233
The traditional return to shareholder focus is a broken model 235
The board needs a makeover 236
Conclusion 237
The last word 237
References 237

Index 240

ABOUT THE AUTHOR

Known as the Consumer Champion and founder of www.customerservice-action.com and www.thecustomerfirstgroup.com, Martin Newman is a force for positive change for both consumers and brands.

He is a constant advocate for consumer rights as well as keeping diversity, social responsibility and employee engagement top of the agenda in his media appearances and through all of the content he produces including on his TV channel, which can be found at www.consumerfocus.tv and on his podcast, *Customer Centricity*, which is available on all main platforms.

He appears regularly on BBC TV and radio, on Sky, Channel 5 and a host of other media channels such as LBC, *The Times* and the *Financial Times* to discuss various consumer issues relating to the retail, travel, casual dining, automotive and financial services sectors.

Martin has almost four decades of experience working in consumer sectors heading up the multichannel operations of some of the world's leading brands, including Burberry, Intersport, Pentland Brands (Speedo, Berghaus, etc), Harrods and Ted Baker. He leveraged this experience to author his first book *100 Practical Ways to Improve Customer Experience*, which was shortlisted for the Business Book of the Year Awards 2019.

A successful entrepreneur, following his career in the consumer sector, Martin founded and scaled a global ecommerce and digital consultancy, Practicology (now called Pattern), to 100 people, with offices across the UK, EU, Middle East and Asia-Pacific, and subsequently sold it in 2018. Martin has since set up The Customer First Group, consumer-facing website Customer Service Action and consumer app ServeOmeter.

Martin delivers keynote presentations and chairs many leading industry events around the world. This has included sharing the stage with Sir Tim Berners-Lee, inventor of the World Wide Web, to discuss the future of the internet and its implications for retailers. He also judges numerous industry awards, such as the World Retail Awards, the Customer Experience Awards, the Retail Insider Awards, the Drapers Digital Awards, the Online Retail Awards of Australia and the Great British Entrepreneur Awards.

Among Martin's many accolades, he has featured in various industry leader lists, including *Retail Week*'s top 50 eTail Power List for five years in a row. He has also been named in the Retail Insiders top 100 Retail Movers and Shakers List for a number of years consecutively as well as the British Vogue Online Fashion 100.

He is a non-executive chairman of the Scout Store, board adviser to Clearpay (Afterpay) and the Mayborn Group, and works with the boards of consumer-facing businesses on their key strategic questions and challenges. He is also a trustee of In Kind Direct and a member of the prestigious KPMG IPSOS Retail Think Tank.

PREFACE

Why I wrote this book

My reason for being is to drive positive change for consumers and brands.

As those of you who know me will be aware, I've been beating the drum for customer-centricity for a long time – 25 years by my reckoning.

I've written a book about it (make that two books!). I've delivered literally hundreds of presentations with this as the key theme. I've created podcasts, interviewed consumers on the high streets of Glasgow, Newcastle, Exeter, Dublin, London, Sydney, Melbourne and New York, talked on TV and radio about it, written umpteen columns and newspaper articles about it. In my client-side roles with Harrods, Intersport, Pentland brands, Burberry and Ted Baker, I've tried to action it as best I could, and I have also done so while advising clients whom I have worked with over the years.

Yet here we are in the 2020s, and you have to look far and wide for anyone who can describe to you what it really means to be customer-centric. What it means to be customer first. What it means to put the customer at the heart of all you do. You'll have to look even harder to find someone who can describe what you need to do to deliver this.

That is what I'm going to attempt to do now throughout this book. I want to create and share a framework that any business can get behind and implement, therefore benefiting from putting customers first.

To be clear, there is a commercial imperative to doing this. Just think about it for a minute. The two financial elements that determine the viability of a business are top-line sales and bottom-line profitability. The customer determines the outcome for both of these measures and yet customers are treated as a cost as opposed to a benefit.

Our focus on customers will determine whether we have a business in the future or not. I really believe that; customer-centricity as a strategy is THE most important and relevant thing we can focus on. To this end, the book is a must-read for many different stakeholders, as every part of the business has some input into driving customer-centricity – from the CEO, CFO and COO to those directly responsible for day-to-day operations that touch the customer, ecommerce directors and heads of ecommerce, multichannel directors, store and branch managers, regional managers, contact centre managers, customer service directors, logistics directors and warehouse managers, chief marketing officers and heads of digital marketing, brand marketing, chief technology officers, chief digital officers, buyers, merchandisers and of course chief customer officers and those who look after CRM.

The book will also be a great opportunity for those who aspire to step up in their careers and to take on more responsibility for customer experience.

To understand where businesses are going wrong, you just need to look at how the customer service team or contact centre is viewed. In the vast majority of businesses, it's seen as a 'cost centre' as opposed to a 'profit centre'. This is a legacy mindset. It's born out of pre-ecommerce times when all consumer-facing businesses held the balance of power. The customer had limited choice. The internet changed all of that and, in 1994, with the first ecommerce transaction, began the democratization of retail, travel, financial services, automotive and other sectors as the proliferation of choice began the shift in the balance of power from the brand to the consumer.

If we view customers as a cost and not a benefit, we're on a very slippery slope. The only way is down. The only question is, how long will it take for us to reach the bottom?

ACKNOWLEDGEMENTS

There are a number of people whom I want to call out for their support during the process of writing the book. My wife Laura and my daughters Antonia and Saskia are always supportive of my exploits and help to keep me grounded at all times!

I will always be indebted to my former executive assistant, Tiffiny (now running The Personal Consultancy), for providing so much help with sources, editing, coordinating with Kogan Page, and also with formatting the manuscript. Thank you Tiff.

I want to thank my good friend Emma Bonar, who is one of the most experienced ecommerce and digital directors around, and now owner of her own fashion boutique, 69BBoutique.com. She is someone who shares my passion for customer-centricity. She has been incredibly helpful in researching case studies of brands in different sectors who stand out from the crowd and are commercially successful as a result of their focus on customer service and customer experience.

I want to thank the publisher Kogan Page and the delightful Stephen Dunnell for his support and feedback. I hope I've done a good job of repaying your confidence in me with the book that I've produced.

Last but not least, I want to thank my colleagues from The Customer First Group. Both for their support during this process as well as for the support they provide our clients in helping them to continually improve the levels of service they deliver for consumers.

Introduction

Whether you're a CEO, CFO, COO or an operational head looking after marketing, ecommerce or other functions, if I told you that if you increase customer retention rates by 5 per cent, you will in turn increase your profitability anywhere from 25 per cent to 95 per cent (Gallo, 2014), would you take customer retention more seriously? Would you then invest in, and focus on, the core drivers of customer retention? This book will provide you with everything you need to know about how to do this as well as provide the business case (yes, you'll still need one of those) to convince the powers-that-be to make the investment.

By reducing churn and keeping your customers, you're not only building your customer base; more importantly, you're most likely creating fans – which in turn means they tend to amplify their thoughts about your brand, both on social media channels as well as face-to-face with family, friends and work colleagues. In essence, they become an extension of your marketing department.

Following on from my first book, *100 Practical Ways to Improve Customer Experience*, which was a practical guide about how to deliver customer-centricity end-to-end across a consumer-facing business, this book is about the value of doing it.

This book is packed full of examples and case studies of consumer-facing businesses from across multiple sectors including retail, travel, financial services, hospitality and automotive, who have been highly commercially successful and the drivers for that success. This is anchored in their culture, levels of service, great experiences and overall consumer engagement.

It seems crazy to have to write a book to prove the value of being truly customer-centric. However, I believe there is a need to do so. I have many conversations with c-suite executives who come from a time when we could take a customer's business for granted and therefore have focused on more traditional business metrics rather than customer-facing ones.

As I mentioned in the Preface, the change that many CEOs missed began in 1994 with the democratization of retail. This is when the first online transaction took place (Grothaus, 2015). It took another 10 to 12 years for broadband penetration to take place in order to deliver a good enough customer experience, which in turn led to consumers beginning to buy online on a regular basis.

But 1994 was when the touch-paper was lit.

The internet has transferred power from brands to the consumer. Whereby in 1994 you had limited choice of your local shops, local restaurant, local car dealer, local bank and local taxi firm, you now have access to brands globally, you can have any food you want delivered to your home, you can configure your car online and buy directly from the car brand, bypassing the dealer altogether. You can manage your finances through a plethora of online banks, including Monzo and Starling, and order a taxi through any number of apps, including Gett, Lyft and Uber. None of these businesses existed pre-internet and pre-digital. But they all have one thing in common. They are laser-focused on how to add value to customers and deliver the best possible experience. This sets them poles apart from most traditional brands in these sectors.

Traditional brands are struggling to keep pace with the change we are seeing.

John Lewis, considered to be one of the UK's leading department store chains and one with better customer service than most, spent £23 million in 2019 on rectifying customer service issues where customers had bad experiences (Bedoya, 2020). To my mind this is like going to the doctors to be given medicine for your symptoms rather than treating the underlying cause – which in this instance relates to many different scenarios where customers were let down from a product or service perspective. To be clear, I'm not singling out John Lewis – far from it. This scenario is repeated across retail and other sectors. The scary thing is that John Lewis does more than most when it comes to focusing on levels of service. They have also made more progress than any other department store when it comes to understanding the need to not only 'sell stuff' but 'deliver services'. That is a big change in outlook.

It's worth including the extract below from my last book, *100 Practical Ways to Improve Customer Experience*, as it clearly highlights the correlation between customer experience and service and commercial performance:

> KPMG Nunwood produced a report in 2017 called the 'connected experience imperative' (KMPG, 2017). It uses research from the Customer Experience Excellence Centre (CEEC), which conducted eight years of ongoing research

with 1,550 detailed brand reviews across 17 markets. During this research and the production of the report, they compared two groups of companies. One the FTSE100 and the other, the top 100 customer experience leaders within the CEEC report. The findings are very telling. Here's what they found the revenue growth comparison to be in three key verticals:

- Financial Services – Top 100 customer experience leader's revenue growth was 2x larger than that of the FTSE100
- Non-grocery retail – Top 100 customer experience leader's revenue growth was 3.5x larger than that of the FTSE100
- Travel and hotels – Top 100 customer experience leader's revenue growth was 1.5x larger than that of the FTSE100

(Newman and McDonald, 2018).

So, the bottom line is that if you deliver good service and customer experience, it will pay off.

Throughout this book I will provide examples of how traditional businesses with legacy people, systems and processes have successfully transformed themselves. In addition, I will highlight how new, disruptive brands alongside the traditional players have been able to drive commercially successful and sustainable businesses as a result of their clear focus on what it means to be truly customer-centric. I will contrast this with lots of examples of brands that have either gone out of business or are sadly on a path to their potential demise and why this has occurred.

I want to finally put to bed the traditional argument made by some legacy CEOs and chairpersons, that it 'costs too much to put customers first'.

The reality is, not only is it the right thing to do, but you have no choice. Failure to do so will see a consumer business die – sometimes a slow death or, increasingly, a rapid fall from grace.

I will also bring a sense of reality to what the future holds. Spoiler alert: I can tell you right now that the high street is not dead. It's also not dying – it's evolving. A great example of this being that for many years in various publications and in my keynote presentations I've talked about my view that Amazon would end up being a multichannel business. They had to. At the end of the day, they need to be where their customers are and that means also having brick-and-mortar stores – as this allows customers to choose how they shop and engage with Amazon.

Suffice to say, I was right. Amazon is now very much a multichannel business, with book stores, Amazon 4* stores, Amazon Fresh, Wholefoods and Amazon Go. If you want to bet against Amazon, be my guest. But if you'd bought their shares in the first year or two, well, you'd be a multimillionaire by now. So, I place a fair amount of faith in their strategy. You should too.

Book overview

To follow is a breakdown of the key points I will cover in each chapter:

Chapter 1 is about the building blocks, all centred around customer-centricity, that drive sustainable commercial success. Within this chapter I will demonstrate that the most commercially successful brands over a sustained period are those that are customer-centric. I will provide case studies to support this and will also call on my framework for customer-centricity, which highlights the key building blocks towards achieving this.

These building blocks are the 10 key customer-centric traits of market-leading brands:

- They are employee-first and focus on creating environments that get the most out of their people.
- They have a clear understanding of core customers and their desired experiences and the need to balance customer wants with unknowns.
- Technology is seen as an enabler and not the end in itself.
- Customer-centric businesses have recognized the need to shift from value to values and the importance of this for their customers.
- They understand the requirement to be present where their customers expect to find them.
- They live and breathe social responsibility and diversity.
- They recognize that consumers don't just want to buy stuff; they're looking to engage with brands that can also be service providers.
- Their operating model and organizational structures are geared towards delivering seamless customer experiences.
- Even when they are large, sometimes global businesses, they focus on delivering hyper-localized products, service, marketing and customer experience.
- More than anything, they are obsessed with customer retention and recognize that a customer is for life, not just for Christmas! They take an approach of maximizing customer lifetime value and see the benefit of doing so.

Chapter 2 is titled, 'Buy less, eat better, experience more'. It addresses the fact that consumer behaviour really is changing. Mindsets are changing. As we become more aware of our own carbon footprint, we see the rise of the conscious consumer.

In this chapter I also explore the impact of the shift towards experiences and away from just buying stuff. I present case studies of brands that successfully deliver great experiences and the effect this has on sales performance.

Chapter 3 brings to life the reasons why brands have failed – those that have sadly bitten the dust and why. I discuss what was broken with their model. Were they too slow to adapt? What were the death knells? I conclude by highlighting the top five lessons learned to help stop other businesses from falling into the same trap.

Chapter 4 brings clarity to brands that have successfully been resurrected. Why do businesses not work in the first place? Who are the brands that have come back from the dead and been successful and why? This chapter culminates with the top six examples of how they've changed and evolved to regain their relevance due to their revised customer value propositions and focus on customer-centricity.

Chapter 5 is about brands that have stood the test of time and why they've been able to do so. Heritage counts – why are some of the brands with history still successful today?

Reinvention is the mother of necessity and most brands have reinvented themselves to stay relevant. I will showcase some that have, as well as demonstrate the top five traits of heritage brands.

Chapter 6 discusses customer-centricity and the fact that it clearly pays to be customer-centric. There is a direct correlation between how customers view and perceive a consumer-facing brand and their commercial performance.

You will get insight into how to more effectively measure the impact of great customer service and experience as well as what the cause and effect of different aspects of customer experience is on profit and loss.

Chapter 7 is, in essence, about the first building block in driving customer-centric transformation, that is, to be 'employee-first'. People-centric businesses are commercially successful and I'll demonstrate why and what it means to put your employees first. You'll get clarity on the top five building blocks towards being an employee-first business.

Chapter 8 discusses the shift from value to values, highlighting the cultural drivers for sustainable success, what constitutes a values-led business and the commercial impact of businesses that put purpose before profit and why it's becoming increasingly important to consumers. While price will play a part in the decision-making process for most consumers, it has to some extent been surpassed by what the business stands for – especially when it comes to younger consumers.

Chapter 9 is about diversity and the requirement for a business to be truly diverse on the outside and the inside in order to successfully meet the needs of its diverse customer base. Diversity covers a broad range of people and requirements and this chapter sets out how best these should be addressed.

Chapter 10 focuses on disruptive business models in consumer sectors and why they are commercially successful. You'll discover case studies of the likes of Rockar, which enables car brands to go direct to the consumer. Or Uber and their impact initially on taxis and more broadly as they've grown their proposition into food delivery.

Chapter 11 answers a big question many are asking, which is, if you were starting a new retail business today, what would it look like? There is no question that there will be many successful retail businesses in the next decade and here you will discover what the core customer experience strategies and building blocks for success look like. An eye-opening chapter, it will also challenge traditional thinking and the return to shareholder model.

Chapter 12 provides a holistic view of what good looks like in automotive/car dealerships, financial services/banks and airlines, and what will make brands successful in these sectors in the 2020s – from the channels to market to the need to shift from being car salespeople or shifting airline seats at the highest possible yield to becoming service providers and what this entails. To maintain relevance, car dealers, airlines and banks have to improve everything, from the channels they use to communicate with customers to focusing more on customer engagement and lifetime value.

Chapter 13 looks at social, as social media is the key to building relationships with customers and taking engagement to the next level. However, social media is also so much more than just a promotional channel. It's key to delivering customer service and is now a core sales opportunity.

Chapter 14, the penultimate chapter, is about Generation Z – Gen Z to you and I. They are the change agents, the ones who will define the future for us all. I map out what I believe these changes will entail. Their input in defining all of our futures is so important that they deserve their own chapter.

Chapter 15 lays out the road map to customer-centricity. I cover the key elements necessary to transform a business to one that is customer-centric.

After this, there can be no excuses as to why any business cannot follow the steps to becoming truly customer-centric. It's the most important thing you'll ever do and will be the strategy that will ensure you have a sustainable and successful business for years to come.

References

Bedoya, D (2020) [accessed 9 April 2020] John Lewis says all 50 of its stores will close on Monday night due to coronavirus – Infosurhoy, *Infosurhoy.com* [Online] https://infosurhoy.com (archived at https://perma.cc/BKR5-7UZ8)

Gallo, A (2014) [accessed 9 April 2020] The value of keeping the right customers, *Harvard Business Review* [Online] https://hbr.org/2014/10/the-value-of-keeping-the-right-customers (archived at https://perma.cc/8RPY-H496)

Grothaus, M (2015) [accessed 13 April 2020] You'll never guess what the first thing ever sold on the internet was, *Fast Company.* [Online] https://www.fastcompany.com/3054025/youll-never-guess-what-the-first-thing-ever-sold-on-the-internet-was (archived at https://perma.cc/8E9E-2E2Y)

KPMG (2017) [accessed 18 December 2017] *The Connected Experience Imperative: 2017 UK customer experience excellence analysis* [Online] https://assets.kpmg/content/dam/kpmg/br/pdf/2017/11/the-connected-experience-imperative-uk-2017.pdf (archived at https://perma.cc/9X2F-R6QZ)

Newman, M and McDonald, M (2018) *100 Practical Ways To Improve Customer Experience*, Kogan Page, London

01

The fundamental building blocks for sustainable commercial success

> **WHAT YOU WILL LEARN IN THIS CHAPTER**
>
> - There is a clear correlation between brands that are successful over a long period of time and their focus on customer-centricity.
> - Most consumers now have a heightened awareness of social responsibility and brands need to demonstrate action here.
> - There are clear steps any business can take to become customer-centric and my framework will help you on this path.

Commercially successful brands over a sustained period are those that are customer-centric

I find it astonishing that anyone in this day and age doesn't get the fact that there is a direct correlation between customer-centricity and commercial performance. Think Apple, Amazon, Alibaba, *et al*. These are brands with a clear understanding of who their core customer segments are, what products and services customers need and how to deliver both great customer experience and highly effective customer service.

You just have to look at the list of the top 100 globally most valuable brands, which includes a number that are consumer-facing (Brandz, 2020). The criteria used to evaluate brand value is a combination of sales, market value and consumer sentiment. There is a direct correlation between all when it comes to being successful over a sustained period of time. There are brands that are pretty much omnipresent on this list. They are businesses that continue to evolve their proposition and centre themselves around their customers. You won't be surprised by the names. Some are consumer-only and others are a combination of business- and consumer-facing. Some of the brands included on the list are: Amazon, Apple, Google, Microsoft, Visa, Mastercard, Facebook, Alibaba Group, Tencent, McDonald's, Coca-Cola, Disney, Home Depot, Nike, Louis Vuitton, Starbucks and PayPal.

Whether you look at Apple (I talk about them more in Chapter 4 as a brand that has been resurrected) or McDonald's, which introduced touch-screen technology into their stores and more healthy eating options in order to maintain their relevance, all of these brands continually seek to be customer-centric in all that they do. They are always evolving, never standing still.

When you consider the pace of change in consumer behaviour, the lack of awareness displayed by so many brands of the importance of putting customers first will ultimately lead to the demise of many consumer-facing businesses. Even more so given the fact that all consumer sectors are going through a huge transition and being disrupted by more innovative and agile businesses.

Retail is arguably going through its biggest ever transition. The fundamental driver for change in the past 25 years is the internet. As previously mentioned, the birth of ecommerce in 1994 began the democratization of retail. It saw the balance of power shift from retailers and other consumer sectors that previously controlled limited channels of distribution, selection and pricing to a world where the consumer has an endless choice of brands to buy from and at what price to pay. Of course, the web gave rise to a plethora of household name brands that didn't exist in the early 1990s. This includes Amazon, ASOS, Boohoo, Missguided, Alibaba, Wayfair, Etsy and eBay, to name but a few.

Fast forward to 2019 and change was occurring at a pace never seen before. Despite increasing awareness of the environmental impact from the retail supply chain, just a year prior, most boards would not have considered this to be a key priority to be addressed in the short term. Then along came Greta Thunberg, a Swedish schoolgirl whose authentic and very visible concerns for the future of our planet and the impact upon it as a result of climate change became the face of the global movement to reverse this (Alter et al, 2019). Capturing the imagination of millions of Gen Z and Millennials and like-minded adults around the world, she provided a vehicle for their concerns to be voiced.

Find me a board of directors today that doesn't have this top of their agenda. If you do, I'd seriously worry about their long-term viability. Why? Because when it comes to what consumers buy and the potential impact of their purchases on the environment, their behaviour is changing and at pace. Underestimate the pace of change at your peril!

In a survey from December 2019, Barclaycard found that 62 per cent of shoppers intended to make fewer purchases because of the potential environmental impact of the production of items. Fast fashion is likely to be the biggest loser, with almost seven out of ten consumers (67 per cent) planning to spend less on cheap clothes (Sky, 2019).

Let's be clear. It was obvious to me at the time that this was not a fad or a short-term trend. This was the start of a movement and one that has accelerated ever since.

It's having a massive impact not only upon fast fashion but on retail as a whole. Why? Because the age of consumerism is at an end. The days of buying stuff just because we can is largely a thing of the past. We've moved headfirst into conscious consumption, which is a term used to describe that we will engage with products and services with more awareness of how our consumption impacts society at large. Therefore, shopping sustainably, with the intent to preserve the environment, is one way to consume products more consciously.

Social responsibility is top of mind

Why do I believe this seismic change occurred in consumer sectors? Because thanks to Greta, Extinction Rebellion and other environmental campaigners, we are rapidly becoming aware of our own carbon footprint. This is the main driver for the change in our values and our behaviour. You might call it 'the shift from value to values'.

As consumers we will increasingly look to engage with brands that have a purpose that centres around the environment and social responsibility – a business that puts its people first, a brand that is authentic and transparent in all that it does and that demonstrates values that are aligned with ours.

There was one additional significant event that acted to further impact consumer behaviour when it came to how we dispose of our discretionary spend – the Covid-19 pandemic. Spending months cooped up in our house, not being able to live our life as we used to, going to shops, eating out, travelling the world, had a big impact upon our behaviour. It made us rethink what was important to us. Prior to the pandemic, consumer behaviour had already begun to shift more towards experiences and away from buying stuff. The pandemic has accelerated this.

So, does all this mean that it's the end for retail, for automotive and other consumer sectors? Of course not. But it's a time for course correction for the majority of brands. Customers will still buy stuff, albeit less frequently. But they'll increasingly want to buy products that are recyclable, derive from recycled or environmentally friendly materials. They'll increasingly purchase electric cars. They'll also increasingly look to rent cars rather than own them. We're moving rapidly into the circular economy. I've always said, 'what goes around, comes around!'

I also firmly believe that consumers will increasingly look to engage with brands whose organizational structures are more representative of them and their needs. Even if they don't, surely having a board that is more representative of the customer base has to be the way to go? Otherwise, how can any brand that targets consumers expect to provide the right products, services and experience for its core customers if it doesn't truly understand them?

We all know that diversity, or lack of it, is still a significant issue. Nearly 20 per cent of the UK population is from an ethnic minority (ONS, 2012), yet 37 per cent of the FTSE 100 boards are all white (Kinder, 2020). Women drive 70–80 per cent of all purchase decisions (Bloomberg, 2019), yet in the FTSE 350 there are approximately 12–14 female CEOs (30percentclub, 2019) – which is a decrease from 18 in 2016! This has to change. There are 14 million consumers in the UK with some form of disability. How many boards have a board member with any disability?

Show them the way and surely, they will follow?

The good news – and yes, there is good news – is that there is a direct correlation between being a truly customer-centric business and commercial performance. Yet too often boards think it's the reverse.

If you adapt your model to address the changes in consumer behaviour I've outlined above, become a purpose-led business, put your people first, maintain authenticity and transparency at all times and, as long as you have products people want to buy, you can be assured of a successful and sustainable future. If you want proof points, here are just a few examples of businesses that tick all or most of these boxes:

- Hotel Chocolat, whose share price increased 140 per cent from 2015 to 2020 (London Stock Exchange, 2020). Its customer-centricity includes having a planet pledge to have fully compostable packaging by 2021. Borne out of a direct mail catalogue and now with a full multichannel business, Hotel Chocolat has a truly personalized approach to marketing. You don't just receive a bog-standard email, moreover the messaging and incentives relate to you, what you've purchased previously, who you are, what you like and what you don't like.
- Kathmandu, the New Zealand outdoor retailer, whose share price rose by 85 per cent from 2015 to 2019 (NZX, 2019). A certified B Corp, they are a brand that strives to be customer-centric in all they do – from being one of the most sustainable retailers on the planet to arguably one of the best in-store experiences with staff who are truly engaged and deliver fantastic customer service.
- JD Sports, whose share price increased 430 per cent over the same period (London Stock Exchange, 2019a). Their product and range is always on the money. They know their customer base so well that their sales are few and far between and they don't have to have the same depth of price cuts that most retailers need to implement.
- Ocado's share price was up 330 per cent from 2015 to 2019 (London Stock Exchange, 2019b). In 2019, Ocado was the 34th most valuable brand in the UK (Marketing Week, 2019). They are the brand that disrupted the retail grocery sector more than any other in recent years. From their use of artificial intelligence to market-leading online experience, they have reset consumer expectations within their category.
- Many of you will not even have heard of Alaska Airlines. Yet for 12 consecutive years, they've been rated number one in traditional airlines for customer satisfaction by JD Power (2019). They are measured across a host of criteria including:
  - overall satisfaction;
  - reservation experience;
  - check-in experience;
  - boarding experience;
  - aircraft experience;
  - staff experience;
  - service experience;
  - cost and fees experience.

They achieved 5 out of 5 ratings for all of the above! Clearly this is not a one-off and they have also won numerous other awards and have been named best US airline by Kayak, and best mid-size airline in North America by Tripadvisor. They have over 1.7 million fans on Facebook – that's a lot of engagement for a regional airline. Their stock price over a 10-year period from 2009 to 2019 increased by around 750 per cent (JD Power, 2019). Customer satisfaction is the output of customer service and experience, and it clearly pays!

I could add dozens of other examples. The bottom line is, a good business is a good business and those that are truly customer-centric are the ones that will win out over the long term.

What it takes to deliver customer-centricity

Customer-centricity is too often thought of tactically – something that can be achieved through marketing communications alone. This is most definitely not the case. To become truly customer-centric, you have to align everything you do as a business, as it touches every part of your organization.

My updated framework (Figure 1.1) for delivering this consists of 10 building blocks, all of which will help any business to move the needle on customer-centricity. But combined, they will help to transform the business to become a truly customer-focused company across its entire value chain and operation. The commercial benefits of doing so are the difference between success and failure.

You must put your own people first

I'm sure many of us have worked for companies where we felt that we were no more than a number. We didn't feel as though we were significant or vitally important to the success of the business. However, my premise is that, how can any organization expect to be customer-centric if it doesn't, in the first instance, put its own people first?

There is a lot of talk about Millennials and Gen Z not wanting to be in a company for any amount of time. However, the reason they leave jobs is that we create environments that they don't want to work in. They're often not empowered to do their jobs to the best of their ability, they're penalized for mistakes as opposed to encouraged to fail fast and we don't pay them particularly well.

FIGURE 1.1   The customer-centricity framework

- Measure what really matters
- Employee-first
- Understand customer wants and needs
- Technologies that empower customers
- Be where your customers are
- Purpose, values and social responsibility
- Diversity and inclusion
- Personalization
- Hyper-localization
- Aligning everyone with the direction of travel

Customer-centricity

They're also looking for brands with a strong sense of purpose: a business that cares about both the environment and the local community, one that provides the ability to learn and take on new tasks, and potentially have a long and fruitful career. Is it any surprise therefore that they choose to leave us when we rarely deliver on these objectives?

Achieve a balance between customer needs, wants and unknowns

We as consumers don't always know what we want. When asked we often give an answer that we think is right, but in reality we behave very differently. Consumer businesses are often too quick to react to this and to implement a new technology solution without really knowing whether or not that's what customers want and will react positively to.

A good example is when many businesses develop mobile apps. You obviously like the idea of consumers increasing their engagement with your brand; however, how many apps can a consumer be expected to interact with? In reality, there aren't many brands that lend themselves to having enough regular customer engagement to warrant having an app.

Technology is there to empower customers and solve their problems

There have been many technology solutions that have not resonated with consumers. They may have seemed a good idea at the time, but the consumer problem wasn't big enough to drive adoption. Think 'the endless aisle', which refers to in-store kiosks offering a broader range of products to consumers to buy from online. Great idea, but when left to their own devices, consumers won't interact with them. If, on the other hand, staff are free and able to provide 'assisted sales', these can work well. I know this from my own experience, as I implemented some of these at Ted Baker when I was head of online back in 2007.

Domino's Pizza is famed for having used innovative technology to deliver pizzas. But they are under pressure from the third-party delivery services that enable every restaurant to be a competitor. They have an innovation lab where they develop new technologies to keep a step ahead of their competitors. To demonstrate their focus, they consider themselves to be an ecommerce company that sells pizza (Maze, 2019). They were first to launch the now ubiquitous tracker that allows customers to see where their order is. Digital orders account for over 66 per cent of all orders, and you can order across multiple platforms, via text, Twitter, smart watch and even voice. Dom is their voice ordering technology, meaning customers are now dealing with AI rather than people taking their orders.

Domino's doesn't use third-party delivery services as they can manage their own deliveries profitably and efficiently. This also allows them to control the customer data, with over 85 million active users and 23 million users of the loyalty programme (PYMNTS, 2020).

You need to be where your customers want to find you

While it may sound obvious, far too many brands in actual fact aren't where customers are, nor where customers expect them to be.

For some brands, being where your customers are, or where they want to be, means offering click and collect. For car dealers, it means offering a virtual test drive or sending me videos of the car I'm interested in. For banks, it means offering the full suite of in-branch financial services online.

Due to the pandemic, and also the increase in working from home (WFH), customers are now spending more time locally and shopping locally. Will national retailers see the opportunity to tap into this with smaller-format stores in more local areas? Why not? Independents are doing well and will continue to do so. Why can't national chains?

Be purposeful, communicate your values and demonstrate social responsibility

Millennials named Patagonia one of the brands they trust the most (Morin, 2020). And you can see why. When US President Donald Trump gave businesses a tax cut in 2018, Patagonia's CEO, Rose Marcario, donated the tax cut to sustainability organizations (BBC, 2018).

Often when you go to the homepage of the Patagonia website, you don't see products; you see an image of the ocean with a statement about protecting fish.

In addition to being a highly trusted brand, Patagonia is a very successful business. It's very much a purpose-led business and there's a direct correlation between its values and its commercial performance. Because when a business behaves like this, you just know it has a great culture, treats its colleagues well and looks after its customers.

I'm sure you all know the saying that it's the little things that count. The Covid-19 pandemic had a dramatic impact on the commercial performance of so many businesses in all consumer sectors – from fashion retailers that had to close not only their stores but also their online business to spinning studios and gyms that had to close, and of course, not forgetting all the hospitality venues, car dealers, airlines. Everything and everyone was impacted.

So, what's my point, I hear you say? Well, some brands got involved. They didn't close their doors and drown themselves in a glass of self-pity, or whisky for that matter.

Psycle, my favourite spinning studio, started running online fitness sessions you could take part in at home. Yoga, Barre and many others did the same. They didn't charge for this. And yet all their income had dried up. Gestures of goodwill like this are relatively inexpensive, but meant so much to Psycle customers like me, who could exercise at home while feeling part of the bigger Psycle community. It brought both physiological and psychological benefits. And it was definitely not forgotten when they were able to open up their studios again! It also led to them launching an online channel with regular classes that you can subscribe to (Arsenault, 2020).

If you want to be taken seriously by customers and colleagues alike, you need to have a clear and believable approach to sustainability. Too many businesses are either kicking the can down the road and claiming they'll be sustainable by a distant time in the future, such as 2025, 2030, 2050, or conducting a tick-box exercise to prove that they are doing something about it. Actions speak louder than words.

An example of one of the most socially responsible businesses globally is the outdoor retailer, Kathmandu. They are ranked number 2 in the world by the textile exchange for preferred materials. They scored an A in the ethical fashion report in 2019. They scored 80 per cent towards their zero waste to landfill target. They recycled 6.7 million bottles into their gear (Kathmandu, 2019).

Their commitment to sustainability very much resonates with their customer base and this can also be evidenced in their commercial performance. Between 2015 and 2020, their share price increased by over 85 per cent (NZX, 2019). A fluke? No. All down to social responsibility? No. But there is a clear correlation to a customer-centric business that demonstrates through its actions that it cares about its people, its customers and the environment.

You need to be both diverse and inclusive

There is still a serious lack of diversity around the boardroom table and in the executive leadership team.

- In the FTSE 350, depending upon when you look at the numbers, there are only around 12 to 14 female CEOs, which is a decrease from 18 in 2016 (30percentclub, 2019).
- In the top 200 ASX companies (Australia), there are only 12 female CEOs, which is a decrease from 14 in 2018 (Waters, 2019).
- In the Fortune 500 US companies there are 33 female CEOs (Zillman, 2019).

Aside from the moral issue, there are also potentially serious commercial ramifications of this. Given the fact that women drive 70–80 per cent of all consumer purchasing (Bloomberg, 2019) decisions, having boards that are often all male or led by males is likely to drive a disconnect between what the business thinks its customers want and what they really want, in terms of product, service and experience. You can have all the data you want but it won't replace having people running a business who reflect or at least have a better understanding of the customer base.

However, diversity doesn't stop at gender. There are an estimated 2 million people with visual impairments and blindness in the UK as a whole, almost 3 per cent of the population (NHS Choices, 2019). The number of people with sight loss is estimated to rise to 2.7 million by 2030.

According to government statistics in the UK, there are an estimated 3.8 million people with a disability (out of a total of 14.3 million disabled people in the UK) who are in the working environment. Given 96 per cent of disabilities are hidden, eg visual impairment, hearing impairment, Crohn's and many others, most businesses will be oblivious to this unless their colleagues have shared this information (Collier, 2018).

Inclusion is both an external and internal challenge. How do we create an environment that works for everyone? I know, from interviewing a number of people with visual impairments for my podcast, that retailers cater very badly for the needs of this customer base. There are still many stores that won't let customers with a guide dog into the store. Even for those who are allowed in, product and merchandising has a long way to go to deliver the information and experience required. Given that there are almost 2 million people in the UK with visual impairments, you'd think that there would also be a commercial imperative to resolve this (NHS Choices, 2019).

Make it personal

You can still count on one hand the number of brands that deliver truly personalized experiences. We've been using the term CRM or customer relationship management since 1997. Yet here we are in the 2020s and what we're still doing is selling stuff, not building relationships.

As mentioned at the outset, increasing customer retention rates by 5 per cent leads to an increase in profits of anywhere between 25 per cent and 95 per cent. Who is it that determined this? It was from research undertaken by the inventor of the Net Promoter Score, Frederick Reichheld of Bain & Company (Gallo, 2014).

Of course, not every product or service lends itself to an ongoing relationship. If you're buying a mattress every eight years, are you going to want to engage with a bed and mattress retailer regularly? You replace your car every three or four years. So, when do you want to hear from the brand you bought from? Well, I 100 per cent believe it should be at regular intervals throughout the lifecycle of the contract or the term you would normally have the product for. This way you can introduce other products or services, tap into the opportunity to sell to the customer's family or friends, and be best placed to secure their next purchase of a car, mattress, BBQ, insurance policy, holiday or whatever it happens to be.

Think about it. When was the last time you received communication from a brand that was truly personalized? It tied in with who you are, what you buy and how frequently, the channels you engage through, the content you like to see and so on? Almost never. You can count on one hand the consumer-facing businesses that are doing this. You can't build relationships if you don't personalize the experience. Otherwise, you just make consumers feel as though they are just a number and their business doesn't really matter to you.

If you look at the business-to-business sector, this will never happen – well, not in most cases. You have account or relationship managers who look after you and whose sole aim is to ensure the business retains your custom and builds the value of that over the years. I fully appreciate that the frequency and/or value of purchase lends itself to this. Of course, I'm not advocating consumer brands trying to manage relationships with account managers. Clearly that would never be commercially viable. It's the sentiment of the focus on customers, doing all you can to ensure they think of you ahead of competitors and giving them reasons to come back.

Localize your proposition

Hyper-localization is where a brand localizes all aspects of its proposition for the specific needs of customers in that locality.

The Hoxton Hotel Group is a UK-based, international chain of boutique hotels. They created a new format aimed at both delivering a great experience for guests while also tapping into the local tech crowd, who have demand for comfy workspaces, excellent coffee and cocktails.

Each hotel has a local vibe and proposition, relevant to their location, using local artists, holding events and providing meeting rooms and workspaces. They promote an 'open house' culture, which is to welcome everyone, not just guests.

They identified the potential for a whole new revenue stream, which is contrary to the traditional hotel model, by enabling non-guests to use their space. Their hotels are the opposite of 'exclusive'. They are very much inclusive.

To some extent it's almost an alternative model to serviced offices. Even one self-employed person in a serviced office could be paying £550+ a month for a desk. These environments generally include free tea and coffee. The alternative is the likes of the Hoxton Group, where you can base yourself for the day and spend maybe £10–12 on teas and coffees but pay nothing for rent. And find yourself in an environment that lends itself to creativity, networking and other associated benefits.

The group has a luxury budget business model. They had a very clear view of how negatively consumers viewed the traditional hotel model and their lack of customer-centricity. The no rip-off policy is core to both the principles and culture of the business as well as the proposition and services customers experience – from flexible check-in and check-out to free breakfast, from rooms with fridges instead of mini bars to free Wi-Fi throughout. On the latter, it never ceases to amaze me how many hotels still charge for Wi-Fi!

The approach to customer-centricity also manifests itself in their communications with highly engaging emails and relevant Instagram content, which is all focused on the location of the hotel, the community and on promoting complementary local businesses (BrandGym, 2015).

Make sure you're all on the same bus

Most consumer-facing businesses still operate in silos. How can any business expect to deliver truly joined-up customer experiences if their own teams are working in isolation of each other?

The result of this is that consumers don't receive the best experience. Whether that's seeing a promotion online that isn't available offline or finding out that the gift vouchers you were given for your birthday are only redeemable in-store and not online, there are so many barriers that are created as a result of working in silos that act to disrupt the customer's journey.

In order to deliver the joined-up experience their customers sought, and to drive an uplift in profitability, in 2020, the luxury department store Neiman Marcus restructured their ecommerce and store teams. They integrated the two teams and put them under the leadership of the chief retail officer. The move was seen as an opportunity to improve customer experience and deepen relationships with customers. The output was improved sales and profitability (Turk, 2020). Everyone's team has to have shared KPIs, or at the very least synergistic KPIs that complement one another.

Conclusion

Measure the inputs, not the outputs

The lack of a framework and an approach to delivering customer-centricity is what motivated me to write my first book, *100 Practical Ways to Improve Customer Experience*. I grew increasingly frustrated at the use of the terms 'customer first', 'put the customer first' and 'customer-centricity', yet when considering the experiences delivered by the brands I worked for and the experiences I had myself as a consumer, it was clear to me that there wasn't a joined-up business-wide approach to delivering this.

The lack of a framework is only part of the challenge. We currently measure or at least pay too much attention to the wrong things. While we need to know what's happening with conversion, sales, return rates, average order values, traffic, bounce rates and so on, these are outputs, not inputs. They don't tell us why we're performing how we are. We need insight, not data. And for that we need to better understand customers and their behaviour. So we measure NPS, customer satisfaction, we talk to different customer cohorts to find out their thoughts on how we're doing, we run surveys. There are many different ways to get under the skin of issues and understand what's really going on in our businesses.

KEY TAKEAWAYS FROM CHAPTER 1

1. Customer-centricity – go big or go home. If you don't do it, your competitors will.

2. Localize and personalize the whole experience. Make it relevant. Consumers are tired of the homogeneous proposition delivered by so many consumer businesses.

3. Start with customer retention and work back from there. If you are to truly drive customer lifetime value, what will it take to achieve that?

4. Think empowerment – how can you empower your people to improve your business and the experience for your customers? And empower your customers to engage with you on their terms.

5. Walk the talk. It is quite simply not good enough to pay lip service to diversity and sustainability. Customers see right through brands that do.

6. If you have a brand, you must have a purpose. That purpose needs to stand for something. Always put purpose before profit and the latter will follow.

References

30percentclub.org (2019) [accessed 13 April 2020] FTSE 350 hits 30% women on boards for the first time in 450 years, *30% Club* [Online] https://30percentclub.org/press-releases/view/ftse-350-hits-30-women-on-boards-for-the-first-time-in-450-years (archived at https://perma.cc/X7E9-XFFF)

Alter, C, Haynes, S and Worland, J (2019) [accessed 20 November 2020] Greta Thunberg: TIME's person of the year 2019, *Time* [Online] https://time.com/person-of-the-year-2019-greta-thunberg/ (archived at https://perma.cc/KE42-TUVD)

Arsenault, B (2020) [accessed 20 November 2020] How a London-based fitness group is helping people transform both body and mind, *Forbes* [Online] https://www.forbes.com/sites/bridgetarsenault/2020/06/02/how-a-london-based-fitness-group-is-helping-people-transform-both-body-and-mind/?sh=1a2c4047c2c0 (archived at https://perma.cc/36LN-QXNY)

BBC (2018) [accessed 9 April 2020] Why this clothes company gave away $10 million, *BBC News* [Online] https://www.bbc.com/news/newsbeat-46386147 (archived at https://perma.cc/CQ59-BNNM)

Bloomberg (2019) [accessed 9 April 2020] Are you a robot?, *Bloomberg* [Online] https://www.bloomberg.com/company/stories/top-10-things-everyone-know-women-consumers/ (archived at https://perma.cc/KH83-XKEH)

BrandGym (2015) [accessed 9 April 2020] The Hoxton Hotel's 'luxury budget' business model, *BrandGym* [Online] https://thebrandgym.com/the-hoxton-hotels-luxury-budget-business-model-1/ (archived at https://perma.cc/7GEF-DLP3)

Brandz (2020) [accessed 9 April 2020] Brandz, *Brandz.com* [Online] https://www.brandz.com/Global (archived at https://perma.cc/5D6N-F35F)

Collier, E (2018) [accessed 9 April 2020] Invisible disabilities in the workplace | supporting employees, The Hub, *High Speed Training* [Online] https://www.highspeedtraining.co.uk/hub/invisible-disabilities-in-the-workplace/ (archived at https://perma.cc/2FHW-DSHL)

Gallo, A (2014) [accessed 9 April 2020] The value of keeping the right customers, *Harvard Business Review* [Online] https://hbr.org/2014/10/the-value-of-keeping-the-right-customers (archived at https://perma.cc/5S7W-EMDD)

JD Power (2019) [accessed 9 April 2020] 2019 North America airline satisfaction study, *Jdpower.com* [Online] https://www.jdpower.com/business/press-releases/2019-north-america-airline-satisfaction-study (archived at https://perma.cc/Q823-DBDL)

Kathmandu (2019) [accessed 9 April 2020] Kathmanduholdings.com [Online] https://www.kathmanduholdings.com/wp-content/uploads/2019/10/Kathmandu_SustainabilityReport_2019_LR.pdf (archived at https://perma.cc/C8HS-RP86)

Kinder, T (2020) [accessed 13 April 2020] A third of FTSE 100 companies set to miss ethnic diversity targets, *Financial Times* [Online] https://www.ft.com/content/945ce30e-4762-11ea-aeb3-955839e06441 (archived at https://perma.cc/NUX7-4DAQ)

London Stock Exchange (2019a) [accessed 14 October 2019] JD SPORTS share price (JD), *London Stock Exchange* [Online] https://www.londonstockexchange.com/exchange/prices-and-markets/stocks/summary/company-summary/GB00BYX91H57GBGBXSET1.html (archived at https://perma.cc/8CCN-9T5H)

London Stock Exchange (2019b) [accessed 14 October 2019] OCADO share price (OCDO), *London Stock Exchange* [Online] https://www.londonstockexchange.com/exchange/prices-and-markets/stocks/summary/company-summary/GB00B3MBS747GBGBXSET1.html (archived at https://perma.cc/7BRS-4XMN)

London Stock Exchange (2020) [accessed 18 January 2021] HOTEL CHOC Share Price (HOTC), *London Stock Exchange* [Online] https://www.londonstockexchange.com/stock/HOTC/hotel-chocolat-group-plc/company-page?lang=en (archived at https://perma.cc/2QNV-T26D)

Marketing Week (2019) [accessed 13 April 2020] Just Eat, Ocado and BrewDog join the club as the UK's 75 most valuable brands are revealed, *Marketing Week* [Online] https://www.marketingweek.com/uk-most-valuable-brands/ (archived at https://perma.cc/4SHJ-45X2)

Maze, J (2019) [accessed 20 November 2020] Domino's works to keep its technology edge, *Restaurant Business* [Online] https://www.restaurantbusinessonline.com/financing/dominos-works-keep-its-technology-edge (archived at https://perma.cc/PZ37-7HUK)

Morin, C (2020) [accessed 20 November 2020] Patagonia's customer base and the rise of an environmental ethos, *CRM.org* [Online] https://crm.org/articles/patagonias-customer-base-and-the-rise-of-an-environmental-ethos (archived at https://perma.cc/797N-LLL2)

NHS Choices (2019) Blindness and vision loss [Online] https://www.nhs.uk/conditions/vision-loss/ (archived at https://perma.cc/CX9A-T4AV)

NZX (2019) [accessed 9 April 2020] KMD Kathmandu Holdings Limited Ordinary Shares, *NZX, New Zealand's Exchange* [Online] https://www.nzx.com/instruments/KMD (archived at https://perma.cc/FC42-MAU2)

ONS (2012) [accessed 15 January 2021] Ethnicity and national identity in England and Wales, *Office for National Statistics* [Online] https://www.ons.gov.uk/peoplepopulationandcommunity/culturalidentity/ethnicity/articles/ethnicityandnationalidentityinenglandandwales/2012-12-11 (archived at https://perma.cc/5XRF-JD9V)

PYMNTS (2020) [accessed 20 November 2020] Domino's hits 25m active loyalty members, *PYMNTS.Com* [Online] https://www.pymnts.com/earnings/2020/dominos-hits-25m-active-loyalty-members/ (archived at https://perma.cc/WU8E-JQQQ)

Sky (2019) [accessed 9 April 2020] Climate change fears and a record Black Friday set to hit Boxing Day sales, *Sky News* [Online] https://news.sky.com/story/climate-change-fears-and-a-record-black-friday-set-to-hit-boxing-day-sales-11895066 (archived at https://perma.cc/2CEQ-2NVS)

Turk, R (2020) [accessed 9 April 2020] Neiman Marcus changes retail strategy, minimizes last call operations, *Fashionunited.uk* [Online] https://fashionunited.uk/news/retail/neiman-marcus-changes-retail-strategy-minimizes-last-call-operations/2020031147927 (archived at https://perma.cc/9SSB-G4CJ)

Waters, C (2019) [accessed 9 April 2020] 'That really hurts': just 12 women CEOs in Australia's top companies, *Sydney Morning Herald* [Online] https://www.smh.com.au/business/companies/that-really-hurts-just-12-women-ceos-in-australia-s-top-companies-20190909-p52pi2.html (archived at https://perma.cc/V9YH-DXH3)

Zillman, C (2019) [accessed 9 April 2020] The Fortune 500 has more female CEOs than ever before, *Fortune* [Online] https://fortune.com/2019/05/16/fortune-500-female-ceos/ (archived at https://perma.cc/X24M-LNTJ)

02

Buy less, eat better, experience more

> **WHAT YOU WILL LEARN IN THIS CHAPTER**
>
> - There is a shift in our behaviour from buying material possessions to wanting to have experiences.
> - Conscious consumption is on the rise and consumers are becoming more aware of their own carbon footprint.
> - What is the impact upon consumer sectors of this change in consumer behaviour?
> - Brick-and-mortar stores are here to stay, and experiential retail will help to secure their future.
> - Case studies of successful brands who deliver great experience and the effect on sales performance.

The shift in consumption from buying material possessions to having experiences

Even before climate change became a focal point, we were starting to see a shift in consumption with consumers seeking out experiences sometimes ahead of buying stuff. As more of us adopt a 'conscious consumption' mindset and approach to what we buy and how we buy it, this has accelerated, as we are tending to seek out experiences that provide us with memories that have the potential to outlast any physical products we buy. Experiences also provide fuel for our social media activity. Instagram, Pinterest, Facebook and to a lesser extent Twitter are populated with millions of examples of us sharing our day-to-day experiences. And the payback we get are the likes, comments and sharing that our friends and family do when they react to our content.

I see this as a trend that will continue. With what the world went through in 2020 and 2021 with Covid-19 and the subsequent impact upon our lifestyle, our inability to socialize and travel, any opportunity to have a leisure, entertainment or travel experience will be a priority for many consumers for some time to come.

This said, the experience economy – a term first coined by *Harvard Business Review* in 1998 to describe how consumers tend to spend more on an experience than a commodity or product – has much to offer product-led businesses.

This has evolved over the years into a lasting change in consumer behaviour whereby we want to experience new emotions and feelings rather than to simply consume something. This relates to products as well as travel or entertainment-related experiences. Think of it in terms of connecting with consumers on an emotional level.

The rise of the conscious consumer – why mindsets are changing

Back in 2018 and 2019, we saw the Greta Thunberg and Extinction Rebellion effect (Nugent, 2020) – climate activists who, through very different means and channels, put the environment and climate change on the front pages. It has largely stayed there ever since. This in turn created heightened awareness among almost all consumers, which in turn led to a genuine concern for, and focus on, one's own carbon footprint – the potential impact our behaviour was having on the environment – what we bought, what we ate, where we travelled to and how we got there.

The impact this will have on all consumer sectors moving forward

Conscious consumption and our move to buy less and experience more has implications for all consumer sectors.

FIGURE 2.1 The four stages of conscious consumption

- Considered consumption
- Conscious consumption
- Conscious consumption when it suits us
- Unconscious consumption

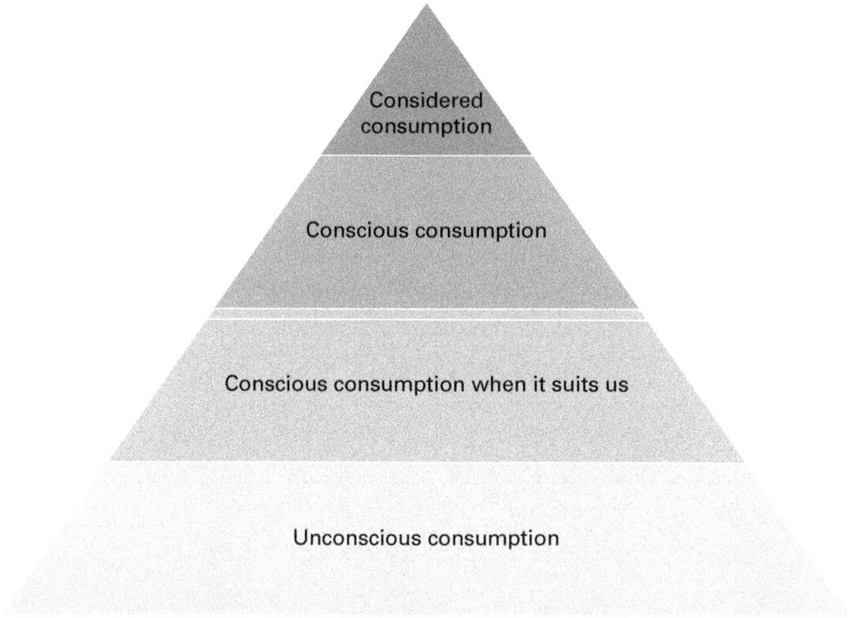

Automotive

A huge shift in purchasing from traditional cars with combustion engines to hybrid and electric cars is highly likely over the coming years. It is also going to be, for all intents and purposes, mandatory as the UK Government has legislated that all cars produced from 2030 onwards must be electric and that all diesel and petrol cars should be removed from our roads (Harrabin, 2020).

At the same time, there has been a reduction in the frequency with which consumers buy new cars. Instead of taking out a contract for three years, they'll look for a four- or five-year contract. If they're buying it outright, they'll keep the car for an average of five or six years as opposed to three or four, maybe longer. This has significant ramifications for the car industry as a whole.

Fashion

Will the same number of consumers be happy with buying from fast-fashion brands and the environmental and supply chain implications of doing so? It is highly doubtful – at least not until they can prove that they are a socially responsible business and have a sustainable supply chain.

It is likely that many consumers' perceptions of fashion and how frequently they need to buy something new will change significantly. 'Do I really need those new sneakers or that new dress?'

Food

The food industry is one where conscious consumption will have a truly transformational impact, as our dietary requirements are changing significantly. This is in part due to the desire to eat more healthily and to our increasing awareness of the environmental impact of our more traditional meat-based diets.

CASE STUDY
Marks & Spencer is one brand that has led the way in this space

Despite its many challenges in defining what its product and customer proposition is and for whom it intends to be relevant, M&S has done a great job of tapping into the move by a significant number of consumers to improve their diets. They clearly understood the importance of vegan, vegetarian and other healthy diets – along with the increasing science that suggests these are not a fad and that they have fundamental health benefits.

And as media attention and content has increased, so has consumer knowledge that you can get all the protein you require from a plant-based diet. By recognizing this and developing their Plant Kitchen range, in 2019 M&S introduced over 600,000 new customers to the brand (Effective Design, 2019).

Despite the obvious success of the Marks & Spencer Plant Kitchen, there are still many people who see veganism and other related beliefs and subsequent changes to diet as a fad. Clearly that is not the case. What we have been experiencing and will continue to experience is a significant shift in consumer behaviour when it comes to our diet. The facts speak louder than words and UK consumers are leading the way in the adoption of plant-based diets.

You only have to take a look at the number of book titles carried by leading book retailers such as Waterstones to get an idea of the insatiable demand for recipes, diets and related books around the subject of veganism. As of December 2019, they carried over 9,303 titles with the term 'vegan' in them compared with less than 950 a year earlier (Vegan Society, 2019).

When you think of takeaways, pizza, Indian, Greek, Turkish and Chinese restaurants probably spring to mind. Therefore, you may be surprised to know that according to the website Food Navigator (Morrison, 2019), vegan meals were the fastest growing choice for takeaways in the UK! Who would have believed that just a few years ago?

This is a sizeable segment of consumers, and the number of vegans in Great Britain quadrupled between 2014 and 2019. In 2019 there were 600,000 vegans, or 1.16 per cent of the population; there were 276,000 (0.46 per cent) in 2016 and 150,000 (0.25 per cent) in 2014 (Vegan Society, 2019).

In the future, consumers who are either vegan, vegetarian or flexitarian will move from the minority and will soon be the majority. According to the Vegan Society (2019), by 2025, around a quarter of the UK population will be vegan or vegetarian, with flexitarians – of which I count myself as one – constituting 50 per cent of the population.

The size of the market is huge – according to Mintel, worth an estimated £740 million in the UK in 2018 (Jones, 2020). But if you consider the rise in adoption of veganism, vegetarianism and flexitarianism, it's most likely in the multiple billions of pounds.

Travel

The travel sector has been at the forefront of concerns around its impact upon the environment. The carbon footprint from airlines is one of the major contributors to climate change – airplane emissions of carbon dioxide, a major greenhouse gas, reached just over 900 million metric tons in 2018 and is expected to triple by 2050 (Tabuchi, 2019).

It has therefore been really pleasing to see some airlines, such as easyJet, commit to being carbon neutral, offsetting the impact by planting trees (easyJet, 2020). While it doesn't eradicate the issue, they at least took pretty significant action to mitigate the impact. Their response also involved investing in projects including renewable energies – in turn offsetting the fuel used from every single flight – reducing the weight of aircraft and taxiing on a single engine.

Small-model electric-powered aircraft have been flown since the 1970s. Over recent years we have seen the introduction of small electric-powered planes, and eventually we will see the introduction of passenger-carrying commercial electric-powered aircraft. The estimated timeline for this is the mid-2020s.

easyJet's commitment to sustainability is clear and will make them the first port of call for many consumers who fly because they have to, not because they want to.

As electric aircraft come into service, the costs of flying on them are likely to be high and place them out of the reach of the average consumer – that is, until they are the predominant aircraft in the market.

Consumer behaviour is changing – not only in relation to what we buy and what we consume, but, as the next section concludes, the channels we engage with in the first place.

Brick-and-mortar stores are here to stay, but the experience needs to step up

The convenience, value and range of sites like eBay, Amazon and Ocado, as well as supermarket and takeaway delivery services, have made online shopping a way of life, and a first choice for many. But the high street is fighting back – and hitting you with all five senses.

The name of the game is 'multi-sensory shopping'. Consumers want and expect to experience their retail on a number of different levels, so everything about your shop has to play its part: the visuals, the soundtrack and interactive opportunities.

In 2019, an international survey of 10,000 shoppers for Mood Media, conducted by Walnut Limited, found that 78 per cent of consumers cited 'an enjoyable in-store atmosphere' as a key factor in the decision to visit a physical store over online shopping (Moore, 2019). That's a huge prize for the brick-and-mortar sector; all retailers have to do is to understand it, then reach out and grab it.

Shopping is a tactile experience, and something that the online experience will never be able to replicate. According to 90 per cent of consumers surveyed, shops that were able to combine music, strong visuals and scent to create a 'multi-sensory' retail experience are more likely to lure them back. And while there are always local nuances to consider, the survey interviewed shoppers from Australia, Benelux, China, France, Germany, Spain, the United Kingdom and the United States, and feedback was consistent in relation to the experiences consumers are looking for (Moore, 2019).

So, what does multi-sensory shopping mean? Well, first, let's understand the obstacles to a good interactive and immersive retail experience. Number one, without a doubt, is long queues: 62 per cent of UK shoppers told the survey that they had avoided or left stores because of long queues. Never mind our cultural attachment to the art of queuing. This is the age of instant gratification, and 15 minutes in a queue can be off-putting for any number of reasons, from the irritating to the impossible – and that's before you even start to consider those with small children, or assistance dogs, or mobility issues. It simply can't compete with one-click ordering and two-hour delivery (Moore, 2019).

Add to the long queues the issue of there never being enough staff to assist. When I interview consumers for my 'fix the High Street' mini-series, this is always the number-one irritant and, in many cases, the reason for shopping online.

You've also got to think about your soundtrack. The music played in shops is really important to customers if you want them to spend any time there. Get it right and it can be a hugely positive factor, putting the customer very much in the right frame of mind. However, the flip side is that 57 per cent said they would disengage if the choice was poor. It's a matter of knowing your customers, judging the demographics and tailoring your music appropriately (Moore, 2019).

While you might make an assumption that most Gen Z (aged 18–24) and Millennial (aged 25–35) shoppers are mainly shopping online, you'd be wrong – 81 per cent of Gen Z prefer to shop in store (Green, 2017). And when it comes to the in-store experience, not surprisingly this segment was the most likely to be influenced by the different aspects of a multi-sensory retail experience (Moore, 2019).

So, what can retailers do to encourage footfall in their brick-and-mortar stores? The key deciding factor for customers in going into a physical site to make a purchase was the ability to touch, feel and try clothes, products or services – 56 per cent of those surveyed tipped this as the winner (Moore, 2019). Products have to be front and centre. If you run a mobile phone store, let the customers see the phones, pick them up, handle them, weigh them. Show them the choice you have to offer. If you sell clothes, make sure the racks are always full so that shoppers can feel the cloth, see the cut and judge the colours. Merchandising is also key. Make sure to merchandise shirts next to suits, blouses next to skirts. There should be plenty of sizes, and clean and plentiful changing rooms to try things on. We all know the basic truth: if you can get someone to try on an item of clothing, they're more than halfway to buying it.

What else? Make the shopping experience interactive. Almost half of customers said they wanted to see in-store special offers on digital screens; 44 per cent said they noticed information about discounts on digital screens; and nearly a quarter told the survey they had recently shared a physical shopping experience online on social media. In China, that proportion rose to over half (Moore, 2019). Make coming to your shop something people can feel good about, communicate with their friends about – the possibility of exponential growth is obvious.

These are the brick-and-mortar stores of the future, the ones that will not only survive the competition from online but will thrive as consumers choose to experience the product in their physical environment – bright, inviting, well-stocked, attractive, active experiences. Shoppers are engaged and involved; they're not passive consumers of a product. They want to feel like going to a store is an event, not just a retail necessity, something they can talk about, show off and enjoy.

None of this is rocket science. The secret of retail success rarely is. It's about being focused, diligent and responsive, seeing opportunities and having the agility to go after them. Stores, chains and brands that get it right will prosper, and will forge a place in tomorrow's market alongside online services (either their own or other people's). Those that don't, that can't see the shape of the future and that miss the boat, will falter and fail.

For all the modernity of the method, the basic process is as old as time. The clever and quick-thinking survive and thrive; the slow, complacent and ponderous lose out, and ultimately go to the wall.

Case studies of successful brands that deliver great experiences and the effect on sales performance

The case studies that follow cover a wide range of businesses operating in diverse consumer sectors, from hospitality to footwear and from mattresses to cooking appliances. But all have one thing in common. They all understand the requirement to create experiences around their products and the commercial opportunity from doing so.

CASE STUDY
Casper

The mattress brand Casper was created on the premise that buying a mattress shouldn't be a difficult process. It's still early in their journey and it remains to be seen how successful they'll be in the long run. With nearly 700,000 fans on Facebook and significant customer engagement, I wouldn't bet against them. They are a great example of what experiential retail should entail, and what they do is even more impressive considering they don't have any stores.

By understanding the issue many consumers have with insomnia, they created their Insomnobot-3000. The bot creates relationships with sleepless customers and brings a human touch (albeit as a bot!) with both humour and personality (Wilson, 2020). This undoubtedly engenders loyalty for the brand, by providing an experience that boosts loyalty through a personal connection with Casper.

While it may not immediately appear obvious how the Insomnobot helps the bottom line, it drives loyalty and retention, and when customers become loyal, they turn from being customers to fans. Then they become advocates and influencers who market on your behalf.

All customers have to do is text Insomnobot-3000 from their mobile phone and share whatever is on their mind. In turn the bot will share sleep advice while empathizing with the customer's inability to sleep (Wilson, 2020).

This initiative is also a great tool for gathering customer data and, more importantly, their contact data as they generate a swathe of mobile numbers, which can then be used to send promotions to. Engaged customers, or in this case fans, are far more receptive to receiving proactive promotional offers.

In addition to this, Casper has opened nap rooms at their 'Dreamery' in New York. You can take a 45-minute nap for $25, while experiencing first-hand the benefits of a Casper mattress (Hartmans, 2019). They lend you pyjamas and provide free snacks and coffee – another great example of how to bring the product and brand to life in a highly experiential and engaging way.

Caspar and the case studies that follow are examples of brands that have recognized the value of the experience economy and of connecting with consumers on an emotional level.

CASE STUDY
The Hard Rock Hotel

The Hard Rock Hotel was the recipient of the JD Power top-ranked hotel in the upper upscale category for 2019 (JD Power, 2019) – achieving a rating of 5 out of 5 for five of the eight categories that are rated. Clearly, the hotel brand is synonymous with the Hard Rock Café brand and therefore consumers will expect a significant level of experience there and one that is different from most generic hotel chains.

The Hard Rock Hotel was rated by customers across the following categories:

- overall satisfaction;
- reservation;
- arrival/departure;
- guest room;
- food and beverage;
- services and amenities;
- hotel facilities;
- cost and fees.

Whichever hotel you go to, just like in the Hard Rock Cafés, you'll find the walls emblazoned with musical instruments and pop and rock memorabilia, from vintage album covers to leather jackets worn by a host of world-renowned stars.

Most of the hotels have memorabilia that is localized. For example, the Palm Springs Hotel has a lamp from Elvis's Graceland home and an honorary policeman's badge presented to Elvis by the local Police Officer Association owing to Elvis's strong association with Palm Springs.

All of the staff in the hotel have their favourite band listed on their name tag, which serves as a talking point to engage with hotel guests.

What's the sum of the parts? Well, the Hard Rock Hotel is part of a group run by the Seminole Tribe in Florida and owns hotels, café's and casinos. It also has various franchise operations around the world. The group is highly profitable, turning over more than $6 billion and with operating profits well in excess of $1.5 billion.

SOURCE Debter (2016)

What the Hard Rock group has been able to do is to tap into our emotional connection with music and engage us through the memorabilia and full music-centric experience they deliver in their hotels.

It feels like a missed opportunity for many consumer brands that don't capitalize on the emotional engagement consumers have with their product category. Whether you're selling nuts and bolts or the latest Nike running shoes, consumers are buying your products for a reason and the opportunity to engage on both experiential and emotional levels is there.

CASE STUDY
There's no place like Home

Home, an entertainment complex in Manchester, is a good example of the experience economy. Built on the site of the former Hacienda Nightclub, it involved the merger of two well-known brands, both of which were in challenging financial situations – the Cornerhouse cinema and gallery, and the Library Theatre Company.

The complex includes two theatres, five cinema screens, an art gallery and a restaurant and bar. Due to its location, state of disrepair and with no main adjacent attractions and no main thoroughfare, many thought it wasn't a viable project.

With over 2.9 million visits since opening in 2015, it's fair to say Home has done a good job of putting to bed those early doubts over its viability (Home, 2020).

The economy and political uncertainty negatively affects retail, particularly when it comes to their impact upon consumer confidence, and therefore what people buy, how frequently and what they spend. Despite this, it appears that regardless of political uncertainty or austerity, consumers are spending more on doing stuff in the experience economy. The pick-me-up we're looking for comes from an experience and one that we can think back on and fondly remember. These are often supported by the video content we created of the memories we shared. These have a lifetime value far greater than an item of clothing or piece of household furniture (Usborne, 2017).

And post-pandemic, this is only going to increase in relevance.

The hospitality sector has an advantage over most others when it comes to delivering an experience, as that is what is at the heart of the proposition that consumers are buying into in the first place. That said, as the examples to follow from Vans and Viking demonstrate, a great customer experience can be, and should be, at the heart of what you do – even when a product is your core business.

CASE STUDY
I'm a fan of VANS

VANS created event spaces in key locations around the world, including London, Chicago and New York. These were branded as 'The House of VANS' and also appeared as pop-ups in multiple locations. With consumer engagement at their heart, these event spaces were very focused on core customers in the skateboarding community with sports, film and music all geared towards this audience.

Subsequently, they leveraged these spaces for many different events and marketing initiatives, from the launch of VANS David Bowie trainers to the promotion of women in skateboarding on International Women's Day, which was aimed at increasing visibility of women in the skateboarding scene.

Its commercial success is proven, with $13.8 billion sales in 2019 (Boardsport SOURCE, 2020), ever-increasing market penetration and how it has successfully maintained its core skateboarding customer while becoming a highly fashionable sneaker brand for everyday wear.

VANS are an example of how to marry up a product and a great customer experience. By integrating these event spaces into many of their locations globally, they have brought the brand and its products to life.

The key to success in these scenarios and the example for other brands to follow is how to get the balance right between delivering a great experience while still selling product and the whole entity being commercially successful. One without the other will only ever be a short-term success.

SOURCE Mulcahy (2019)

Over time we will see more and more examples of retailers and other consumer sectors seeking to create experiences rather than just selling products.

Just think of the coffee shop environment. From the mass-market brands such as Starbucks, Costa Coffee and Café Nero to the artisanal independents, the coffee shop is so much more than just a cup of coffee or tea. With free Wi-Fi, charging points for your laptop and phones, pleasant background music and an increasing range of food, they have become home to business meetings, social gatherings and an office environment for self-employed consultants and others.

In addition to VANS, sneaker stores have become increasingly experiential. The brand Veg-NonVeg, India's first multi-brand sneaker store, has understood the desire for its core Millennial and Gen Z target customer to shop from a curated range of all the best sneakers from around the world in a cool and hip environment, with art deco architecture, a café, live events and parties. The store is a hub and meeting place for fans of the brand. It's so much more than just another retail outlet.

Again, you'd be forgiven for thinking that a great customer experience is easier to deliver in a fashion-led sector than in the following example of a leading kitchen appliance manufacturer. But you'd be wrong. In actual fact, they have arguably done an even better job of creating a lifestyle brand with experience at the very heart of their DNA.

CASE STUDY
The Vikings still have the power

If you're outside of the US, you probably won't have heard of the brand Viking Range. Based in Greenwood, Mississippi, unlike the traditional way to market kitchen-related products, which focuses very much on the product itself, they market their range of kitchen appliances and accessories to promote a culinary lifestyle. They bring the culinary lifestyle to life by engaging with customers at their cooking schools, which take place throughout the United States.

In the UK and EU, a brand like Miele, founded in 1899, does something similar. If you're looking at buying their appliances, you are invited to the Miele Experience Centre, where you will be shown by professional chefs how to create fantastic culinary experiences using their cooking appliances. Miele will also come to the customer's house to give personal demonstrations on how to get the most from their appliances. Miele is a €4.2 billion company (Allianz Global, 2018).

At Viking Range, the number of consumers who have participated in their cooking schools is getting on for close to 80,000. For everyone who attends, there is an incentive to acquire an appliance. Every dollar they spend on attending the school earns customers discounts on Viking Range products.

The idea for the cooking schools at Viking Range emanated from the founder and CEO Fred Carl, who asked various colleagues to visit a Land Rover dealership in Dallas that offered test drives over a rocky terrain that really highlighted the strengths and benefits of the SUV. This inspired Fred and his team to do the same with the Viking Range kitchen products by bringing them to life through their cooking schools.

The schools were so successful that the business franchised them as a standalone concept to upmarket grocery stores and hotels. You can find a Viking Cooking School at Harrah's Casino in Atlantic City, New Jersey, as well as at Hubbell & Hudson, a high-end gourmet food market near Houston, Texas.

Viking Range was sold to Middleby Corporation for $380 million in 2013.

SOURCE Roner (2012) and Tadena (2013)

Conclusion

So, there you have it. The world over, the most successful consumer brands are continually thinking about how to leverage and integrate experience into their products and services. They recognize the shift in consumer wants, needs and behaviour as they seek to buy less and experience more. These businesses are agile and move quickly to embrace the changes and to be front and centre for consumer demand.

KEY TAKEAWAYS FROM CHAPTER 2

1 The shift in consumption from buying material possessions to having experiences has implications for all consumer businesses. This is also aligned with conscious consumption and the focus consumers have on sustainability. This is something you must act on now.

2 Delivering a great experience has a very tangible payback – in revenue, repeat business and customer lifetime value.

3 Experience-led brands are more sticky. Customers are more engaged and therefore become loyal to the brand, as they behave more like fans than customers.

4 You can be a product company but still have a whole new revenue stream from delivering services.

5 We are going through a seismic shift in consumer behaviour like we've never experienced before. The changes we're seeing in consumption, the move to veganism, are permanent. They're not fads and they're inextricably linked to sustainability and other key aspects consumers increasingly care about.

References

Allianz Global (2018) [accessed 7 January 2021] *Allianz Global corporate and specialty SE annual report* [Online] https://www.agcs.allianz.com/content/dam/onemarketing/agcs/agcs/about-agcs/AGCS-Annual-Report-2018-EN.pdf (archived at https://perma.cc/Z7BW-3PCC)

Boardsport SOURCE (2020) [accessed 21 November 2020] Vans revenues +24% & set to become $4 billion co. by 2020, *Boardsport SOURCE* [Online] http://www.boardsportsource.com/2019/05/23/vans-maintains-momentum-reports-24-revenue-increase-in-fy2019/ (archived at https://perma.cc/BT24-43CH)

Debter, L (2016) [accessed 27 November 2020] An alligator wrestler, a casino boss and a $12 billion tribe, *Forbes* [Online] https://www.forbes.com/sites/laurengensler/2016/10/19/seminole-tribe-florida-hard-rock-cafe/?sh=1597a9e25bbc (archived at https://perma.cc/F4AN-ZJLL)

easyJet (2020) [accessed 27 November 2020] Carbon offsetting, *Easyjet.com* [Online] https://www.easyjet.com/en/sustainability (archived at https://perma.cc/5UAC-89J3)

Effective Design (2019) [accessed 15 January 2021] How M&S Plant Kitchen has helped plant based eating go mainstream, *Effectivedesign.org.uk* [Online] https://effectivedesign.org.uk/sites/default/files/521%20Plant%20Kitchen.pdf (archived at https://perma.cc/DH9C-JETN)

Green, D (2017) [accessed 20 November 2020] Gen Z has a completely different shopping preference from millennials – and it's good news for retail, *Business Insider* [Online] https://www.businessinsider.com/generation-z-vs-millennials-in-shopping-2017–10?r=US&IR=T (archived at https://perma.cc/283U-RY4Y)

Harrabin, R (2020) [accessed 27 November 2020] Ban on new petrol and diesel cars in UK from 2030 under PM's green plan, *BBC News* [Online] https://www.bbc.com/news/science-environment-54981425 (archived at https://perma.cc/A5NK-2MP9)

Hartmans, A (2019) [accessed 10 April 2020] Inside Casper's Dreamery nap room in New York City, *Business Insider* [Online] https://www.businessinsider.com/casper-dreamery-nap-room-nyc-review-photos-2018-7?r=US&IR=T (archived at https://perma.cc/P3MX-DKAS)

Harvard Business Review (1998) Welcome to the experience economy, *Harvard Business Review* [Online] https://hbr.org/1998/07/welcome-to-the-experience-economy (archived at https://perma.cc/L53W-CFN2)

Home (2020) [accessed 27 November 2020] About, *HOME* [Online] https://homemcr.org/about/ (archived at https://perma.cc/K64M-6LUN)

JD Power (2019) [accessed 10 April 2020] 2019 North America hotel guest satisfaction study, *JD Power* [Online] https://www.jdpower.com/business/ratings/study/North-America-Hotel-Guest-Satisfaction-Study/10149ENG/Upper-Upscale/1437 (archived at https://perma.cc/K2ST-2MYL)

Jones, L (2020) [accessed 27 November 2020] Veganism: why are vegan diets on the rise?, *BBC News* [Online] https://www.bbc.com/news/business-44488051 (archived at https://perma.cc/KA8W-JPST)

Moore, A (2019) [accessed 13 April 2020] Sensory experiences increase in-store sales by 10 percent, finds new research from Mood Media, *Mood Media* [Online] https://moodmedia.co.uk/mood/sensory-marketing/ (archived at https://perma.cc/S7PH-PHWF)

Morrison, O (2019) [accessed 27 November 2019] Vegan meals are 'UK's fastest growing take-away choice', *Foodnavigator.com* [Online] https://www.foodnavigator.com/Article/2019/09/02/Vegan-meals-are-UK-s-fastest-growing-take-away-choice (archived at https://perma.cc/N6AM-NLPJ)

Mulcahy, E (2019) [accessed 27 November 2019] Experiential marketing: 9 examples of brilliant brand experiences, *The Drum* [Online] https://www.thedrum.com/news/2019/05/22/experiential-marketing-9-examples-brilliant-brand-experiences (archived at https://perma.cc/Z5Y5-C4YE)

Nugent, C (2020) [accessed 20 November 2020] How Extinction Rebellion is changing its climate activism, *Time* [Online] https://time.com/5864702/extinction-rebellion-climate-activism/ (archived at https://perma.cc/HME7-EJ2E)

Roner, L (2012) [accessed 10 April 2020] Thriving in the experience economy, *Compass Magazine* [Online] https://compassmag.3ds.com/special-reports/the-age-of-experience/thriving-in-the-experience-economy/ (archived at https://perma.cc/Y9WQ-BV6V)

Tabuchi, H (2019) [accessed 27 November 2020] 'Worse than anyone expected': air travel emissions vastly outpace predictions, *Nytimes.com* [Online] https://www.nytimes.com/2019/09/19/climate/air-travel-emissions.html (archived at https://perma.cc/Q4TY-W8XG)

Tadena, N (2013) [accessed 27 November 2020] Middleby buys appliance maker Viking for $380m, *MarketWatch* [Online] https://www.marketwatch.com/story/middleby-buys-appliance-maker-viking-for-380m-2013-01-01 (archived at https://perma.cc/ZQ4S-ZJB2)

Usborne, S (2017) [accessed 20 November 2020] Just do it: the experience economy and how we turned our backs on 'stuff', *Guardian* [Online] https://www.theguardian.com/business/2017/may/13/just-do-it-the-experience-economy-and-how-we-turned-our-backs-on-stuff (archived at https://perma.cc/CS6W-HSFG)

Vegan Society (2019) Statistics, *Vegan Society* [Online] https://www.vegansociety.com/news/media/statistics (archived at https://perma.cc/2AN4-6PBW)

Wilson, M (2020) [accessed 10 April 2020] The best customer experience examples in retail & shopping, *Business 2 Community* [Online] https://www.business2community.com/customer-experience/the-best-customer-experience-examples-in-retail-shopping-02274045 (archived at https://perma.cc/8EPL-KYUA)

03

The fallen

The brands that have sadly bitten the dust and why

WHAT YOU WILL LEARN IN THIS CHAPTER

- What stops a business from being successful?
- Why do businesses that once seemed as though they'd be around forever go to the wall?
- What are some of the prime examples of consumer brands from different sectors that failed?

Why do businesses not work in the first place?

There are lots of reasons why a business fails. Don't get me wrong – business failure is not an exclusive club for established businesses. There are many more start-ups and early-life businesses that fail every year.

Key issues to consider

- Supply and demand – they could be selling a product or a service that consumers don't want any more. The old rule of supply and demand never goes away. This also applies to start-ups. History is littered with some fantastic ideas that unfortunately there wasn't enough demand for. Entrepreneurs can be guilty of creating something that solves a problem only they see.

FIGURE 3.1 The business failure avoidance checklist

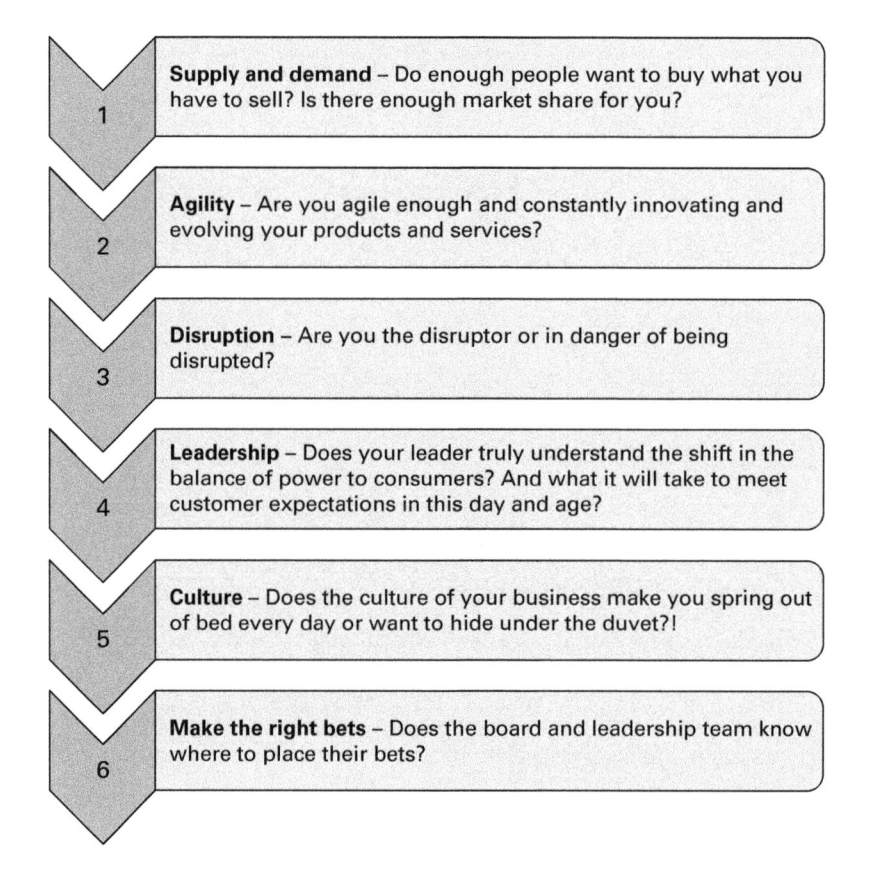

1. **Supply and demand** – Do enough people want to buy what you have to sell? Is there enough market share for you?

2. **Agility** – Are you agile enough and constantly innovating and evolving your products and services?

3. **Disruption** – Are you the disruptor or in danger of being disrupted?

4. **Leadership** – Does your leader truly understand the shift in the balance of power to consumers? And what it will take to meet customer expectations in this day and age?

5. **Culture** – Does the culture of your business make you spring out of bed every day or want to hide under the duvet?!

6. **Make the right bets** – Does the board and leadership team know where to place their bets?

- Move with the times, ideally ahead of them! – they could have been too slow to move with the times and to recognize the changes in consumer behaviour and what that meant for their business. Think Blockbuster Video. Saying that, don't get ahead of yourself – some start-up businesses were just ahead of their time and the market wasn't ready for them. One example is Boo.com, a fashion retailer that burnt through $135 million of investment capital in 18 months and went bust in 2000 (Jones, 2017). ASOS was formed in 2000! What if?

- Beware of the disruptors – a business could find itself disrupted by new, more agile, digitally led businesses that have worked out how to leverage technology to serve customers in a way that established players can't. Think Uber, Deliveroo, Just Eat, Monzo Bank, etc.

- You need a leader who is fit for the age we're in – they could have ineffective leadership. As Confucius said, a journey of a thousand miles begins with a single step (Confucius, circa 551 BCE – circa 479 BCE), and it's vital that step is in the right direction. If the business has a leader at the helm who doesn't get the new world, the strategy is most likely going to be flawed. The business could well be placing its bets in the wrong areas. Think of all the established retail businesses that were too slow to reduce their store portfolios after seeing a large percentage of sales go online. Or too slow, for that matter, to digitize their businesses and pursue online growth and greater business efficiencies.

- Culture comes from the top – their culture could be toxic and not a place where people really want to be. This often manifests itself in significant staff churn and poor levels of customer service.
- Look after the money – it could have mismanaged its finances. Sometimes this is accelerated by placing bets in things that don't pay off. As the saying goes, cash is king. Run out of cash and it's almost always all over. There are few lenders prepared to prop up a business, particularly if it has a flawed model.

Examples of a number of failed consumer brands from a range of sectors

The list of casualties in consumer sectors in recent years is long, and it includes brands that you would never imagine would go out of business.

Sadly, the Covid-19 pandemic played a big part in the demise of a multitude of well-known brands. For the purposes of this chapter, I'm not going to highlight those who fell by the wayside during the pandemic. The focus is on brands that got into trouble due to their lack of customer focus and understanding of how the market was changing.

In the US, some of the big names to have filed for Chapter 11 bankruptcy protection or that have gone out of business include JC Penney, Blockbuster, Toys R Us, Staples, Borders and Forever 21. In the UK, brands that have gone bust include many well-known names, from Thomas Cook, the once leading tour operator, to BHS, Barratts Shoes, Beales, Pretty Green, Patisserie Valerie and Phones 4U. There is then a longer list of brands that went through company voluntary administrations (CVAs), where they were able to close their loss-making stores, and those that went into prepack administrations. The former includes Arcadia, Debenhams and Mothercare; the latter includes Clintons Cards, Bonmarché, Links of London and Jack Wills.

What was wrong with their model?

Before I go on, I should stress that we shouldn't get too carried away with the list above. Throughout history you'll find business casualties that were too slow to adapt to meet the changing needs of consumers or to adapt their business models and cost structures. In the UK, think Woolworths, Tandy, Rumbelows, Freeman Hardy and Willis, Dixons, MFI, Focus, C&A, Borders, Comet, JJB Sports, Tie Rack and Athena. Many of these brands suffered from being too slow to react to changes in consumer behaviour. For some, it was that their product was no longer desirable or relevant. For others, they were too slow to pursue ecommerce and multichannel. Some had been disrupted by online businesses in their space (eg Borders and Amazon). Some were too slow to adapt their operating models and reduce their store count as more and more sales went online. In the US, names include: Circuit City, Levitz Furniture, Compaq, Pan Am, Tower Records and F.W. Woolworth.

While each of these brands will have had mitigating circumstances affecting them, I firmly believe that a good business is a good business. To my mind that equates to good leadership, an employee-first culture (appropriate remuneration, learning and development, succession planning), a clear strategy and differentiation, the right operating model and a clear purpose – and of course, products or services that enough people actually want to buy in the first place.

Were they too slow to adapt?

In my previous book, *100 Practical Ways to Improve Customer Experience*, we talk about Blockbuster, the global video and DVD retailer you used to see on every high street in the UK and US. They didn't see online ordering and the potential threat of LoveFilm and other ecommerce players until it was too late.

CASE STUDY
Blockbuster Video

In 2008 Blockbuster had 650 stores, a turnover of around £300 million and were making a healthy profit (Hobbs, 2017). Although it started an online rental business, the company didn't really take it seriously that the future would be in digital downloads and online ordering, because the company's executives all had a retail background and the priority seemed to be to save the high street shops at all costs. They even introduced food lines, such as popcorn and ice cream.

This online division appeared to have been treated as something inferior to traditional retailing with the possibility of cannibalizing high street sales. Even sadder is the fact that Blockbuster had millions of members' details about purchasing behaviours and their customers were very fond of the company.

However, the message here is that you have to evolve to meet customer priorities or progress will catch you out sooner or later. It is only by understanding the future picture of individual activity across online and offline that you can really understand customer behaviours and preferences.

SOURCE Newman and McDonald (2018)

I'm sure the then board of Blockbuster wished they had acquired Netflix when it was offered to them for $50 million in 2000 (Chong, 2015). If only we all had a crystal ball!

What about Toys R Us? It's incredible to think they went bust – a household name and market leader in the UK toy industry for so many years. So, what happened? Well, I believe their lack of customer-centricity is what happened. They were an old-school retailer that took their customers for granted.

Their stores were tired, unimaginative and, for a toy retailer, entirely lacking in customer experience. They were huge sheds in out-of-town retail parks, devoid of atmosphere, engagement or entertainment – all of which you'd expect from a toy retailer (BBC, 2018), and exactly why so many consumers continue to flock with their children to Hamleys.

Toys R Us has since made a comeback with much smaller, experiential led, mall-based stores. This model certainly has a much better chance of sustained success, second time around.

CASE STUDY
Why did Jamie's Italian restaurants not last the course?

Unfortunately, retail is not the only consumer sector to see well-known brands bite the dust. Jamie's Italian, run by the well-known chef and TV presenter Jamie Oliver, went bust in 2019 (Naylor, 2019). Not all the reasons for its demise were of its own making.

We're eating out less and therefore the casual dining sector has been heavily affected. In the UK, visits to restaurants were up 2 per cent in Q1 2017 and down 2 per cent in 2018 (MCA, 2019). That trend has continued in recent years. Of course, this sector was decimated by the Covid-19 pandemic. It was terribly sad to see some very successful businesses go to the wall as a result of the lockdowns. Post-pandemic, I anticipate our restaurants will struggle to keep up with demand as we all make up for lost time! Pre-pandemic, you can also argue that the casual dining market was saturated with oversupply when demand was falling.

Another contributing factor was 'consumer promiscuity'. There is no real loyalty to casual dining brands, but also not enough effort on the part of the brand to drive loyalty in the first place (Lalla, 2016). Nando's is one of the few casual dining brands that have a meaningful loyalty programme.

This sector has also had to face increased competition from disruptors – Deliveroo, Just Eat and Uber Eats opening up home delivery for many consumers.

While Jamie's expanded quickly, they had a lack of scale compared with core competitors so wouldn't be first choice for many consumers, who had more awareness and experience of other brands such as Ask Italian, Zizzi, Bella Italia and Carluccio's (the latter another casualty of the pandemic).

Jamie's Italian also faced increasing costs including business rates and labour costs: the national Living Wage and apprenticeship levy (0.5 per cent tax) (Espiner, 2018).

But I believe one of the biggest issues was around the product and proposition and the overall impact upon the customer experience. You can trade off a celebrity's brand for a period of time, but not forever. Consumers often complained of an inconsistent experience across different restaurants. The key to success in any dining chain, whether eating in the restaurant or getting a takeaway or home delivery, is knowing that what you're going to get is consistent and as you remember it. That in turn delivers a good customer experience.

There were limited healthy eating options and catering for vegans, and therefore you could argue they were also a little too slow to adapt to market trends.

There are a number of well-known car brands that have disappeared over the years – all of which suffered in some shape or form from a decline in customer experience. This related to the design of the vehicles not being aligned to customer desires or the cars being poorly manufactured and suffering negative impact upon brand equity as a result of product failure.

CASE STUDY
To have mass-market appeal, cars need to look the part and be practical

The car industry has been less impacted than retail and hospitality when it comes to established brands failing. But there have been some significant exceptions.

Hummer, the large truck and SUV brand once popularized by the American military, was in circulation from 1992 to 2010. Concerns over its safety and fuel consumption led to its demise. However, it has since been repurposed by GMC, which have launched a more consumer-centric proposition that is electric (Hawkins, 2020).

SAAB, the Swedish car brand, went bust in 2011, partly due to having different owners in a short period of time with no clear strategy. I'd also argue that the brand wasn't popular enough. The design failed to move with the times and didn't excite consumers. It is tipped to make a comeback as an electric vehicle under the ownership of National Electric Vehicle Sweden (NEVS) (Saarinen, 2017).

In the case of both Hummer and SAAB, the real underlying reason for their demise was lack of consumer demand. The reason for that was a product that wasn't enticing enough. The reason for that was a lack of understanding of what customers really wanted.

It remains to be seen whether or not electric versions of these brands can be successful, but they're likely to have more chance of being so as they're tapping into significant consumer awareness of the more sustainable environmental impact of electric cars.

History is littered with the names of brands we would once have thought were here to stay. One such brand is Mothercare.

CASE STUDY
Mothercare

Unfortunately, we didn't care enough about Mothercare. Founded in 1961, Mothercare went from being *the* destination for new mums and mums-to-be to administration in 2019.

In the early stages of the business, they were renowned for their technology offer, and in 1962 were early adopters of mail order.

Despite being the category leader more than 50 years on from their formation, they found themselves being disrupted by pureplays (internet-only businesses with no physical presence) and a huge increase in the channels of distribution of their products. You can buy many of the core baby- and infant-related products in a host of retail environments, from Amazon to Asda.

New parents are frequently unable to go to the shops, so online should be a critical channel in this space. Mothercare could have reduced their high street footprint to invest more online and in the logistics infrastructure in order to meet customer expectations and compete with Amazon and the supermarkets.

Also, a lot of their stores were in out-of-town retail parks, not ideal with brand adjacencies next to DIY sheds and electrical retailers.

One of their biggest challenges I believe was that their core customer was only interested in buying from them over a relatively short window of time – a year or two at best. They then sold the Early Learning Centre, which, in hindsight, provided them with the opportunity to extend the relationship with parents well beyond the formative years of their children. Had Mothercare integrated the two propositions, or at least created a loyalty mechanism between the two, they would have stood a much better chance of defending their market share against the disruptors and mass market grocers who entered their space.

SOURCE Clark (2019)

Mothercare is a business that ran for nearly 60 years before hitting the wall. It's an example of how a once very successful business can make a few bad decisions that ultimately lead to its demise. I believe that the longer a business has been established, the more at risk it becomes of ultimate failure. Take the next example, Thomas Cook, a business established in the mid-1800s.

The saying that nothing lasts forever very much rings true when it comes to consumer-facing businesses. My addition to this is if you think you'll last forever, you won't. It leads to a business taking its eye off the ball. Whereas if you continually review your approach to people, product, price, values, relevance and your overarching levels of customer-centricity, I think a business has a much better chance of long-term sustainability.

CASE STUDY
Thomas Cook overcooked their model

The international tour and airline operator and one of the travel sector's oldest brands, Thomas Cook went bust in 2019 after operating for 178 years. When they went bust, they required £1.1 billion to recapitalize their business and couldn't raise the investment to do so.

The company provided a one-stop-shop for travellers, providing everything from flights to hotels to tours and meals. It operated its own hotels and airline. They were considered to be a reputable, trusted brand for decades.

Their problems grew as they were too slow to adapt to significant changes in consumer behaviour. As travel bookings moved online, Thomas Cook's business was still very much focused on high street stores, with 600 stores worldwide.

They failed to realize the importance of being in the game in terms of search, where Expedia and Booking.com dominate the market. As it became easier for customers to design their own holidays online at a good price, the package holiday market became less relevant. This personalization element was completely alien to their business strategy, but increasingly important for consumers. They found themselves disrupted by a plethora of online players from Expedia and LastMinute.com to Booking.com and Airbnb.

Other key factors in their demise were the expense of running an airline, and its inability to compete effectively with the low-cost carriers such as easyJet and Ryanair.

SOURCE Simms (2019)

It was a real shame to see a brand of Thomas Cook's standing and longevity go to the wall. But it should serve as a lesson to any business that you must always be evolving, never standing still. Most importantly, you need to understand consumer behaviour and their needs and wants and how best your business can cater for this in an ever-changing world.

The brands that die invariably have a mindset that emanates from a time when they held the balance of power. That is long gone.

CASE STUDY
They've not fallen over, but they've been slowly treading water for some time

I've always been fascinated by Marks & Spencer – perhaps because I've never worked there. I've often looked from the outside in to try and imagine what they could do to get the brand back to past glories of yesteryear.

Let's be clear – with the exception of the financial results during the pandemic, Marks & Spencer still makes a profit. That cannot be said for a lot of other retail businesses.

The brand is still strong and well established, but their image is tired and arguably in need of reinvigorating, if not reimagined. Despite store closures, they have a large footprint of stores. They have an ageing estate.

I admire them greatly for their continued efforts to transform the business. A good example is their partnership with Ocado to give them a credible online food proposition. This said, my sense is that they haven't gone far enough. What they need is revolution, not evolution. They need radical transformation, as well as the implementation of new initiatives. They need to do all they can to be the mothers of reinvention.

If it were me, I would close anywhere from 25 per cent to 50 per cent of the larger, least profitable stores. Then make the brand even more accessible with a curated range and take it into a number of local high streets with small-format stores and pop-ups, much as they've done by franchising the food proposition to petrol forecourts. I'd invest savings in digital, both in-store and online, and refit the remainder of the stores to be far more modern in design and merchandising.

Their food business continues to prosper and, as I mentioned previously, their Plant Kitchen range and strong focus on vegan, vegetarian, flexitarian and food intolerances has brought them a new and younger customer base. The challenge is, how do they make the rest of their fashion and general merchandise proposition relevant for this customer?

I believe they have a window of opportunity to steal a march on the large fast-fashion players who are struggling to meet the sustainability requirements consumers have of them across their supply chain. Marks & Spencer could start a standalone brand that is sustainable from the get-go and not impacted by any negative perception of the core mother ship.

They have also been acquiring brands such as Jaeger and broadening their offer by adding other established brands more popular with a younger consumer. This is a smart play and they should add more relevant brands to their offer. A combination of other desirable brands and a new standalone sustainable fast-fashion brand would make M&S more relevant to a younger consumer.

The biggest mistake anyone selling fashion always makes is not recognizing when the brand has gone off and what to do about it. If consumers don't like your brand so much anymore, but they still like some of your designs, these could still sell if you removed the branding. Alternatively, you could create a sub-brand that consumers don't associate with the core brand that's lost its desirability.

Product is at the heart of customer experience. If customers don't desire what you sell anymore, that is going to be a slippery slope from which you may never recover.

What were the death knells?

A decline in customer experience in most cases was the beginning of the end for these brands. But customer experience is far reaching and has broader implications than most businesses realize. It's not just about the manifestation of an experience. It's about the product, the levels of service, marketing communications and more. As was the case with Mothercare, the product proposition wasn't relevant beyond the first year or two of a baby's life. So the customer value proposition was no longer relevant. Or the fact many of their stores were in retail parks adjacent to DIY retailers didn't create the experience expectant mothers and their partners were looking for.

Thomas Cook could have improved customer experience by personalizing it more and rewarding loyalty, thus encouraging repeat bookings and discouraging consumers from booking their own trips. But they could also have encouraged consumers to use them for flights instead of going to a budget airline.

Despite many organizations talking about being customer first or putting the customer at the heart of all they do, they are making it increasingly difficult for us to contact them directly. We've all been there. You call the contact centre and you end up on this automated call answering system. Press 1 for this and 2 for that and 3 for the other! Then, you're often met with another layer of options. If you're really lucky, after about 10–20 minutes you might actually get through to a human being. Often when you do get through, you just know that you're going to be met by a total inability to resolve anything for you.

Added to this, many consumer-facing brands are removing the ability for you to email them. They'd rather you 'chatted' online through live chat. The issue with that is that in most cases nowadays, you're actually 'chatting' to a chat bot, otherwise known as artificial intelligence! Well, there's nothing wrong with my intelligence, and it most certainly isn't artificial. So, if I want or need help from customer service, I expect that to come from a real-life person – be that over the phone, via email or face-to-face.

I fully appreciate that consumer-facing businesses are trying to cut costs, but you cannot afford to do that at the expense of the customer, as that is a completely false economy. All you will do is drive the customer away. In the trade we call that 'customer churn'.

I can genuinely never understand the mentality of a business that sells to consumers and doesn't get this. After all, we're all consumers. We've all suffered our fair share of really poor levels of service. It honestly feels to me as though some brands are going out of their way to make it as hard as possible for you and I to contact them. How can that possibly be a recipe for success? Why would you expect to increase the customer's propensity to engage with you when you treat them with such disdain? I've never yet come across a business where technology and artificial intelligence can provide better, more relevant, more personalized levels of service than human beings.

The bottom line is that as consumers, we have the power. We live in an increasingly democratized world. The power is at the click of a mouse or voting with our feet. Or, even worse, telling our friends and family on social media about the terrible experience we went through at the hands of a consumer brand. Many of the brands listed previously that no longer exist failed to understand the impact of poor service.

A decline in customer experience is not the only reason for the demise of brands that were previously highly successful. Often it can be down to poor stewardship. This in turn is not always as a result of poor leadership and can be down to all the focus being on short-term commercial performance and little to no medium- to long-term approach.

CASE STUDY
CEOs need to play the long game

Most CEOs are needing to reinvent their firms, identify and access new markets, deal with shrinking margins and pay out dividends. In such situations, it isn't surprising c-suite captains invariably find themselves walking the plank.

But perhaps the biggest danger here, to CEOs, shareholders and customers alike, is the spectre of short-termism. This is not to say planning for the short term is inherently bad, but everyone in the industry should understand how the pressure to keep share prices alive and investors happy can lead to dangerous tailspins.

If you've been putting off the need to invest in a new digital platform to save costs, or if you've delayed selling off floor space to keep market confidence, you're only going to make the eventual hit harder when it comes. But if your brief is to deliver and maintain a certain valuation above all else, you're in a bind.

This is one reason we see firms failing, having seemed profitable just a quarter or so before. CEOs might not know whether they can maintain profit for four consecutive quarters, but they will know they won't reach two consecutive quarters if they can't reach one. In that environment, unfortunately, short-termism trumps any long-term planning.

Short-termism leads to short-termism and, more often than not, all the things you don't want: a volatile share price, a compromised service and a lack of emphasis on innovation and product improvement. Retail is all about brand, but the stability we associate with the best retail brands is powered by some furious duck paddling below the water and a serious long-term vision.

Boards that back CEOs with a plan tend to be rewarded over the medium to long term. Those that equate dividend payouts with customer satisfaction are making a mistake. Both are important, but only one is essential.

SOURCE Newman (2019)

Conclusion

You're never too big to fail. The list of failed businesses over the past decade include household name brands you'd have assumed would be around forever. Maybe if these brands had a checklist of the various factors that could lead to their demise, it would have enabled them to make the changes necessary and at pace. We're talking good business principles to maintain success – effective and inspiring leadership, the right products and services, a good culture and engaged workforce, continual innovation and a clear, customer-driven plan of what to invest in.

> **KEY TAKEAWAYS FROM CHAPTER 3**
>
> So, what could Mothercare, Jamie's Italian, Thomas Cook, Hummer, SAAB and Blockbuster have done to avoid Armageddon?
>
> 1 First of all, they needed to be closer to their customers, their wants, needs and changing behaviour. It is clear that all suffered as a result of not being relevant to enough customers.
>
> 2 They needed to be more focused on customer retention and lifetime value – finding ways of keeping customers loyal and giving them tangible reasons to keep coming back.
>
> 3 They needed to be more agile and quicker to change and adapt their business model to the better experiences being delivered by disruptive brands in their sector. As the saying goes, keep your friends close and your enemies closer. Business can be like a war at times, and if you don't know what your closest competitors are up to, you could easily lose the fight.

4 More attention could have been paid to ensuring their proposition was delivered consistently across all of their channels and touchpoints.

5 They should have behaved more like service providers and not just product providers. This would have ensured they were on top of the full customer experience.

6 Hyper-localization and personalization – local and personal is where it's at. They would have increased retention and increased customer lifetime value if they'd been able to deliver more relevant local and personalized experiences.

7 Their CEOs needed to be given the opportunity to make strategic and investment decisions that may not have paid back until the longer term.

8 Costs should always be managed effectively. However, the culture of the business needs to be one of test and learn and failing fast. To do this, failure must not be penalized. Otherwise, the business will always lag behind the competition, who are more agile and prepared to take risks.

References

BBC (2018) [accessed 21 November 2020] Five reasons Toys R Us failed, *BBC News* [Online] https://www.bbc.com/news/business-43210854 (archived at https://perma.cc/P3F6-J5R2)

Chong, C (2015) [accessed 21 November 2020] Blockbuster's CEO once passed up a chance to buy Netflix for only $50 million, *Business Insider* [Online] https://www.businessinsider.com/blockbuster-ceo-passed-up-chance-to-buy-netflix-for-50-million-2015-7?r=US&IR=T (archived at https://perma.cc/9F64-CV73)

Clark, J (2019) [accessed 10 April 2020] Three reasons behind Mothercare's fall into administration, *CityAM* [Online] https://www.cityam.com/mothercare-collapses-after-failure-to-adapt-to-changing-consumer-behaviour/ (archived at https://perma.cc/FK2U-9WBJ)

Espiner, T (2018) [accessed 26 February 2021] What's eating the restaurant trade? *BBC News* [Online] https://www.bbc.com/news/business-42923499?SThisFB (archived at https://perma.cc/PLV9-8MMZ)

Hawkins, AJ (2020) [accessed 26 February 2021] The Hummer is back as a 350-mile range 'electric supertruck' that can drive diagonally, *The Verge* [Online] https://www.theverge.com/2020/10/20/21525290/hummer-ev-electric-truck-gmc-price-specs-range (archived at https://perma.cc/NL2A-P5KR)

Hobbs, T (2017, July 7) [accessed 5 December 2017] From iconic to punchline: Blockbuster's CMO reflects on failure, *Marketing Week* [Online] https://www.marketingweek.com/2017/07/03/blockbusters-cmo-failure/ (archived at https://perma.cc/2LZP-6DNY)

Jones, H (2017) [accessed 27 November 2020] Are tech stocks in danger?, *The National* [Online] https://www.thenationalnews.com/business/are-tech-stocks-in-danger-1.93196 (archived at https://perma.cc/ZT4Y-RR7Y)

Lalla, A (2016) [accessed 21 November 2020] What consumer promiscuity means for brands, *Economic Times* [Online] https://economictimes.indiatimes.com/what-consumer-promiscuity-means-for-brands/articleshow/51597486.cms?from=mdr (archived at https://perma.cc/YK5V-PFJ7)

MCA (2019) [accessed 21 November 2020] UK restaurant market report 2019, *MCA* [Online] https://www.mca-insight.com/market-reports/uk-restaurant-market-report-2019/597394.article (archived at https://perma.cc/HRE9-A68A)

Naylor, T (2019) [accessed 27 November 2020] No wonder Jamie's went bust: Brits have lost their appetite for samey chains, *Guardian* [Online] https://www.theguardian.com/commentisfree/2019/may/23/jamie-oliver-restaurant-chain-bust-brits (archived at https://perma.cc/Z539-5FED)

Newman, M (2019) [accessed 10 April 2020] CEOs need to go long, *Martin Newman* [Online] https://martinnewman.co.uk/ceos-need-to-go-long/ (archived at https://perma.cc/CV47-95L5)

Newman, M and McDonald, M (2018) *100 Practical Ways to Improve Customer Experience*, Kogan Page, London

Saarinen, M (2017) [accessed 10 April 2020] Saab: the cars, the history and what went wrong, *Auto Express* [Online] https://www.autoexpress.co.uk/saab/98267/saab-the-cars-the-history-and-what-went-wrong (archived at https://perma.cc/6UT2-2P6P)

Simms, S (2019) [accessed 21 November 2020] How could travel giant Thomas Cook fail?, *Nytimes.com* [Online] https://www.nytimes.com/2019/09/23/travel/why-thomas-cook-travel-collapsed.html (archived at https://perma.cc/T5N2-W864)

04

The resurrected

> **WHAT YOU WILL LEARN IN THIS CHAPTER**
>
> - How any business can turn itself around and avoid going bust.
> - The best examples of how different brands have managed to resurrect themselves and have regained their relevance as a result of revised customer value propositions and a focus on customer-centricity.

Brands that have bounced back

There are many examples of brands that have successfully been resurrected – in many cases, brands that were very nearly out of business and have made spectacular comebacks. The most notable of these is Apple, which at the time of writing is the most valuable company in the world (Popkin, 2020).

The common thread when you look at brands that came back from the dead or those that were on their knees is customer experience: product, brand, customer service, delivering on the customer promise, listening to the voice of the customer, staff engagement, in-store experience, online experience, visual merchandising, marketing, last-mile logistics/delivery – the list goes on. It's the sum of the parts. When a brand does all of this well, it delivers a great customer experience. And that is what sets it apart from the competition.

All of the brands I can think of that have come back from the dead have had the same focus:

FIGURE 4.1 The four pillars of brand resurrection

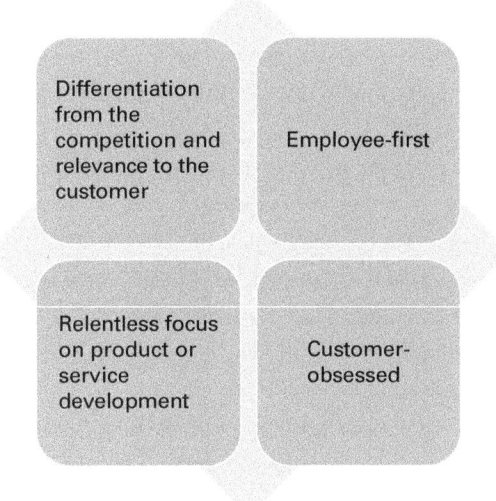

- Differentiation from the competition and relevance to the customer
- Employee-first
- Relentless focus on product or service development
- Customer-obsessed

1 They ensured that they had key points of difference from competitors while maintaining their relevance to customers.
2 They were employee-first and understood the importance of their people to all that they did.
3 They had a relentless focus on product and service development.
4 They were customer-obsessed and truly customer-centric.

CASE STUDY
Apple

Yes, believe it or not, one of the most successful brands in the world, a household name, with a market cap of $trillion plus, very nearly went out of business.

As hard to imagine as that is, Apple nearly went out of business in 1997. It was on life support when Steve Jobs returned to save the business in June of that year.

It was announced just three months later at the fiscal year end that Apple had lost over $1 billion – in part fuelled by its move to expand its range with new products that simply didn't resonate, including the Newton MessagePad, which was a handheld device not dissimilar to the Palm Pilot. In Walter Isaacson's biography of Steve Jobs, he wrote that Apple was 90 days from going out of business. Hard to believe, isn't it?

With a peace offering from Microsoft of a $150 million investment, Apple began its recovery, and within a year its turnaround was very much under way with the launch of the iMac. It was an extremely customer-centric product. Beautifully designed, easy set up for internet usage and great to use, in less than six months it sold close to 800,000 units, and in 1998, contributed significantly to Apple making its first profit for three years.

The now legendary designer, Jony Ive, designed the iMac and subsequently the iPod and iPhone. The rest, as they say, is history.

It's a well-known fact that neither Jony Ive nor any of the product designers at Apple did any market research. Often consumers don't know what they need. And if you asked a consumer what they'd want their music device to look like, when we were all walking around with Walkmans, would anyone have conceived the iPod? Of course not.

This said, I am a fan of at least validating with existing customers the path you're thinking of heading down. But not doing so clearly hasn't held Apple back!

SOURCE CB Insights Research (2019), Isaacson (2012) and Muriuki (2020)

Many of you probably don't even remember the time when Burberry was on its knees. Yes, even some of the best-known and most successful brands in the world today, such as Apple and Burberry, came very close to disappearing altogether.

CASE STUDY
Burberry – from checking out to check this out!

Burberry lost its way as a brand in the early 2000s. Like many fashion-led brands before and since, they became mass market. Their core check design became a staple of the masses. To cash in, the brand made more and more products with a check design and subsequently took the brand downmarket, where it had too much visibility and on the wrong core customer.

The then CEO Rosemary Bravo led the turnaround of the brand. The subsequent arrival of creative director Christopher Bailey and chief executive officer Angela Ahrendts led to a parallel growth strategy of taking the brand back to its heritage from a design perspective refocusing on a new core customer base while leveraging digital technology and social media to drive consumer engagement and sales.

I had the privilege of driving some of the digital transformation during my tenure as head of ecommerce and launched Burberry's first ecommerce presence in Europe in 2006. The commercial output of Bailey and Ahrendts' strategy was a breath-taking triple-digit increase in Burberry's share price over a seven-year period.

Today, there are few more customer-centric brands than Burberry. They lead with a strategy that has customer and digital at its heart. They leverage digital to drive brand inspiration and activation across all channels and touchpoints, including online, stores and live-streaming runway shows. Social media underpins the brand's communication with consumers and they continually invest in data science and analytics to provide the insight required to enable the brand to make more informed decisions across retail, ecommerce, customer service and marketing.

They have a multichannel proposition (collect in store) available worldwide. The implementation of local distribution centres improves stock availability and reduces delivery times. Burberry is personalizing its customer communication, editorializing its website and creating digital-first platform collaborations to drive consumer engagement. Burberry has over 17 million fans on Facebook and Instagram. Its share price has increased by around 750 per cent since its troubled times in the early 2000s.

SOURCE Rigby (2015) and Roy (2019)

As was the case with Burberry, fashion brands are more cyclical than most and too often lose sight of their core customers. They often are the cause of their own fall from grace. When you take a brand that is not accessible to all, it remains aspirational to many, but when you increase its availability and take it to the masses, it loses its cachet.

Airlines have a different set of challenges. That said, product, service and experience are very much at the heart of their success or failure.

CASE STUDY
Delta Air Lines

The terrorist attacks of 9/11 had a catastrophic impact upon all the major established US airlines. They faced the perfect storm of reduced demand from consumers, rising fuel costs and the growth of budget airlines that were offering cheaper fares. This ultimately led to Delta Air Lines declaring bankruptcy in 2005.

Delta came out of bankruptcy in 2007 and made a number of bold moves to improve its performance – from adding new routes and buying their own oil refinery to putting their people at the heart of all they did.

To this end, the starting point for their turnaround was to focus on their employees. This was a recognition that to be customer-first you need to be employee-first at the outset. They invested in employee training and development and also instigated a profit-sharing scheme for employees, which paid out over $1 billion in 2018.

SOURCE Anderson (2014)

It goes to show that an approach of 'employee-first' in turn puts your customer first and can even revive a bankrupt business, as was the case with Delta.

I can't think of any sustainably successful business that doesn't have a people-first culture. To be successful, any business needs to have motivated employees who always want to go the extra mile, be that for their customers or their colleagues.

CASE STUDY
The building blocks of LEGO®

LEGO® is a household name with global brand awareness and visibility. And it has managed to continually reinvent itself in order to maintain relevance and has been a constant in the lives of millions of children over the years.

However, you may not be aware of this, but in 2003, the company was on the verge of going out of business. As a result of various issues from decreasing consumer demand to new business ideas that failed to deliver, they found themselves $800 million in debt.

Their diversification into lines of business including TV shows, video games and theme parks was largely unsuccessful. While the leadership had the insight for the opportunities, their lack of experience in these areas led to the end product not being fit for purpose.

In 2004, Jorgen Vig Knudstorp became CEO. His turnaround plan involved a number of key initiatives, from reducing the product range by 46 per cent from 13,000 to 7,000 LEGO® parts and moving manufacturing to less expensive locations to selling a majority shareholding in the theme parks to Merlin Entertainments.

But the key driver in the turnaround was understanding core customers and the potential to form deeper engagement with the brand. This manifested itself in the highly successful smash hit LEGO® Movie, produced by Warner Brothers in 2014, leading to a 15 per cent year-on-year uptick in profits. It has also seen LEGO® open flagship stores in major cities and key locations around the world.

Their turnaround has been so spectacular that by 2015 the company overtook Ferrari to become the world's most powerful brand, and with profits of £660 million also became the number-one toy company in Europe and Asia and the third largest in North America.

LEGO® leverages its fans in product development by enabling them to submit their own design ideas. Once the product has been developed and taken to market, the winning entries get 1 per cent of sales. What's not to like about that? What a fantastic way to engage and incentivize core customers to help you drive more sales and profitability. And customers end up being able to buy the products they really want. It truly is a win-win.

Listening to customers and involving them in product development and design has undoubtedly paid dividends. Another example came in 2011, when LEGO® undertook customer research that highlighted that 91 per cent of LEGO® users were boys. They subsequently launched LEGO® Friends in 2012, tripling sales to girls.

LEGO® also invests heavily in digital, with LEGO® Life providing a safe social platform for kids too young for Facebook or Instagram to share their creations. Again, a great example of a brand that caters effectively for a range of customer segments.

SOURCE CB Insights Research (2019) and Davis (2017)

I hope that you see the pattern emerging. In almost every case I can think of, a business that went bust just didn't have a deep enough understanding of its customers and of how best to create products, services and experiences they desired. The reverse can be said for successful brands as well as those that have been able to reverse their decline, such as with LEGO®, Netflix and the other case studies in this chapter.

Despite Apple not researching new products with customers, it is clear that they continue to identify customer-related problems that are fixed through the design and development of technology solutions that deliver better customer experiences.

CASE STUDY
Netflix was nearly no flix!

You may not realize this, but Netflix has been around since 1997, when it started as an online DVD rental service.

They first introduced a monthly rental subscription in 1999. Seeing the fallout from the dotcom boom and bust in 2000, they offered themselves for sale to

Blockbuster for $50 million. They were turned down. I'm sure Netflix are delighted they were rejected! As for Blockbuster? Well, sadly as we have already discussed in the previous chapter, it was the beginning of the end for them.

Netflix listed the business in 2002 at around $1.20 per share and, in 2003, reached 1 million subscribers. In 2007, they launched their online streaming service.

In 2011, Netflix said it would split its business into a streaming service and a separate DVD service. In November 2011, Netflix's share price crashed after 800,000 subscribers quit in protest. Some businesses would have been so bloody-minded in believing their strategy to be right that they would have persisted down this path. Thankfully for Netflix, they listened to customers and swiftly reversed their decision and decided to keep both entities together.

This very nearly led to the demise of the business and just shows how quickly things can unravel when you make a strategic decision that is inward-looking rather than something that reflects the needs and wants of your customer base.

Since that time, Netflix has gone from strength to strength. In 2013, they launched their first *House of Cards* series. In 2015, Netflix's stock price was nearly $100 a share, a rise of 574 per cent in five years. In 2016, it went global, launching into 130 new territories.

As of 2020, Netflix had 195.2 million global subscribers (Schomer, 2020) and a stock price of over $480 (Yahoo, 2020) – obviously boosted by the Covid-19 lockdown, but nonetheless, a quite remarkable performance for a business that nearly went bust only a decade earlier. Initial investors have received a whopping 41,000 per cent return on investment since their IPO (NewsBreak, 2020).

SOURCE Product Habits (2018)

It may seem a little surreal moving from the example of how Netflix turned around their business with a more customer-centric proposition to how Greggs, the UK's leading baker, became the success that it is today. But both are equally compelling examples. Both of these businesses understand their customer wants and needs and deliver consistent levels of customer experience across all that they do.

CASE STUDY
Greggs – they're on a roll!

Started as a door-to-door bakery sales business in 1939, Greggs opened their first store in 1951. By 2016, Greggs had a bigger UK presence than McDonald's and

Starbucks. By 2019, they had over 1,850 branches in the UK. They have gone from being a regional brand in the north-east of England to a takeover of the UK – helped in some form by having a plethora of celebrity fans, including Milla Jovovich, Thomas Turgoose and Jake Gyllenhaal.

While the business has never been on its knees, it has had to come back from numerous setbacks throughout its history. One of these was in 2013 when Greggs realized that they couldn't compete against supermarkets for take-home baked goods, so they repositioned as a brand offering food-on-the-go. This also had the effect of increasing the potential frequency of purchase and demand: breakfast, lunch, dinner and snacks.

They know their customers extremely well and adapt quickly to demand. The best example being when, in 2019, they launched a vegan sausage roll to complement their traditional sausage roll offer. This was a huge success, generating significant media coverage, sales and introducing the brand to a new customer base.

They have a very positive public image and are clearly focused on social responsibility through the Greggs Foundation and the Greggs Breakfast Club, which was set up to ensure local children were given an adequate first meal of the day.

They pay their staff well and often profit-share through staff bonuses, while providing them with 50 per cent discount cards. They have around 750,000 fans on Facebook. That's pretty good engagement for a business selling sausage rolls – be those pork or vegan!

SOURCE Heasman (2019), Econsultancy (2019) and Cumming (2016)

Conclusion

The first step towards salvation for a brand is recognizing that it's in trouble in the first place, as this isn't always immediately obvious. A brand could go quickly, or it might die a death from a thousand cuts.

The best chance of avoiding this is to ensure that what it does is suitably different from any competitors, that its people are at the heart of all it does, it has a relentless focus on improving products and services, and that it is truly customer-obsessed.

These steps should be part of a continual process, not something that is revisited every three years as part of a strategic review.

KEY TAKEAWAYS FROM CHAPTER 4

1 Understand customer wants and needs – there can be no better example of a business that understands its customers than Greggs. They and their customers have a mutual respect and admiration for each other. This is evidenced through their significant following on social media: three-quarters of a million fans on Facebook (Econsultancy, 2019) – not bad for a purveyor of sausage rolls! They have done what most local or regional players have been unable to do and that is to take their business and prove its relevance throughout the UK while also maintaining the feel and positioning of a local bakery. They also recognize that shift happens and, as such, they continually roll with the times, and nothing demonstrates that better than the success of their vegan sausage roll.

2 People make the difference – it's near impossible to be customer-centric and commercially successful over a sustained period of time without being employee-first. There are some great examples in this chapter of brands that do so, none more so than Greggs and Delta Air Lines, both of which regularly profit-share and distribute bonuses to their staff.

3 Join up the experience – businesses must be able to deliver joined-up customer experiences across all channels and touchpoints. Silos belong on farms and not in consumer-facing businesses.

4 Digital was at the heart of the turnaround plans of most of these brands. Digital provides an opportunity to do business more efficiently. Colleagues can communicate and collaborate more effectively. Customers can benefit from more joined-up and rewarding experiences and many parts of the organization can work more productively and cost-effectively.

5 Know when to pivot – to be customer-centric, you need to listen to customers, and you need to be quick to pivot when you realize that you've made the wrong decision. If you are one of the fortunate early investors in Netflix's IPO and you've held on to your shares through the volatility of them nearly going bust in 2011, you will have enjoyed a huge return on your investment!

6 Leadership – last but definitely not least, these brands had leaders who understood the importance of the first five points: understanding who the most important segments of customers are, the importance of putting your own people first, creating organizational structures that lend themselves to delivering joined-up experiences for customers and the opportunity presented by digital technology to engage both internal and external customers more effectively and to improve productivity and efficiency.

References

Anderson, RH (2014) [accessed 21 November 2020] Delta's CEO on using innovative thinking to revive a bankrupt airline, *Harvard Business Review* [Online] https://hbr.org/2014/12/deltas-ceo-on-using-innovative-thinking-to-revive-a-bankrupt-airline (archived at https://perma.cc/8F5A-8J75)

CB Insights Research (2019) [accessed 18 January 2021] 18 companies that battled bankruptcy, scandal, and more, *CB Insights Research* [Online] https://www.cbinsights.com/research/corporate-comeback-stories/ (archived at https://perma.cc/5TLM-3JDW)

Cumming, E (2016) [accessed 21 November 2020] How Greggs conquered Britain: 'Nobody can quite believe how well it has done', *Guardian* [Online] https://www.theguardian.com/global/2016/mar/05/greggs-conquered-britain-bakery-profit-sausage-rolls (archived at https://perma.cc/MP4N-9SA6)

Davis, J (2017) [accessed 21 November 2020] How Lego clicked: the super brand that reinvented itself, *Guardian* [Online] https://www.theguardian.com/lifeandstyle/2017/jun/04/how-lego-clicked-the-super-brand-that-reinvented-itself (archived at https://perma.cc/9FS5-T67F)

Econsultancy (2019) [accessed 18 November 2019] 18 companies with brilliant digital strategies, *Econsultancy* [Online] https://econsultancy.com/18-companies-with-brilliant-digital-strategies/ (archived at https://perma.cc/7P8L-GKFD)

Heasman, C (2019) [accessed 11 April 2020] The untold truth of Greggs, *Mashed.com* [Online] https://www.mashed.com/144759/the-untold-truth-of-greggs/ (archived at https://perma.cc/FQ34-2HYD)

Isaacson, W (2012) [accessed 13 March 2021] The real leadership lessons of Steve Jobs, *Harvard Business Review* [Online] https://hbr.org/2012/04/the-real-leadership-lessons-of-steve-jobs (archived at https://perma.cc/GPZ3-2E52)

Muriuki, W (2020) [accessed 11 April 2020] Apple net worth 2020, *Wealthy Persons* [Online] https://www.wealthypersons.com/apple-net-worth-2020-2021/ (archived at https://perma.cc/3L78-6RPV)

NewsBreak (2020) [accessed 21 November 2020] If you invested $10,000 in Netflix's IPO, this is how much money you'd have now, *News Break* [Online] https://www.newsbreak.com/news/2041372378866/if-you-invested-10000-in-netflixs-ipo-this-is-how-much-money-youd-have-now (archived at https://perma.cc/H83W-4962)

Popkin, B (2020) [accessed 21 November 2020] Apple just became the first U.S. company worth $2 trillion, *NBC News* [Online] https://www.nbcnews.com/business/business-news/apple-now-worth-2-trillion-making-it-most-valuable-company-n1237287 (archived at https://perma.cc/T37V-884E)

Product Habits (2018) [accessed 21 November 2020] How Netflix became a $100 billion company in 20 years, *Product Habits* [Online] https://producthabits.com/how-netflix-became-a-100-billion-company-in-20-years/ (archived at https://perma.cc/5ECV-WBJV)

Rigby, C (2015) [accessed 11 April 2020] Burberry digital investment pays off in double-digit sales growth, *InternetRetailing* [Online] https://internetretailing.net/rxuk/rxuk/burberry-digital-investment-pays-off-in-double-digit-sales-growth (archived at https://perma.cc/D4AP-LZZK)

Roy, S (2019) [accessed 11 April 2020] How Burberry is leveraging technology to lead in the digital age, *Tech Wire Asia* [Online] https://techwireasia.com/2019/04/how-burberry-is-leveraging-technology-to-lead-in-the-digital-age/ (archived at https://perma.cc/TZM6-5N6F)

Schomer, A (2020) [accessed 15 January 2021] Netflix's subscriber gains slowed in Q3 after two consecutive quarters of gangbuster growth, *Business Insider* [Online] https://www.businessinsider.com/netflix-q3-subscriber-growth-slows-content-pipeline-remains-healthy-2020-10 (archived at https://perma.cc/NW7J-5S8D)

Yahoo (2020) [accessed 21 November 2020] Netflix share price, *Finance.yahoo.com* [Online] https://finance.yahoo.com/quote/NFLX (archived at https://perma.cc/N2YT-RM68)

05

Brands that have stood the test of time and why

> **WHAT YOU WILL LEARN IN THIS CHAPTER**
>
> - Heritage stands for something. There are many brands with history that are still successful today. Why is that?
> - Reinvention is the mother of necessity – brands that have reinvented themselves to stay relevant.
> - Top five traits of continually successful brands.

For any business to stand the test of time, it has to meet some basic requirements. First of all, there has to be an opportunity in the market for the brand. Any business hoping to be sustainable also has to have sufficient resources to drive growth. The business needs to have a good leadership team and of course the baton will need to be passed from one team to another successfully over many years. At the heart of any successful brand is understanding the needs of its core customers and how best it can help to meet customer needs and wants.

For a brand to be relevant over a long period of time, it has to be authentic. It must be perceived by consumers as being reliable, trustworthy, consistent, respectful and real. We become emotionally invested in brands that are authentic and we continue to buy from them even when there are cheaper or other alternatives around (Kakroo, 2016). In essence, we have bought into their brand values and have become part of their brand equity.

A great example of this is Harley-Davidson. Technologically, their motorcycles were surpassed by the Japanese brands such as Honda and Kawasaki, whose bikes had reverse gears, rear speakers, air conditioning and other technical advancements. However, what they didn't have was the emotional connection that Harley-Davidson had with its fans.

The customer experience with Harley-Davidson emanated from the top. The leadership team actively demonstrated their passion for their customers by forming the Harley Owners Group (HOG). The leaders were always up front supporting customers. Then outings were always sponsored by the Harley-Davidson dealerships, bringing together the employees, dealers and customers (Mehlape, 2019).

Brands that are successful over a sustained period of time are more innovative. They are always looking to improve the customer experience and often reinvent themselves to maintain their relevance. They also out-resource the competition by investing in product and service development and evolving at a quicker pace.

The authenticity of a brand always ensures that employees stand behind it. The brand is something they can be proud of. Being proud to work for a brand also means you work harder, are more committed and also emotionally invested in the business.

Harley-Davidson is a brand with a rich heritage. Another is Selfridges. They both have significant heritage which is known worldwide. They are iconic brands within their own sectors.

Heritage counts – brands with history and why they're still successful today

CASE STUDY
Selfridges

Despite the retail climate, in which traditional retailers (and particularly department stores) are struggling to survive, Selfridges remains a success story. (By 2018, for instance, there were 25 per cent fewer department stores in England than a decade previously (Lendy, 2018).)

Selfridges has made significant investment in both their physical stores and digital platforms to improve the customer experience. Their stores are always being evolved. They never stand still. As a brand, Selfridges has come to define the term 'experiential retail'. By continuing to invest in their stores and creating great in-store experiences and retail theatre, they have managed to maintain the relevance of the brick-and-mortar stores.

Rather than opening multiple stores, they are limited to four physical locations and are therefore able to invest in improving the store experience. Selfridges stores are not just about shopping – the Oxford Street store offers restaurants, bars, a flower market and cinema, pop-up ice rinks, exclusive products and a huge accessories hall.

The continual drive to differentiate and to deliver great retail experience can be evidenced by this quote from Selfridge's Group MD Anne Pitcher: 'We will strive to remain at the forefront of experiences as we disrupt and reimagine the world of retail, where sustainability and creativity are at its heart' (Rigby, 2019).

They continually look to remove barriers for customers. A good example is when they invested in improving the delivery experience with the Selfridges Plus subscription – £10 annual fee for free next day delivery. This is a key driver for customer retention. Clearly, they recognized the success that Amazon had with its Prime membership. Nonetheless, they were the first big UK retailer to offer a similar delivery proposition.

ITV's lauded drama *Mr Selfridge* depicted the early years of the business, from 1908 to 1928. What it did was highlight the attention to detail Harry Selfridge had and his understanding of what retail theatre was all about. Yes, he knew they had to have the finest products, but he recognized the importance of great customer service, visual merchandising and customer experience.

It is clear to this day that the current owners of Selfridges understand the importance of this as they continue to ensure that Selfridges has the best brands and products, highly effective customer service, retail theatre and they continually evolve the store and the digital proposition. With profits up year on year and significant engagement on social media (over 1 million fans on Instagram), it is clear that their customer-centric strategy pays off, year after year.

SOURCE Rigby (2019) and Halstead (2020)

You may not automatically think of banking as a sector that has brands that understand the importance of customer-centricity. You'd also be forgiven for thinking that banks have enjoyed customer loyalty by default rather than by design – particularly as, historically, and until recent times, it has been extremely difficult to change your bank.

When you think of successful banks, you tend to think of the household name brands such as HSBC, Lloyds and Barclays. Or, if you're in the US, then Morgan Stanley, JP Morgan, and Bank of America. But there are small, regional, sometimes local banks that have stood the test of time when other big names such as Lehman Brothers have not. One such successful, local bank is Citizen's Bank.

CASE STUDY
Citizen's Bank – a bank for the people

Not all successful banks are the national players. Nor is it all about the disruptors.

With assets of over $160 billion and sales of over $6 billion, Citizen's Bank is a regional player based out of Providence, Rhode Island, with branches across eastern states in the US. The bank was established in 1828 under the brand 'the High Street Bank', changing its name to Citizens Savings Bank in 1871.

Customer experience and customer-centricity is at the very heart of their thinking every day. Customer journey mapping, a discipline often referred to in relation to the online customer experience, is a practice they undertake regularly. Their team adopt different customer personas in order to determine where the barriers and sticking points might be along the customer's journey and to think through how they might streamline. In essence, they try to determine the customer's entire experience with Citizen's Bank, from the very first point of contact right the way through to problem resolution.

They have over 170,000 fans on Facebook – not bad for a regional bank! They were ranked third in the overall list of Temkin customer experience ratings across all categories and numbers in banking.

SOURCE CXFS (2019) and Temkin (2018)

Another sector that has seen many brands come and go and very few stand the test of time is the automotive sector. There are few car brands that have managed to consistently be an aspirational choice for consumers the way BMW has for nearly a century.

CASE STUDY
BMW

Founded in Germany in 1916, BMW was a manufacturer of aircraft engines and subsequently became an automobile manufacturer in 1928. Fast forward to the 2020s and they're undoubtedly now a world-class brand manufacturing luxury cars and motorcycles. They have become one of the world's most recognized brands, with a reputation for great craftsmanship, reliability and quality.

While we've all talked about personalization for decades, BMW were the first car brand to create a configurator so that customers could choose modifications and accessories in advance of buying their car.

Their success is ultimately down to their customer, or in this case driver, focus. Their focus on the driver manifests in them producing consistently designed aspirational vehicles, with petrol caps and badges, switches and dials in the same place on every vehicle. The BMW 'feel' is a deliberate objective, so whichever model you drive you get a sophisticated but accessible engineering quality.

They've been around for more than 100 years, and to maintain their relevance they are now focusing on mobility, connectivity and personal experiences. They have also demonstrated their innovation and customer focus with the move into electric vehicles with their stunning i8 and i3 models.

With over 20 million fans on Facebook, over 26 million on Instagram and a market capitalization of over €57 billion, it is obvious that their strategy and focus on the customer continues to pay off.

SOURCE Chamat (2016) and Duncan (2016)

While BMW has managed to pretty consistently maintain its position as a leading automotive brand throughout its history, you might be surprised to know that has not always been the case with Rolls-Royce.

CASE STUDY
Rolls-Royce

While Rolls-Royce has enjoyed iconic status as a brand for much of its 117-year existence, it has not always been a smooth ride. Under the ownership of BMW, the brand has gone from strength to strength. Their cars are a thing of beauty inside and out and have a performance to match.

The Rolls-Royce Phantom has been one of their top-selling models, along with the Wraith, Cullinan and Dawn models. Rolls-Royce has seen a significant increase in the demand for more personalized and customized cars. Their vehicles are customized at their bespoke department at Goodwood in the UK.

Rolls-Royce has also done a great job of reinventing its range with the addition of its Black Badge cars, aimed at making them more interesting and relevant to a younger affluent consumer. The cars in this range have more power and, instead of chrome, have dark metal detailing. Even the iconic Spirit of Ecstasy is high-gloss black on this range of vehicles.

In 2018, they sold 4,107 cars, making it their most successful year ever at that point. Clearly, their sales have been affected by Covid-19, but the brand's customer-centric focus will see it continue to go from strength to strength for many years to come. Despite their ups and downs over the years, Rolls-Royce is most definitely a brand that has stood the test of time.

SOURCE Dobie (2016) and Banks (2019)

In contrast to the sectors outlined above, fashion has its own unique challenges – not least because, by definition, a brand is either fashionable or it isn't. Therefore, fashion brands are among the hardest to maintain success with over a prolonged period of time, as both their designs and the brands themselves go in and out of fashion periodically.

CASE STUDY
Gucci

It's not that long ago, around the mid-2010s, when Gucci was losing its sparkle.

Fast-forward to 2019. Of Gucci's $8 billion in sales, 62 per cent came from Millennials. Add to this the fact that Gucci's fastest growing demographic is 24 years old or younger, they have demonstrated probably better than any other high-end brand how to successfully connect with younger, fashion-hungry consumers.

One reason for their success is that they invested heavily in digital. In 2016 and 2017 they were described as the 'best performing digital fashion brand' by L2 Research. They have transitioned a legacy business into one where digital is the core driver. Their digital-first approach has seen them bring ecommerce, social media, digital marketing and mobile apps together to deliver the digitally led experience this younger consumer demands. It has led to a stellar commercial performance.

Their focus on driving engagement with younger consumers can also be evidenced by their investment in ArtLab, which is a factory blending artistic experimentation with state-of-the-art production. This has also given Gucci far greater agility and enabled them to go from concept to product much faster than their competitors.

Gucci achieves what most brands struggle to do. They manage to stay true to their heritage while making their storytelling relevant to today's consumer. The creative director, Alessandro Michele, moved the brand forward from the overt sexiness and extravagant branding of the Tom Ford era to a more modern androgynous, casual and sensuous feel. Michele has maintained the core elements of Gucci's heritage. He resurrected the GG logo from the company archives and used it to embellish accessories, and even invited a graffiti artist (Trevor Andrew) to reinvent the logo for one of the brand's collections but with a bold new point of view that resonates with today's luxury consumers.

You may have noticed how popular belts with the GG logo are. They've almost become the must-have accessory to complete your outfit.

Their distinctive branding is consistently expressed across advertising, product and in store, creating a cohesive brand message that particularly resonates with Chinese customers. Digital IQ rates Gucci as the fourth most popular luxury brand in China. Thirty-eight per cent of Gucci's revenues come from the Asia-Pacific territory and their sales have been growing in double digits year-on-year. With 19 million fans on Facebook, over 40 million on Instagram and a market capitalization of over $10 billion, Gucci truly belongs in an all-too-small club of brands that stand the test of time.

SOURCE Danziger (2017), Statista (2020) and Langer (2019)

You might not think of sports events as being iconic brands that have stood the test of time. However, they are among the most successful. Just like any other brand, the more successful ones continually look to improve their product and the customer experience in order to maintain their success.

CASE STUDY
Wimbledon

For those of you lucky enough to attend, you probably realize that the Wimbledon experience is almost the same as it was when the tournament was founded in 1877. It is set apart from other tennis tournaments by its reliance on its heritage and tradition – the grass courts, strawberries and the uniforms. It has a unique DNA, much as the Masters or Open Championship have in golf.

Despite only running for two weeks a year, it has the second highest brand awareness of a sporting event in the world (number one is the Super Bowl). However, the Super Bowl is still largely a US-centred event, whereby Wimbledon has true global coverage and interest. Wimbledon's brand is based on tradition and heritage, but they are leveraging digital to transform their relationship with tennis fans. They have huge engagement online, because they have adapted to the new media landscape that requires short, mobile-optimized content. The traditional broadcast model of extended periods of tennis coverage has been replaced by a stream of short content clips that are related to the brand but attention-grabbing. This content appeals to tennis fans, but also to people who are interested in Wimbledon as an event. In 2019, they had 33 million pre-event views of video and 380 million championship video views.

They use AI (IBM Watson) to analyse player emotion, movement and crowd noise to capture the most engaging moments to include in highlights and use a 'competitive margin' metric to identify the matches that will be closest fought and are likely to be the most dramatic. This content can be served almost immediately. Wimbledon is successfully retaining the heritage aspects of the tournament but using technology to transform the way fans engage with the brand.

With turnover in excess of £260 million and profits north of £40 million, Wimbledon knows how to create a winning formula, and deliver it consistently year after year.

SOURCE Newsroom (2018), Wimbledon (2020), and Arnold (2018)

Reinvention is the mother of necessity – brands that have reinvented themselves to stay relevant

One thing that pretty much all successful brands do time and again is reinvent themselves. In order to stay ahead of the competition and maintain relevance to customers, you need to reinvent.

CASE STUDY
Emirates

One of the world's leading airlines – in actual fact, they were voted number five in the world's best airlines in 2019 (Skytrax, 2019) – Emirates has continually worked to reinvent itself. They have been operating since 1985, but have over time turned themselves into an iconic brand.

Along with Virgin Atlantic, they were one of the first major airlines to offer a chauffeur-driven limousine to first class and business class customer transfers to and from both the departure and arrival airports for both outbound and inbound journeys. Their airport lounges are among the best in the industry and the inflight experience is top notch – from your own mini bar in business class to a suite with a door in first class. You can even take a shower at 40,000 feet in their A380.

Their significant and very tangible focus on customer service is in addition to an eye-watering investment in new aircraft. They have recently invested $9 billion on 30 Boeing 787 jets (Reuters, 2019). It is this constant, customer-focused innovation and product development that keeps them at the top of the industry.

They have also invested heavily into sports marketing by sponsoring Arsenal's football stadium and renaming it as the Emirates and with their shirt sponsorship of the biggest football team in the world, Real Madrid. Emirates recognizes the value of close association with iconic sports brands.

SOURCE McNutt (2019) and Alkhaisi (2019)

Ultimately, most of Emirates' success comes down to a great customer experience, one that they continually evolve. Another such brand that has very successfully reinvented itself in the electricals sector is LG.

CASE STUDY
'Life's Good'

LG has become a household name brand and yet very few consumers probably know what the LG letters stand for. They were originally called the Lucky Goldstar Group, but were rebranded to LG in 1995. The aim was to aid their expansion into Western markets and to make them more competitive. Fast-forward to today and the brand LG is associated with the company's tagline; 'Life's Good'.

With global sales in excess of $53 billion, the company is valued at over $28 billion – quite an achievement for what was once a very localized East Asian brand. It's a great example of one whose consumer focus and constant reinvention has enabled it to build a global brand. They have consistently and relentlessly built a reputation for product innovation, reliability and quality. In doing so, they have elevated the brand and it is viewed by consumers the world over as a high-quality brand.

SOURCE lgnewsroom (2020)

Top five traits of continually successful brands

It is rare for a brand to be commercially successful for a prolonged period and not be obsessed with its customers and with its people in the organization, as one doesn't work without the other.

FIGURE 5.1 The top five traits of successful brands

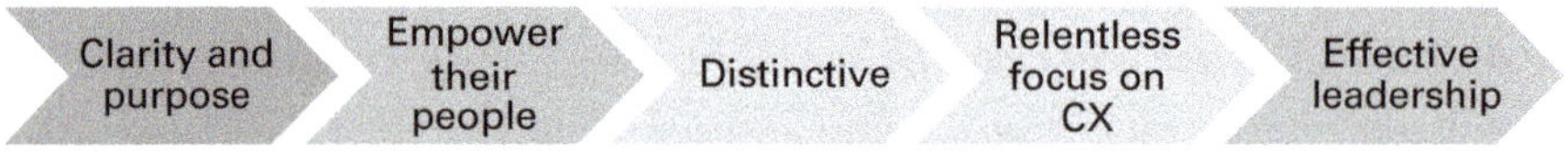

Clarity and purpose → Empower their people → Distinctive → Relentless focus on CX → Effective leadership

1 Continually successful brands have clarity and purpose. Consumers know and like what they stand for.
2 They have the confidence to empower all of their people and not let hierarchy get in the way of doing the right thing for their customers.
3 They are distinctive within their own category. However, they continually look to reinvent themselves in order to maintain their relevance.
4 They are relentless in delivering a great and consistent customer experience.
5 They have highly effective leaders who make it their job to facilitate others to do their job to the best of their ability.

Conclusion

It is not an accident that a business is successful year after year or even over many decades. Of course, every brand has peaks and troughs. The path is never smooth. But the success of a business in the long term is often determined by how it reacts to a crisis. All of the brands in this chapter have had to come through extremely difficult periods in their history.

Many have had to reinvent themselves in order to become relevant again. Despite its iconic heritage, from design and performance perspectives, Rolls-Royce is a brand that had to do just that. But it took new ownership from BMW to inject the reinvention, innovation and customer experience that was required to make the brand truly relevant again.

Selfridges would never have made it through its more than 11 decades of history had the culture of innovation, retail theatre, differentiated products and first-class customer experience not been instilled in it by Harry Selfridge over a century ago.

KEY TAKEAWAYS FROM CHAPTER 5

1   Every brand that has stood the test of time truly understands the wants and needs of its customers. They also understood what the problems were in their sector and how they could evolve their products and customer experience to help customers overcome barriers to engagement. The prime example is how they've all leveraged digital to great effect – not only in helping them to operate more efficiently but moreover by empowering customers to choose how they want to engage with the brand.

2   Reinvention is the mother of necessity. All brands that are successful over a prolonged period of time have reinvented themselves along the way. Sometimes it's just been a small evolution. While other times they've had to pivot and become a different proposition entirely. Sometimes they've done it through necessity, other times simply by recognizing the need to offer customers something new. A great example of a brand that has continually reinvented itself is Dyson. Once renowned for having revolutionized the vacuum cleaner market, we now think of them as also being the leaders in fans, hand-dryers, humidifiers and hair dryers (Burton, 2011).

3   Products and services have to be desirable. They also have to live up to the promise made to customers. All truly successful brands have had a relentless focus on product efficacy as well as having a very strong service proposition at the heart of their over-arching customer value proposition – both of which feed through directly to the brand values. Service-led brands tend to have the most customer-centric cultures. Take Dyson, as outlined above: they have fantastic products and a relentless focus not only on product development but on ensuring that their products work and stand the test of time. They also have a very strong service ethos. When a product stops working, their engineers will often come to your house to fix it. And if they can't fix it, they'll replace it (Watkin, 2020). As you can immediately tell, this is a very different and far more customer-centric approach and experience than you'd have with 99 per cent of other brands, whereby you'd have to send the product back to the brand and then find yourself in a discussion, possibly even an argument, over why they won't replace it or repair it. Dyson's sales are in the region of £5–6 billion and they make north of £750 million profit every year. Added to that, James Dyson is one of the world's richest people (Metcalf and Stupples, 2019).

4   Sustainably successful businesses are constantly investing in product and service development and looking to improve how they do what they do.

Although I haven't called them out in this chapter, due to their relatively young age, there can be few better examples of this than Amazon. Every day, across every part of their business and in every project, they are looking at how they can raise the bar for customers and deliver a better experience. I don't think there is another brand that does a better job of driving customer lifetime value than Amazon. Prime is the best example of how they recognized the value of driving frequency of purchase and its impact upon customer lifetime value (Malachard, 2020).

5 Businesses that have stood the test of time over many years have clear brand propositions that resonate with customers. But even the best brands recognize that their brand values have to evolve. Not only did Rolls-Royce have to evolve their product in order to be relevant, but they had to evolve the brand. It was stuck in a bygone era, and while it was still associated with luxury, it didn't talk to performance and innovation. This is what BMW brought to the brand. It dragged it out of the history books and turned it from a brand most of us thought fondly of, but would never consider as aspirational, to once again being one of the most iconic and desirable brands in the world.

References

Alkhaisi, Z (2019) [accessed 21 November 2020] Emirates hands Arsenal $280 million in record sponsorship deal, *CNNMoney* [Online] https://money.cnn.com/2018/02/19/news/companies/emirates-arsenal-record-sponsorship-deal/index.html (archived at https://perma.cc/5663-9988)

Arnold, D (2018) [accessed 27 November 2020] Wimbledon: creating the ultimate digital experience, *London Business School* [Online] https://www.london.edu/think/wimbledon-creating-the-ultimate-digital-experience (archived at https://perma.cc/Z2HE-JCC9)

Banks, N (2019) [accessed 21 July 2020] Luxury Marque Rolls-Royce reveals record sales in its 115-year history, *Forbes* [Online] https://www.forbes.com/sites/nargessbanks/2019/01/10/rolls-royce-2018-sales/#456cf56727ac (archived at https://perma.cc/JL8Q-XRHX)

Burton, C (2011) [accessed 21 November 2020] The seventh disruption: how James Dyson reinvented the personal heater, *Wired UK* [Online] https://www.wired.co.uk/article/the-seventh-disruption-james-dyson (archived at https://perma.cc/5XXR-9R9Z)

Chamat, R (2016) [accessed 21 July 2020] The secrets to BMW's marketing success, *8ways.ch* [Online] https://www.8ways.ch/en/digital-news/secrets-bmws-marketing-success (archived at https://perma.cc/MQ9K-ZHBU)

CXFS 2020 (2019) [accessed 12 April 2020] Here's how Citizen's Bank is mapping a journey to great customer experiences, *CXFS* [Online] https://cxfinance.wbresearch.com/blog/citizens-bank-great-customer-experience-journey-strategy (archived at https://perma.cc/AMP8-MJ5Q)

Danziger, P (2017) [accessed 21 July 2020] Gucci's cracked the luxury code with millennials, thanks to its dream team of Bizzarri and Michele, *Forbes* [Online] https://www.forbes.com/sites/pamdanziger/2017/11/16/guccis-cracked-the-luxury-code-with-millennials-thanks-to-its-dream-team-of-bizzarri-and-michele/#39f1d0321523 (archived at https://perma.cc/BTJ3-MTF3)

Dobie, S (2016) [accessed 21 July 2020] Rolls-Royce launches more powerful Black Badge models, *Top Gear* [Online] https://www.topgear.com/car-news/british/rolls-royce-launches-more-powerful-black-badge-models (archived at https://perma.cc/75F7-WPQ7)

Duncan, A (2016) [accessed 21 July 2020] As BMW turns 100, what does the next century hold for the ultimate driving machine?, *The Drum* [Online] https://www.thedrum.com/news/2016/03/24/bmw-turns-100-what-does-next-century-hold-ultimate-driving-machine (archived at https://perma.cc/4THE-RC2W)

Halstead, M (2020) [accessed 21 July 2020] Selfridges: a success story, *Red Flag Alert* [Online] https://www.redflagalert.com/articles/risk/selfridges-a-success-story (archived at https://perma.cc/U93H-2JQW)

Kakroo, U (2016) [accessed 21 November 2020] Which emotions do authentic brand stories evoke?, *Brandanew.co* [Online] http://www.brandanew.co/emotions-authentic-brand-stories-evoke/ (archived at https://perma.cc/277V-3H5X)

Langer, D (2019) [accessed 21 July 2020] Learning from Gucci's wild success with millennials and Gen Z, *Jing Daily* [Online] https://jingdaily.com/gucci-success-millennials-gen-z/ (archived at https://perma.cc/9TE6-TAF7)

Lendy (2018) [accessed 21 July 2020] Lendy – the crowdfunding marketplace for loans secured on UK property, *Lendy.co.uk* [Online] https://lendy.co.uk/media/number-of-department-stores-falls-25-in-less-than-a-decade (archived at https://perma.cc/4D3F-38FS)

lgnewsroom (2020) [accessed 21 November 2020] LG announces 2019 financial results, *Lgnewsroom.com* [Online] http://www.lgnewsroom.com/2020/01/lg-announces-2019-financial-results/ (archived at https://perma.cc/65UT-FVUV)

Malachard, V (2020) [accessed 21 November 2020] Why winning companies (Amazon, IKEA,…) focus on retention, *BossData* [Online] https://bossdata.be/resources/why-winning-companies-focus-on-retention/ (archived at https://perma.cc/Q459-UX5G)

McNutt, E (2019) [accessed 21 November 2020] Virgin Atlantic unveils swanky new upper-class suite, *The Points Guy UK* [Online] https://thepointsguy.co.uk/news/virgin-atlantic-upper-class-suite/ (archived at https://perma.cc/H838-5FMP)

Mehlape, P (2019) [accessed 21 July 2020] Why do some brands stand the test of time while others fade away?, *Brandsandbranding.co.za* [Online] https://www.brandsandbranding.co.za/why-do-some-brands-stand-the-test-of-time-while-others-fade-away/ (archived at https://perma.cc/7J6K-4ZV6)

Metcalf, T and Stupples, B (2019) [accessed 21 November 2020] Are you a robot?, *Bloomberg.com* [Online] https://www.bloomberg.com/news/articles/2019-01-22/dyson-tops-list-of-richest-brits-on-vacuum-maker-s-record-profit (archived at https://perma.cc/8EUR-ZR35)

Newsroom (2018) [accessed 21 July 2020] Innovation vs heritage: can your brand speak to both?, *Marcommnews.com* [Online] https://marcommnews.com/innovation-vs-heritage-can-your-brand-speak-to-both/ (archived at https://perma.cc/ACQ2-D3CG)

Reuters (2019) [accessed 27 November 2020] Emirates orders 30 Boeing 787, reduces 777X order to 126 jets, *Reuters* [Online] https://es.reuters.com/article/idCND5N1Y301O (archived at https://perma.cc/E9Y2-2VMA)

Rigby, C (2019) [accessed 21 July 2020] How Selfridges is reimagining the department store as retail changes, *InternetRetailing* [Online] https://internetretailing.net/location/location/how-selfridges-is-reimagining-the-department-store-as-retail-changes-20349 (archived at https://perma.cc/6AQE-BL5Z)

Skytrax (2019) [accessed 21 July 2020] The world's top 10 airlines of 2019, *Skytrax* [Online] https://www.worldairlineawards.com/worlds-top-10-airlines-2019/ (archived at https://perma.cc/77TJ-BM89)

Statista (2020) [accessed 21 November 2020] Gucci: revenue share by region worldwide 2019, *Statista* [Online] https://www.statista.com/statistics/267733/global-revenue-share-of-gucci-by-region (archived at https://perma.cc/UVY7-NXTY)

Temkin, B (2018) [accessed 11 April 2020] Wegmans, H-E-B, Citizens, Credit Unions, Publix, and Subway receive top customer experience scores across 318 U.S. companies, *Qualtrics* [Online] https://www.qualtrics.com/docs/xmi/XMI_TemkinExperienceRatings-2018.pdf (archived at https://perma.cc/MPQ4-6A66)

Watkin, J (2020) The Real Reason You Purchase A Dyson Vacuum Cleaner | Customerthink, Customerthink.com [Online] https://customerthink.com/the-real-reason-you-purchase-a-dyson-vacuum-cleaner/ (archived at https://perma.cc/5DEY-3FFX) [accessed 21 November 2020]

Wimbledon (2020) [accessed 27 November 2020] Wimbledon.com [Online] https://www.wimbledon.com/en_GB/atoz/faq_and_facts_and_figures.html (archived at https://perma.cc/5G48-6WAR)

06

Customer-centricity – it all adds up

> **WHAT YOU WILL LEARN IN THIS CHAPTER**
>
> - Commercially successful businesses over a sustained period of time are customer-centric. That is the common denominator.
> - The shift from selling stuff to delivering services presents great opportunities to extend customer lifetime value.
> - How different aspects of customer experience directly affect profit and loss.

The direct correlation between how customers view and perceive a consumer-facing brand and their commercial performance

I feel strongly that too many brands still view customer service, customer experience and all things customer-centric as something they're forced into doing, as opposed to it being the right thing to do. That is clearly evidenced by the fact that the vast majority of businesses see it as a cost and not a benefit.

I have been on the advisory board of a brand that thought that putting in a contact centre would just add a layer of cost to the business. They were trying to use technology to answer all customer service issues. There's also a clue in the word 'issues' as to the shortfall of this approach. This business, like so many others, only sees problems when customers contact the customer service team. I'm the polar opposite. I see opportunities – opportunities to sort out customer problems and ensure they buy from us again, opportunities to cross-sell, up-sell or just sell more to the customer, opportunities to delight the customer and have them tell their friends, family and social media networks how good we are. The opportunity this more positive approach offers compared with the traditional process of just trying to make 'awkward customers go away' is incomparable.

If you only look at the cost of serving customers, that's how you're likely to view it. You'll look to remove costs, remove headcount and take away jobs and processes where staff serve customers, and all of that will ultimately lead to greater levels of customer dissatisfaction, poorer levels of service, an increase in customer churn, an increase in negative sentiment and amplification of negativity towards your brand on social media and of course a reduction in sales and profitability.

Whereas if you measure customer lifetime value (CLV), net promoter score (NPS), word of mouth, customer satisfaction (CSAT), sentiment analysis and so on, you would take a very different approach. Your perspective would be all about delivering great service and experience in the recognition that this would give you the best opportunity to convince customers to come back and to maximize their lifetime value to your business.

It would be central to everything you do and all the big decisions you make for your brand.

FIGURE 6.1 Viewing customer service as a cost as opposed to a benefit

Cost	Benefit
Remove ability for customers to contact you and/or make it difficult	Enable customers to contact 24/7 via various channels
Front-line staff pass customer issues up the chain of command	Front-line staff are empowered to make decisions
KPIs measured are about quantity and not about customer satisfaction	KPIs measured are about quality/issue resolution
Focus on the cost to serve	Focus on customer lifetime value

CASE STUDY
Tesla – you'd be mad to bet against them

Does anyone really believe that it is by chance that Tesla has become the most valuable car brand in the world? It used to be Ford for many years. Why are Ford not the most valuable car company in the world any longer? It is partly because their market has been disrupted. Also, like many long-established previous market leaders, they have been slow to innovate and slow to react to the changes in consumer needs and behaviour.

Tesla has rewritten the rulebook and completely disrupted the traditional car industry model – from disintermediating and removing the need for a middleman and selling direct to the consumer to opening showrooms where customers actually spend time, eg shopping centres, as opposed to big sheds five miles outside of town!

When it comes to servicing and repairs, they're also streets ahead of the industry. None of this, 'you bring your car to us and we'll fix it for you.' They do the opposite and come to your house to fix any issues with the car.

In the 2019 list compiled by Consumer Reports of the automotive brands that were the most popular, Tesla's customers were more satisfied than any other car brand – and for the third year running. Owner satisfaction is rated out of 100, with Tesla scoring 89. The consumer scores their satisfaction on various factors, including price, the overall driving experience as well as comfort, sound system/audio and styling.

Like most successful brands, when your customers are happy, they often amplify their delight on social media channels. It's what we call 'word of mouth'. Or in this day and age, you might think of it as 'word of web'. From 5 million followers on Twitter to 7.2 million followers on Instagram, the brand has huge engagement with consumers. It's fair to say that they don't have customers; they have fans.

Is it therefore any wonder that they're the most valuable car company in the world? Tesla are now valued in the hundreds of $billions and worth many times more than Ford and General Motors put together! I wouldn't be in the least bit surprised if Tesla were to become the most valuable consumer brand in the world.

SOURCE Matousek (2019) and Kaemingk (2019)

It doesn't matter what category you operate in or where you are in the world, brands that are truly customer-centric have the best financial performance over a sustained period of time – as is the case with Etsy.

CASE STUDY
Etsy

Etsy tapped into all that's good about the internet – the opportunity to create a global community around a shared passion or hobby of art and craft designs that was previously not well catered for, either offline or online. They carved out a niche for themselves. By only offering handcrafted and vintage goods, they were able to firmly position as the number-one place to go for artist-made products. This is a defendable position, particularly when you consider the Amazon model. While you can buy anything from Amazon, you wouldn't go to them as your first choice if you were serious about crafting.

But there's another aspect to the Etsy model that differentiates it. Etsy creates value for both buyers and sellers. For the former, Etsy offers the largest variety of handmade goods available that can be delivered anywhere around the world. As for sellers, Etsy provides the opportunity for artists to make a living. They can build their personal brand and sell their goods way beyond their local area.

Etsy has created a commercial model around the buyer and seller interactions, charging a listing fee to sellers while also selling advertising and SEO services to help sellers reach more customers. As a result of tapping into this niche community-led sector, Etsy grew largely through word-of-mouth to become a very successful global brand in the arts and crafts sector.

It's a hugely popular brand and was recently listed as number one on Brandwatch's list of brands with the best customer experience (Brandwatch, 2020). Etsy has become the most trusted, respected and engaging platform for anyone in the arts and crafts sector and, as it increases the range and category profile, it further increases customer lifetime value.

In terms of proof points, Etsy is a listed business whose share price has grown by nearly 500 per cent since it listed. Its market capitalization is over $16 billion (Nasdaq, 2020), with approximately 60 per cent of traffic being direct, demonstrating a large, loyal customer base (Zilvera, 2018).

CASE STUDY
Wagamama

There are few stars in the casual dining sector, which has been in decline for quite some time, even well before the Covid-19 pandemic. With Byron Burger, Jamie's Italian, Prezzo, Carluccio's, GBK and Strada either forced to restructure and close restaurants or go into administration, Wagamama is an exception.

Wagamama has continued to grow, opening seven new restaurants in 2018 and more in 2019. CEO Emma Woods has commented on the fact that great businesses, and therefore the Wagamama business, are built by dedicated colleagues, a commitment to always be on the side of their customers and a clear sense of purpose.

With consumers increasingly wanting to eat at home, Wagamama has expanded into Deliveroo, delivery-only kitchens, click and collect, and food-to-go (meal kits). They have a test kitchen in Soho (the 'noodle lab') to try new menu ideas on customers before launching them and have responded to changes in customer preferences with an extensive vegan menu.

Market Force Information surveyed customer experience in the UK's casual dining restaurants in early 2019 and found Wagamama led the way across many key metrics. They are top in six out of ten categories and top in two of the top three main drivers for consumers: food quality and friendly service. Others include the overall highest customer satisfaction in addition to Wagamama having the biggest propensity to gain recommendations from diners and most loyal customers (Marketforce, 2019). Wagamama focus on the customer experience, with good food, value for money, well-trained staff, efficient service and a varied menu, which helps to create a loyal customer base.

The company was acquired for £559 million in 2018. With its relentless focus on customers, location, quality, menu innovation and its people, it can only be a matter of time before Wagamama becomes a £1 billion business. They have nearly 600,000 fans on Facebook. With that level of engagement, there's only one way the success of this business will go – and that is up.

SOURCE Coghlan (2018) and Lake (2019)

Measuring the impact of great customer service and experience

Over the past decade, we have moved from the goods era to the services era (Table 6.1).

The disruptive brands such as Ocado have understood better than the established players how to democratize the experience for consumers, either by removing middlemen or by leveraging technology to empower staff and customers alike. Think also Uber, Just Eat, Airbnb, Rockar (which are providing the tech to enable car brands to go direct to the consumer). They see themselves as service providers much more so than a brand that sells stuff.

TABLE 6.1 The shift from the goods era to the service era

The goods era	The service era
We sold stuff	We look to deliver experiences
The focus is on competitors	The focus is on the customer
Management had to be certain	Being entrepreneurial, we need to be confident
We outsourced a lot of what we did	We engage employees
Hierarchical structures	Collaborative structures
Big, loud brands	Authentic brands
Incremental improvement	Game-changing innovation

Brands that move from just selling products to delivering services adopt a different mindset that permeates the entire organization. The culture is one of serve rather than sell.

Brands that do this also tend to have a strong purpose, and while they may not be perfect, they are often further evolved on tackling key customer-facing issues such as diversity and social responsibility.

They have a can-do mindset in the business. They have empowered their people to get stuff done and to always go the extra mile when it comes to customer service and customer experience. The shoe repairer and key cutting business Timpson empower their team on the front line to make customer decisions up to £500 without having to go up the chain of command to management (PPN, 2020).

Sometimes going the extra mile involves surprising and delighting customers. This is a gesture-based marketing approach that goes a long way with customers, but that not nearly enough brands adopt. My own personal highlight of this is when I procured Lab Series skin cream for the first time. They sent me a very luxurious bathrobe/dressing gown. Being Scottish and mildly cynical (I hear you), I thought I bought it by accident! After a short time, I realized it was a gift with my purchase, but not one that was promoted, hence it being a random act of kindness. Of course, it's not too random! It's considered. But I wasn't expecting it and therefore it meant more to receive it. I subsequently went on to be a loyal customer for the best part of a decade until I realized that I had received no personalized communication nor any other random acts of kindness since! I then decided to switch to another brand.

During the early days of the pandemic, I bought some Levi's online. When my order arrived, they had included a Levi's designed face mask. I loved this – such a simple and cost-effective gesture. But the nature of it really resonated with me. It was a very kind and timely gift.

CASE STUDY
Going the extra mile

There's a great story of a customer who was flying on JetBlue in the US when he tweeted that he was unable to get his favourite Starbucks coffee before the flight because he was flying out of Logan Airport's smaller terminal in Boston. Guess what happened next? Within a few seconds of receiving his tweet the JetBlue and airport customer service teams conspired to deliver a Starbucks mocha to the customer's seat on his flight! Suffice to say, said customer, Mr Brown, amplified his delight on Twitter. And so he should, as well. This is such a great example of a customer-focused team doing something that doesn't appear anywhere in their job description, but that has such a big impact. And the positive word of mouth this created was well worth the effort (Brown, 2013). Often, it's the small things that have the biggest impact on customers.

The cause and effect of different aspects of customer experience on profit and loss

The points below give you an idea of the potential positive impact of great customer experience and service – and the correlation of this on commercial performance:

1 **Cause:** In person: Having enough staff to serve

 Effect:
 - customers buy rather than abandoning their purchase;
 - they return more frequently.

 P&L and KPI impact:
 - increase in sales and profitability;
 - increase in customer satisfaction;
 - increase in lifetime value.

2 **Cause:** In person: Efficient, helpful and friendly staff in the physical environment

 Effect:
 - customers buy rather than abandoning their purchase;
 - they return more frequently;
 - social media amplification.

P&L and KPI impact:
- increase in sales and profitability;
- increase in average order values;
- increase in customer satisfaction;
- increase in customer lifetime value;
- increase in social media engagement.

3 **Cause:** An inclusive environment: An environment that caters effectively for all customers, including those with disabilities (visible and hidden)

Effect:
- customers buy rather than abandoning their planned purchase;
- social media amplification.

P&L and KPI impact:
- increase in sales and profitability;
- increase in customer satisfaction;
- increase in social media engagement.

4 **Cause:** Online: A website that delivers the expected experience with minimal barriers – whether you're buying something or just looking for information

Effect:
- customers buy rather than abandoning their planned purchase;
- they return more frequently.

P&L and KPI impact:
- increased conversion rates across all channels;
- increased average order values;
- increased sales and profitability;
- increase in customer satisfaction.

5 **Cause:** Self-service: Online or in-store, with technology that is usable

Effect:
- easier for task-rich, time-poor customers to purchase.

P&L and KPI impact:
- increase in sales;
- increase in customer satisfaction.

6 **Cause:** Personalization: Communication that reflects your wants, needs and customer history

   Effect:

   - customers buy more frequently.

   P&L and KPI impact:

   - improved email response levels;
   - increase in customer lifetime value.

7 **Cause:** Ways to contact: The ability to contact the brand as you desire – by phone, email, live chat; the brand responds to any communication within a timely fashion, eg an hour or two

   Effect:

   - social media amplification;
   - word of mouth;
   - customers buy more.

   P&L and KPI impact:

   - reduction in churn, increase in retention;
   - improvement in issue resolution;
   - customer satisfaction/NPS;
   - increase in social media engagement.

8 **Cause:** Availability: Stock or service availability is promoted consistently across all channels and touchpoints

   Effect:

   - customers buy rather than abandoning their planned purchase;
   - they return more frequently.

   P&L and KPI impact:

   - increase in sales and profitability;
   - increase in average order values;
   - increase in customer satisfaction;
   - increase in customer lifetime value.

9 **Cause:** Order fulfilment: Delivery and returns propositions are customer-centric – same day, next day, specified time and day, click and collect, free returns

Effect:
- customers buy rather than abandoning their planned purchase;
- they return more frequently.

P&L and KPI impact:
- increase in sales and profitability;
- increase in average order values;
- increase in customer satisfaction;
- increase in customer lifetime value.

10 **Cause:** Loyalty: Loyalty is rewarded and promoted across all channels

Effect:
- customers aim to achieve loyalty thresholds and therefore buy more frequently and across more channels.

P&L and KPI impact:
- reduction in churn and increase in customer retention;
- increase in sales and profitability;
- increase in average order values;
- increase in customer satisfaction;
- increase in customer lifetime value.

11 **Cause:** Staff empowerment: Front-line staff are focused on and empowered to resolve customer issues

Effect:
- social media amplification.

P&L and KPI impact:
- reduction in churn and increase in customer retention;
- increase in customer lifetime value;
- increase in social media engagement;
- increase in NPS and CSAT.

12 **Cause:** Socially responsible: The brand is actively pursuing social responsibility and communicating its progress

Effect:
- social media amplification;
- customers engage more.

P&L and KPI impact:
- customers buy more frequently;
- increase in sales and profitability;
- increase in customer satisfaction;
- increase in customer lifetime value;
- increase in social media engagement;
- increase in NPS and CSAT.

13 **Cause:** Diversity and inclusion: The brand is actively pursuing diversity and inclusion across its workforce and leadership and communicating its progress

Effect:
- social media amplification;
- word of mouth;
- customers engage more;
- customers buy more frequently.

P&L and KPI impact:
- increase in sales and profitability;
- increase in customer satisfaction;
- increase in customer lifetime value;
- increase in social media engagement;
- increase in NPS and CSAT;
- reduction in employee churn;
- increase in employee happiness.

14 **Cause:** Technology: The brand has leveraged technology to improve the customer experience

Effect:
- customers engage more;
- customers buy more frequently.

P&L and KPI impact:
- increase in sales and profitability;
- increase in customer satisfaction;
- increase in customer lifetime value;
- increase in social media engagement.

15 Cause: Issue resolution: Customers' issues are resolved more effectively

Effect:
- social media amplification;
- customers buy more frequently.

P&L and KPI impact:
- reduction in churn, increase in retention;
- improvement in issue resolution;
- customer satisfaction/NPS;
- reduction in customer service costs.

Of course, not only is there a direct correlation between brands that deliver great customer service and experience and their commercial performance; the reverse also holds true of those that don't. There is a direct link between the commercial performance of brands that deliver poor experiences and poor customer service.

Different sectors are affected more than others when it comes to customer reactions to a poor experience. According to a Brandwatch survey of over 9,000 consumers across different countries, 55 per cent of consumers said that following a bad experience in the household goods sector, they were highly unlikely to give a brand a second chance (Brandwatch, 2020). That's no second chances for more than one in every two customers who have had a bad experience!

Household goods are not the only sector to suffer the wrath of customers who have been on the wrong end of a bad experience. Of the beauty customers who responded to the survey, 51.3 per cent would be unlikely or highly unlikely to make another purchase from a brand they'd had a bad experience with. Women are less likely than men to forgive a beauty brand for a bad experience, with 54 per cent saying they wouldn't give a brand a second chance (Brandwatch, 2020).

Therefore, being customer-centric is not only the number-one strategy for driving sales and profitability, as a result of increasing customer lifetime value, but it's also the best way to avoid customer churn. As the research above suggests, when you get customer service wrong, you rarely get a second chance.

Marketing communications can be a powerful driver in the move towards customer-centricity. While we have moved very much towards performance-based marketing, and in my opinion, not done enough to communicate brand values, there is one brand I feel has done this particularly well – and that is Iceland.

CASE STUDY
Iceland

Iceland produced one of the best, and most effective, TV campaigns of all time in 2018. The predominantly frozen food supermarket used an animated orang-utan to highlight the impact of palm oil production on the environment.

It very cleverly positioned Iceland as the leading supermarket on environmental and wider societal issues. It also elevated Iceland to the main consideration for consumers of all supermarket brands, something it had never achieved before.

The campaign was an amended version of Greenpeace's *Rang-tan* film. It was viewed more than 65 million times across social media as well as on Iceland's own channels and was one of the most viewed Christmas campaigns of all time.

It also had a big impact upon sales – in particular mince pies, which was the hero product of the campaign. Iceland produced its mince pies using butter instead of palm oil. Year-on-year sales of mince pies grew by over 11 per cent!

Their MD, Richard Walker, is a passionate environmentalist and this can be evidenced by their pledge to eliminate plastic packaging for all Iceland branded products by 2023.

Iceland was named as the UK's top supermarket for customer satisfaction for the second time in 2019 by the UKCSI. Ranked at 83.2, they were way ahead of the national average of 77.7. They were measured across more than 30 customer-facing measures, including how helpful staff were, products, pricing and quality.

SOURCE Hickman (2018) and Iceland (2019)

Conclusion

You must not treat customer experience and customer service as a cost centre. It is the common denominator in all consumer-facing businesses that are successful year after year. By treating it as a profit centre and understanding the commercial impact of different aspects of service and experience, you can make far better investment decisions that will result in securing a successful future for your business.

KEY TAKEAWAYS FROM CHAPTER 6

1 Focus on the issues highlighted, which are the drivers of 'cause and effect', as these provide the insight required to tell you what to prioritize and improve. We all spend far too long measuring and even obsessing about metrics that don't actually tell us anything about what's happening in our business.

2 Think of your business as a service provider, not as a product company, and determine how you might leverage a service-based approach to improve all aspects of customer experience. It's not only about what you sell; it's how you sell it and how you serve customers before, during and after the sale that will ultimately determine whether or not they come back and give you their business in the future.

3 Empower your people to go above and beyond for customers. This is as much about culture as it is about empowerment. You also need to make sure you've got the right people in the business in the first place who have a natural propensity to go the extra mile. The next time you're on a recruitment drive, why not say that you have customer service roles and you're looking for candidates who are customer- and service-obsessed to fill them? You'll have a better chance of them moving the needle on customer service and experience.

4 Customer satisfaction pays. Be sure to measure it regularly and act on feedback. There are lots of ways to ascertain how customers feel about your business, your products and your levels of service – from walking the floor and talking to customers to measuring NPS and CSAT as well as softer measures around sentiment analysis, what customers say about your brand when you're not in the room and what they say about you in focus groups.

5 The brands I outline in this chapter all have fans rather than customers. There is a big difference in the value to a business of having a fan over a customer. As I'm sure will be obvious, the former spends more and engages more frequently; the latter infrequently and has little loyalty to the brand.

References

Brandwatch (2020) [accessed 11 April 2020] The best brands and industries for customer experience 2020, *Brandwatch* [Online] https://www.brandwatch.com/reports/2020-best-brands-for-cx/view/ (archived at https://perma.cc/9R27-848L)

Brown, P (2013) [accessed 27 November 2020] The time JetBlue treated me to Starbucks, *Pb* [Online] https://paulgordonbrown.com/2013/12/06/jetblue/ (archived at https://perma.cc/D56X-TSQZ)

Coghlan, A (2018) [accessed 27 November 2020] Wagamama is a success story in a hard-hit market, *Eater London* [Online] https://london.eater.com/2018/10/30/18041760/wagamama-noodle-restaurant-sale-restaurant-group-casual-dining (archived at https://perma.cc/B8YB-F2R2)

CSM Newsdesk (2019) [accessed 26 February 2021] Wagamama is king of customer satisfaction, *CSM* [Online] https://www.customerservicemanager.com/wagamama-is-king-of-customer-satisfaction/ (archived at https://perma.cc/N5L7-W7K5)

Hickman, A (2018) [accessed 27 November 2020] Iceland's Rang-tan campaign delivers 65m views, sales and consideration lift, *Prweek.com* [Online] https://www.prweek.com/article/1520088/icelands-rang-tan-campaign-delivers-65m-views-sales-consideration-lift (archived at https://perma.cc/E454-9ZXW)

Iceland (2019) [accessed 12 April 2020] Iceland named UK's top supermarket for customer satisfaction for second time running, *Iceland* [Online] http://sustainability.iceland.co.uk/news/iceland-named-uks-top-supermarket-for-customer-satisfaction-for-second-time-running/ (archived at https://perma.cc/2RAG-F3TT)

Kaemingk, D (2019) [accessed 12 April 2020] 7 examples of good customer service practices, *Qualtrics* [Online] https://www.qualtrics.com/blog/customer-service-examples/ (archived at https://perma.cc/C3BR-354G)

Lake, E (2019) [accessed 12 April 2020] Wagamama's success continues as like-for-like sales grow by 6.3%, *The Caterer* [Online] https://www.thecaterer.com/news/wagamama-q2-2019-like-for-like-growth (archived at https://perma.cc/A3BZ-63K3)

Matousek, M (2019) [accessed 12 April 2020] Tesla owners are more satisfied than any other auto brand's, according to Consumer Reports, *Business Insider* [Online] https://www.businessinsider.com/tesla-tops-consumer-reports-owner-satisfaction-list-2019-2?r=US&IR=T (archived at https://perma.cc/39E5-9E9F)

Nasdaq (2020) [accessed 15 January 2021] Etsy stock is up almost 300% in 2020: Here's why it's still worth buying, *Nasdaq* [Online] https://www.nasdaq.com/articles/etsy-stock-is-up-almost-300-in-2020%3A-heres-why-its-still-worth-buying-2020-12-16 (archived at https://perma.cc/8CHV-7RKS)

PPN (2020) [accessed 21 November 2020] Trust proves key to success at Timpson, *Purchase to Pay Network* [Online] https://www.p2pnetwork.org/business/937-trust-proves-key-to-success-at-timpson.html#:~:text=t%2C%20John%20Timpson%20says%20that,amount%20of%20money%20over%20time (archived at https://perma.cc/74V7-2FYM)

Zilvera (2018) [accessed 21 November 2020] Almost all traffic to my Etsy shop is direct traffic, *Community.etsy.com* [Online] https://community.etsy.com/t5/Managing-Your-Shop/Almost-all-traffic-to-my-Etsy-shop-is-direct-traffic/td-p/19948652 (archived at https://perma.cc/RQ67-HQWD)

07

Employee-first

The first building block in driving customer-centric transformation

> **WHAT YOU WILL LEARN IN THIS CHAPTER**
> - Organizational culture is the key to building a business that outperforms its competitive set.
> - There are key drivers to becoming a people-centric business as well as clear benefits from doing so.
> - What it means to put your employees first.

I have worked for, and with, some of the world's best-known brands. Despite their success, they do not all put their employees at the heart of what they do. We often hear the phrase 'put your customers first'. But if you don't start with putting your own people first, don't expect them to put your customers first! I've often thought about how much more successful a business could be if it was more people-centric.

The different types of organizational culture

What a crazy concept. Look after your people and they'll look after your customers! Not only will it make them feel valued; it'll also make you more profitable. Apologies for the sarcasm, but let's be honest, how many of us have worked for organizations that you can count on more than one or two fingers who have been genuinely focused on putting their employees first? Much of this is determined by the culture of the company.

To follow is an interesting model that describes the different types of organizational culture and how you can essentially categorize pretty much all businesses into one of four types. It has been created by Robert E. Quinn and Kim S. Cameron from the University of Michigan at Ann Arbor.

According to Quinn and Cameron, there are four main types of organizational culture. I'm sure we can all identify with each and think of businesses we've worked for in our careers that fit into each of these descriptions:

1 The first is a business with a 'clan-oriented culture', which is family-oriented with a very strong focus on nurturing and developing its people and working in collaboration and doing things together. It has more of an internal than external focus and tends to empower its people. It would be easy to imagine how the focus on people development and collaborative working would lead to a business being successful. The warning would be to also keep an eye on the market, as businesses that look inwards too much are exposed to being disrupted or usurped by competitors.

2 The second culture type involves a company that has an 'adhocracy-oriented culture'. It is fast-paced, agile and dynamic in its approach. Entrepreneurialism is at the heart of its ethos and, as such, it is innovative, risk-taking and focused on being first to market with new initiatives. It's more focused externally than internally while empowering its people to go the extra mile. These types of businesses can grow fast and also fail fast. It becomes harder to maintain the same levels of entrepreneurship and agility as the business scales. One of the key points of failure for these types of businesses is 'the founder syndrome' – when the founder doesn't recognize that it's time to hand over the reins to someone else.

3 The third culture describes companies that have a 'market-oriented culture'. They are more external than internal in their outlook. They are laser-focused on results, on competitors and on high achievement. They have a 'get the job done' mindset. Businesses with this approach and culture are prone to having high staff turnover, as their focus is extremely competitive but more concerned with what's going on in the market than with its people. It's not a recipe for sustainable success.

4 The fourth culture is one where businesses have a 'hierarchy orientation'. These companies are internal-looking and extremely focused on efficiency,

doing things the right way and in a highly controlled fashion. These organizations often have a micromanagement approach. This becomes a core driver for staff churn as employees don't feel trusted to get the job done.

SOURCE Tipster (2013)

Too often businesses fear empowering their employees

There's something about giving power to someone and not having full control of what happens. That is when a business tends to have a culture of penalizing mistakes as opposed to encouraging them and learning from them. There are a number of benefits to giving your colleagues the autonomy to make decisions:

- By empowering your colleagues, you create an employee-centric culture.
- Companies that adopt this type of culture foster a lot of goodwill and pride.
- Employees go the extra mile as they feel valued and encouraged to contribute ideas and make a difference.

We've all worked in jobs at some point in our careers where either we or colleagues we work with are just turning up for the pay cheque. They're not emotionally bought into the business. They feel disengaged and increasingly often even hate working for the company.

It's not rocket science, is it, really? Whether it's a large corporate enterprise or a small business, there are a number of things that stifle employees and act to kill off any hope they had of it being a place they really want to work in the long term.

Bureaucracy, lack of empowerment and micromanagement are just three of the elements that leave many employees feeling highly disillusioned. Even those who are high-performers get very frustrated and suffer from burnout.

Employee-centric businesses have a very different approach from more 'conventional cultures', where the approach is still often one of 'management is always right'. When addressing weaknesses in the business, too few companies start by asking those on the shop floor or the front line. Decisions are made and pushed top–down when the answer could well be sitting with front-line employees – if only they were given a voice and a say.

Companies that do get all of this understand the benefits of employee happiness and the impact that an employee-centric business has.

How do you define and articulate an employee-centric culture?

First of all, and in complete contrast to more hierarchical and 'traditional' cultures, in an employee-centric organization, people feel totally safe making suggestions or coming forward with new ideas. This stimulates engagement and drives innovation. The business culture fosters idea-generation and creativity, communication is open and inclusive, and employees are positively encouraged to challenge how the business operates.

In this culture, employees feel a strong sense of connection to the business, their team and their colleagues as well as having a clear and secure sense of identity. Feeling valued, having a voice and being able to express their opinions openly are key drivers for most employees. When you add career development opportunities to that you create an environment where employees take great pride in their work and in the business.

In my framework to deliver customer-centricity, being an employee-first business is the first step to achieving that. Can any business truly deliver sustainable and profitable growth without putting its people first? I really don't think so. Aside from the commercials, it's so clearly the right thing to do. Every business is about its people first and foremost.

The benefits of being an employee-centric business are many:

- Happy employees deliver better levels of customer service. That makes for happier customers who spend more, buy more frequently and who also tell their friends and family what lovely people and what a nice business they're buying from. This extends the customer lifetime value and it all adds up to a better top line and a more profitable business.
- Happy employees who are invested in the business and its success are more productive.
- Happy employees stay longer – that saves time, effort and costs on recruitment, performance management and so on.
- Happy employees attract other new talent, which saves money on recruitment.
- A good employee-first culture attracts talented people. That helps to up-skill capabilities and the performance of the business.
- Projects are delivered more effectively on time and on budget as the right people are matched up with the right task.
- Employee-first businesses encourage their teams to submit ideas on a regular basis for how to improve things, develop new products, serve

customers more effectively, communicate better and so on. They reward this behaviour. Whereby many traditional businesses penalize failure either by telling an employee off or even by reducing their ability to make their bonus.

- People-first businesses often need fewer layers of management, as they have created cultures where people can get on with their job.

CASE STUDY
Timpson

There can be no better example than Timpson, the cobbler and key-cutting business. They stripped away almost all of the middle management of the business. They empower their staff on the front line, serving customers – to the extent that they are all able to spend £500 resolving a customer issue. This level of trust and empowerment creates not only great levels of service but the ability and agility for the business to execute new initiatives or any business change far quicker than 99 per cent of other organizations (PPN, 2020).

Therefore, it is no surprise that Timpson makes many millions per annum in profits and has grown both the top and bottom line consistently over recent years. Its 2018–19 profits grew from £12.6 million to £14.2 million (Ord, 2019).

Unfortunately, and unlike the example of Timpson, too many businesses see their shareholders as the most important group of stakeholders, even ahead of their own employees.

Just Capital, an organization set up by Deepak Chopra, Arianna Huffington and others, was set up to review how effectively different companies perform against ethical measures. They ran a survey in 2019 and discovered a huge disconnect between the perception of American consumers of a business's priorities versus their own. Whereby 60 per cent perceived that a business prioritizes its shareholders versus 20 per cent who thought it prioritized customers and 20 per cent thought businesses prioritized their staff (Ward, 2020). It is clear that the survey respondents care most about how an American business treats their people when it comes to their benefits, working conditions and fair pay than how they treat their shareholders.

In my humble opinion, and as evidenced by a multitude of consumer brands, any business that prioritizes its shareholders over its people will fail at some point. When I say fail, I mean they will go bust.

Subsequently, Just Capital worked with the not-for-profit Robert Wood Johnson Foundation, whose purpose is the creation of healthy communities, to identify companies that are people-first businesses. The output of this was a list of 100 businesses that focus on delivering health and well-being benefits for their people while simultaneously investing in the community and reducing levels of pollution. Unsurprisingly, some of the top 10 can be found in the list of the world's 100 most valuable brands, including Microsoft, Salesforce and Intel (Anzilotti, 2019).

People-centric businesses that are commercially successful

CASE STUDY
Pret A Manger

Pret A Manger (Pret), the highly successful sandwich chain, differentiates itself in three main areas:

- menu;
- customer service;
- dedication to sustainability and social responsibility.

These have all helped it to become a global success. Their employees like working there and are rewarded for performing at or above expectations, hence customers get great product and service, which keeps them coming back. Marketing strategy is focused upon driving word-of-mouth, listening to customers and leveraging advocacy.

Much of the word-of-mouth is generated by small gestures such as random acts of kindness. Staff are empowered to give out a free cup of tea or coffee to a customer when they think it's relevant. It could be someone who looks as though they're having a bad day and would welcome a pick-me-up or to a loyal, regular customer who comes in every day and is thankful for the recognition of their loyalty.

Pret's core values are:

- Happy teams make for happy customers.
- Never stand still – always innovating and evolving.
- Amazing standards every day.
- Doing the right thing.

Their daily team meetings provide feedback on the previous day's service, which helps to make staff feel engaged. Their team is encouraged to contribute ideas for new menu items or changes. If an idea is adopted, there is an award for the person or team who came up with the idea (Pret, 2020).

They used customer feedback when planning their first veggie Pret in Soho, London, in 2016. Sales figures showed a marked shift towards meat-free choices. They asked customers what they thought of a veggie store idea in a blog piece and then asked people to vote in an online poll. 10,000 people responded and it was clear that just under half (44 per cent) liked the shop idea. Following their acquisition of EAT, they began converting these stores into Veggie Prets (Fleming, 2019).

A majority stake in Pret was acquired by private equity firm Bridgepoint for £345 million in 2008 (Harrington, 2008). It sold the business for £1.5 billion in 2018. Along the way, it enjoyed healthy profits generated by the business as well as a £1.15 billion profit from the sale of the business (Jahshan, 2018). Who says employee-first and customer-centric businesses don't pay?

Another business that walks the talk when it comes to putting its own people first is international lingerie brand and retailer Hunkemöller.

CASE STUDY
Hunkemöller

The Dutch-based lingerie retailer Hunkemöller is a business that understands the value of putting its people at the heart of what it does. They very much see their colleagues as being brand ambassadors.

They hold large-scale brand events annually with staff from 15 countries, with a fashion show showcasing the next season. Social is at the heart of their approach and all of their colleagues are encouraged to participate in the amplification of the brand through social channels and create genuine engagement with consumers.

This approach permeates much of what they do. They use content marketing for recruiting staff, with video and blog posts highlighting what it's like to work at Hunkemöller. They developed an employee engagement app to inspire staff, schedule tasks and for staff to book holidays. They have a strong focus on learning and development, training and up-skilling their colleagues. They measured engagement as 39 per cent higher among employees after six months.

Their strategic aim is to deliver 'world class service' in their stores. This talks to the culture of the business, which is focused on exceptional service and making genuine contact with customers. All relevant KPIs are increased and improved as a result of their focus on staff and service. Average transaction values, the number of units sold per transaction, conversion and customer lifetime value increased across the board as a result of implementing the training programme.

Hunkemöller is a hugely successful business. It has been sold many times over to different private equity owners and has grown from a Dutch retail business to a pan-European brand and the market leader in lingerie.

SOURCE Hunkemöller (2018)

If you track the commercial performance of people-centric brands, you see a very clear pattern of success emerge. Take Google. As of 2019, their share price has increased by 400 per cent since their IPO in 2009 (Hecht, 2019). Is that all down to being people-centric? No, of course not. But their people and culture are a huge part of their long-term, sustainable success.

CASE STUDY
Google

Google has a very motivated and loyal workforce. They also walk the talk when it comes to how they treat their employees.

They offer market-leading benefits including competitive salaries, genuine opportunities for career development, employees can spend seven days every year volunteering for a charity and they have a transparent and innovative company culture.

In addition to the benefits listed above, they offer their staff free food, medical services on site, great parental benefits, haircuts, gaming centres, gardens and laundry services as standard, but much more besides.

As you'd pretty much expect them to do, Google use data to understand issues within the business, eg Google identified that mothers were leaving the company at a higher rate than other employees. So what did they do? They improved their parental leave benefits, resulting in a 50 per cent reduction in the attrition rate.

Employees describe Google as a 'safe and inclusive' workplace, a sentiment ascribed to the staff town hall meetings, support for transgender Googlers and unconscious bias workshops. They also offer a Global Education Leave programme, a sabbatical allowing employees to take leave for education, which is also paid for by the company.

Google's former senior vice president of people said: 'What's beautiful about this approach is that a great environment is a self-reinforcing one: All of these efforts support one another, and together create an organization that is creative, fun, hardworking and highly productive.'

It can be no surprise, therefore, that they consistently come top in the best companies to work for lists worldwide.

I think I'll just leave my book and contact Google HR to see if they've got any room for me…

All joking aside, don't get me wrong: Google is no holiday camp. Their team work extremely hard and obviously have to be at the top of their game. But you can see the attraction for top talent to want to work there.

The results of their employee focus? Their stock price has increased by nearly 400 per cent over a nine-year period. Staff retention pays as does being employee-first.

SOURCE Fortune (2017), Investopedia (2019) and Gillett (2016)

What it means to put your employees first

I created a model for businesses to create a plan for how to engage their colleagues more effectively. One of the drivers for me doing this was to combat the general perception that Millennials don't want to work anywhere for more than a year or two. Whereby the issue is that we don't create environments where they want to stay. We often pay them a minimum wage, unlike the case with Hunkemöller, they aren't offered any training or development, there's no succession planning or real opportunities for them where they can see potential for career progression over many years and they're not empowered to make decisions.

I recommend that all businesses adopt these guidelines for their employees:

- Remuneration – pay them a fair and proper wage.
- Understanding – empathize and demonstrate this through business culture and the environment you create.
- Learning and development – look to offer continual opportunities for growth.
- Empowerment – give them the tools to do the job and the trust and freedom to make decisions that don't need management approval all the time.
- Succession planning – show them there's a career path available to them in the business.

- Another 'S' worth noting is shared success. Make sure your employees get to share in your success. One of the best examples of this is John Lewis. Their partnership model ensures that all employees benefit when the business does well. It also engenders a sense of ownership among all of the employees.

Every year there are lists created of the best companies to work for. I had the privilege of being on the board of the multichannel fashion retailer White Stuff for four years as a non-executive director. They were featured for many consecutive years in the *Sunday Times* list of the 100 best companies to work for (Sunday Times, 2020). There are lots of positive reasons for businesses to want to appear on this prestigious list. It gives the employees a sense of pride, it's a great recruitment advert and it also talks to customers about the values of the business.

Another such list is *Forbes* magazine's list of America's best employers. Within the travel and leisure category in 2019, Hard Rock International was recognized as the top employer. This was the fourth year running they had earned this inclusion. The research was conducted by Forbes and Statista, the market research company. They ran a survey of more than 50,000 US employees to determine who merited a place on the list of best US employers (HrNxt, 2020).

CASE STUDY
The John Lewis Partnership

As previously mentioned, John Lewis's employees are essentially partners in the business. The John Lewis Partnership, which consists of John Lewis and Waitrose, is the UK's largest employee-owned business. Their team are empowered, which, in addition to the partner model, promotes a shared responsibility for customers and business results. All of this adds up to their team being highly motivated employees. Their colleagues are all involved in decisions and strategy to help create the best customer experience.

The John Lewis Partnership was founded over a century ago by John Spedan Lewis, who created a whole new way of doing business. Involving staff in decision-making, he laid out a constitution that defined their rights and responsibilities as co-owners of the business. This constitution sets the happiness of employees (through worthwhile and satisfying employment) at the heart of the business. 'The Partnership's ultimate purpose is the happiness of all its members, through their worthwhile and satisfying employment in a successful business.' The constitution set out seven principles, which include:

- Deal honestly with customers.
- Conduct business relationships with integrity.
- Contribute to the well-being of local communities.
- The purpose is the happiness of its members.
- The power is shared by the Partnership Council, the Partnership Board and the chairman.
- Their aim is to distribute a share of profits each year to its members.
- Relationships are based on mutual respect and courtesy, with as much equality between its members as differences of responsibility permit.

Because employees are engaged in the aims and success of the business, they take pride in serving customers and the community. They view it as a great place to work, deliver great service and customers feel valued when they shop there.

To further emphasize the importance of their employees being partners in the business, Waitrose and John Lewis rebranded to Waitrose & Partners and John Lewis & Partners respectively.

While like all department stores and many other retailers they have had a tough time commercially, their focus on customer-centricity, staff empowerment and staff engagement will see them come good in the long run, and unlike others who have fallen by the wayside, even as their operating model evolves, theirs is a business I believe will stand the test of time.

SOURCE Employee Ownership Association (2020) and Culture Consultancy (2020)

CASE STUDY
Amazon

In 2019, Amazon topped the list of LinkedIn's best companies to work for in the UK. Despite rumblings of discontent in the warehouse, Amazon is doing more than most to prove that they look after their people – to the point that they offer tours of their distribution centres, which many tens of thousands of people have undertaken.

The business has more than half a million employees globally and is on a well-stated mission to become the world's 'most customer-centric company' – if, indeed, it's not there already.

Amazon has six core values that it lives by: customer obsession, frugality, bias for action, ownership, high bar for talent and innovation.

Employees are expected to adhere to 14 Leadership Principles, a few of which include the following:

- Never say 'that's not my job'.
- Examine their strongest convictions with humility.
- Do not compromise for the sake of social cohesion.
- Commit to excellence even if people may think these standards are unreasonably high.

In contrast to Google, Amazon employees are encouraged to be frugal – instead of free gourmet meals, they are provided with free coffee and bananas. Amazon claims to be 'frugal on behalf of our customers'.

Despite its size, Amazon aims to behave like a start-up and avoid bureaucracy. One of the leadership principles is 'speed matters'.

Jeff Bezos describes the management style as Day One Thinking – treating each day as if it was the first day of business.

Amazon pay (US employees) more than minimum wage in most places (whatever their employment status), and give them access to the same health and retirement plans as executives.

HR tenets include: 'Employees come to Amazon to do meaningful work, and we make that easier by removing barriers, fixing defects, and enabling self-service. Applying to, working at, and leaving Amazon should be frustration-free experiences.'

The results speak for themselves. As of 2020 Amazon is the fourth most valuable business in the world (Forbes, 2020).

SOURCE Duhigg (2019) and McCracken (2019)

Conclusion

Being an employee-first business is the first and most important building block upon which to build the foundations for being a customer-centric business.

Employee-centric businesses are invariably more successful over a sustained period of time. After all, every business is only as good as its people and the decisions they take and the service they provide.

Take the US grocery retailer Wegmans. 2019 marked the 22nd anniversary of the *Fortune* 100 Best Companies to Work For, a list that Wegmans has made it on to *every year since its inception*. In 2019, it was ranked third. They've been on the list of the top 10 companies for 16 out of 22 years, which in itself is a remarkable achievement and clear recognition of their focus on their employees. They were also rated number one in the Temkin customer experience ratings out of all consumer categories. Their sales are approaching $10 billion and they're highly profitable. Like Greggs, they don't just have customers; they have fans (Temkin, 2018).

By creating an employee-first culture, empowering staff, providing opportunities for learning and development and career progression, businesses retain their staff for longer. This in turn leads to greater consistency of customer service and customer experience as well as a workforce that wants to make a difference and continually strives to improve.

KEY TAKEAWAYS FROM CHAPTER 7

1 Empower your people – give them the tools to do the job and the freedom to make decisions. The former proves that you understand what they need to do their job to the best of their ability, while the latter demonstrates that you trust them.

2 Implement the rest of the 'rules' model highlighted above – prove to your colleagues that you really care by providing training, learning and development opportunities, by paying them well or, even better, enabling them to share in your success. Create career progression opportunities. Always be empathetic.

3 Enable the 'voice of the employee' – encourage everyone in the business to contribute ideas on everything from how to improve ways of working to new products or services. No matter what their role or what level of the organization they work at, everyone should have a voice.

4 Prioritize your employees over your shareholders – the best way of ensuring that you can deliver the best possible return for your shareholders is to be an employee-first business. Put your people first and they will go the extra mile. Those extra miles are the difference between success and failure.

5 Walk the talk – you must ensure that all the managers and leaders in the business are demonstrating and delivering their part in being a people-first business.

References

Anzilotti, E (2019) [accessed 20 July 2020] These are the 10 big companies that treat their employees the best, *Fast Company* [Online] https://www.fastcompany.com/90355524/these-are-the-10-big-companies-that-treat-their-employees-the-best (archived at https://perma.cc/N9CY-2DTL)

Culture Consultancy (2020) [accessed 20 July 2020] So what can you learn from John Lewis, *Culture Consultancy* [Online] https://www.cultureconsultancy.com/blogs/so-what-can-you-learn-from-john-lewiss-culture/ (archived at https://perma.cc/97SE-M7XV)

Duhigg, C (2019) [accessed 20 July 2020] Is Amazon unstoppable?, *New Yorker* [Online] https://www.newyorker.com/magazine/2019/10/21/is-amazon-unstoppable (archived at https://perma.cc/PM3L-3KHV)

Employee Ownership Association (2020) [accessed 20 July 2020] John Lewis Partnership, *Employee Ownership Association* [Online] https://employeeownership.co.uk/case-studies/john-lewis-partnership/ (archived at https://perma.cc/EE3K-BXX8)

Fleming, M (2019) [accessed 21 November 2020] Pret confirms the end of the Eat brand to 'turbocharge' Veggie Pret, *Marketing Week* [Online] https://www.marketingweek.com/pret-turbo-charge-veggie-pret/ (archived at https://perma.cc/7TYL-ZAXE)

Forbes (2020) [accessed 21 November 2020] The world's 22 most valuable brands, *Forbes.com* [Online] https://www.forbes.com/the-worlds-most-valuable-brands/#5545e9fa119c (archived at https://perma.cc/NB37-8LBC)

Fortune (2017) [accessed 27 November 2020] Google, *Fortune* [Online] https://fortune.com/best-companies/2017/google/ (archived at https://perma.cc/5AM3-M47R)

Gillett, R (2016) [accessed 20 July 2020] 5 reasons Google is the best place to work in America and no other company can touch it, *Business Insider* [Online] https://www.businessinsider.com/google-is-the-best-company-to-work-for-in-america-2016-4?r=US&IR=T#more-than-one-quarter-of-googlers-telecommute-at-least-some-of-the-time-4 (archived at https://perma.cc/HV5M-PPNW)

Harrington, M (2008) [accessed 20 July 2020] Pret A Manger sold for £345m, *Telegraph.co.uk* [Online] https://www.telegraph.co.uk/finance/newsbysector/retailandconsumer/2784891/Pret-a-Manger-sold-for-345m.html (archived at https://perma.cc/8SEL-YRT3)

Hecht, A (2019) [accessed 21 November 2020] If you invested $1,000 in Google 10 years ago, here's how much you'd have now, *CNBC* [Online] https://www.cnbc.com/2019/10/08/what-a-1000-dollar-investment-in-google-would-be-worth-after-10-years.html (archived at https://perma.cc/HY5J-8DRM)

HrNxt (2020) [accessed 20 July 2020] Hard Rock International recognized by Forbes as one of America's best employers for diversity in 2020, *Hrnxt.Com* [Online] https://hrnxt.com/news/hard-rock-international-recognized-by-forbes-as-one-of-americas-best-employers-for-diversity-in-2020/14942/2020/02/23/ (archived at https://perma.cc/9AWX-9K59)

Hunkemöller (2018) [accessed 20 July 2020] Our brand journey, *Hkmi.com* [Online] https://www.hkmi.com/wp-content/uploads/2019/02/Brand-Journey_GB_jan18.pdf (archived at https://perma.cc/DV6N-7EGN)

Investopedia (2019) [accessed 20 July 2020] 10 reasons Google is one of the best employers, *Investopedia* [Online] https://www.investopedia.com/articles/investing/060315/top-10-reasons-work-google.asp (archived at https://perma.cc/FLM7-VNK2)

Jahshan, E (2018) [accessed 21 November 2020] Pret A Manger sold for £1.5bn to German billionaires, *Retail Gazette* [Online] https://www.retailgazette.co.uk/blog/2018/05/pret-manger-sold-german-billionaires-jab/ (archived at https://perma.cc/T72W-RD6N)

McCracken, H (2019) [accessed 20 July 2020] These are Amazon's 38 rules for success, *Fast Company* [Online] https://www.fastcompany.com/90334069/these-are-amazons-38-rules-for-success (archived at https://perma.cc/3PQE-PJPF)

Ord, M (2019) [accessed 21 November 2020] Strong year at Timpson group, *Insider Media Ltd* [Online] https://www.insidermedia.com/news/north-west/strong-year-at-timpson-group (archived at https://perma.cc/HJ5X-KVUW)

PPN (2020) [accessed 21 November 2020] Trust proves key to success at Timpson, *Purchase to Pay Network* [Online] https://www.p2pnetwork.org/business/937-trust-proves-key-to-success-at-timpson.html#:~:text=t%2C%20John%20Timpson%20says%20that,amount%20of%20money%20over%20time (archived at https://perma.cc/673Y-7S4G)

Pret (2020) [accessed 21 November 2020] About Pret, *Pret.co.uk* [Online] https://www.pret.co.uk/en-GB/about-pret (archived at https://perma.cc/A9VA-WEJL)

Sunday Times (2020) [accessed 20 July 2020] The *Sunday Times* best companies to work for list, *Best Companies* [Online] https://www.b.co.uk/the-lists/ (archived at https://perma.cc/3X6S-SM7V)

Temkin, B (2018) [accessed 11 April 2020] Wegmans, H-E-B, Citizens, Credit Unions, Publix, and Subway receive top customer experience scores across 318 U.S. companies, *Qualtrics* [Online] https://www.qualtrics.com/docs/xmi/XMI_TemkinExperienceRatings-2018.pdf (archived at https://perma.cc/B52Y-M7HZ)

Tipster, T (2013) [accessed 20 July 2020] 4 types of organizational culture, *ArtsFwd* [Online] https://www.artsfwd.org/4-types-org-culture/ (archived at https://perma.cc/M8RZ-LPL4)

Ward, M (2020) [accessed 21 November 2020] One chart shows worker satisfaction is quickly becoming a top priority for executives, *Business Insider* [Online] https://www.businessinsider.com/one-chart-shows-what-people-think-about-stakeholder-capitalism-2020-10?r=US&IR=T (archived at https://perma.cc/56HJ-MSWB)

08

Purpose before profit

The shift from value to values

> **WHAT YOU WILL LEARN IN THIS CHAPTER**
>
> - Purpose is another key driver of commercial success, even more so when a business puts its purpose before its profitability.
> - The cultural drivers for sustainable success.
> - Examples of what it means to be a values-led business.
> - The commercial impact of businesses that put purpose before profit and why it's becoming increasingly important to consumers.
> - Consumers see through purpose greenwashing. It's vital to avoid this at all costs.

Purpose is a key driver of profitability

Similarly to social responsibility and customer-centricity, the commercial value of the purpose of an organization is hugely underestimated.

Brands such as Nike, Walmart and Google, all of which have a strong, well-communicated and well-understood sense of purpose, have enjoyed a 175 per cent increase in their brand valuation over a 12-year period. Contrast this to a medium growth rate of 86 per cent and a rate of 70 per cent for brands with a low sense of purpose (Kantar, 2020).

Consumers recognize when a brand has a genuine commitment to purpose and those that have, have grown at twice the rate of other brands.

There have been many drivers and reasons for brands turning to purpose as a commercial opportunity. From the global financial crisis of 2008 to the impact of social media and the amplification of consumer dissatisfaction and cynicism, to fake news, companies have seen purpose as an answer to the challenges they face in the market.

The problem, according to creative content agency Verity London, is that companies are too often jumping on the 'purpose bandwagon' and, as a result, find themselves being named and shamed across social and other media channels when they get called out for doing so (Verity London, 2019).

A prime example of this is Pepsi's commercial featuring Kendall Jenner. The core narrative was that racial tensions between communities and the police could be solved with a soft drink. The advert was pulled 48 hours after launch, following significant ridicule and derision on social media (Smith, 2017).

Starbucks suffered a similar issue with their #RaceTogether campaign, the proposition of which asked their baristas to engage customers on the same challenging subject of racial tension. It was subsequently deemed inauthentic and superficial and was widely criticized and lambasted across the media and social media. It too was removed in short order (BBC, 2015).

There are many issues for brands that get accused of purpose washing. They don't only risk a backlash from consumers, but their employees also see through hypocrisy and inauthenticity. This can also be a driver for disengagement, a drop in productivity and an increase in employee churn.

You might define brand purpose as having a bigger reason to exist, a higher purpose. In the absence of this, and as the examples above demonstrate, brands should not jump on the purpose bandwagon, as it's highly likely to backfire. It may be easier to think of it as having a 'societal commitment'. Think back to the Covid-19 pandemic: there are so many examples of brands that demonstrated this. One is Burberry, which leveraged their machines to produce PPE gowns for NHS patients and staff (Independent, 2020).

Role-modelling is another approach to demonstrating brand purpose and a societal commitment. One great example is the pharmacy and grocery chain in the US, CVS, which promoted the fact that they were 'quitting too'. They removed cigarettes from sale. Subsequently, a study revealed that customers who purchased cigarettes exclusively at CVS stores were 38 per cent less likely to buy tobacco after CVS stopped selling cigarettes (Cohen, 2017).

Another example of role-modelling was when one of the US's largest retailers, Dick's Sporting Goods, removed assault rifles from sale, but not only that, they destroyed $5 million worth of guns (Holson, 2019).

The cultural drivers for sustainable success

The culture of a business is essentially at the heart of everything the business does. It's much more than a philosophy. It's very much about interaction, how people act, behaviour, communication and so much more. A great framework produced by Paul Spiegelman that does a good job of highlighting the core elements of company culture is called the 10Cs of company culture (Spiegelman, 2020).

This framework is a great example of how to create a culture that has purpose and values at its heart and that all the employees of the business can get behind. I have expanded on this framework below and in Figure 8.1.

FIGURE 8.1 The 10Cs of company culture

#	
1	Core values
2	Camaraderie
3	Celebrations
4	Community
5	Communication
6	Caring
7	Commitment to learning
8	Consistency
9	Connect
10	Chronicles

Core values

The values of a business are not just sound bites to be hung on the wall. They are inextricably linked to the purpose of the business. They are principles the business wants to live up to and therefore they act to guide and shape everyday decision-making. They can be a great source of reference in helping to make decisions. For example, 'does this decision meet our core values as a business?'

To be effective, they need to be lived and breathed and become part of everyday life within the organization. They also need to be executed consistently. Core values don't change, irrespective of what's happening in the market or within the business or how the business might have changed over time. Its values remain at the heart of what it does and how it behaves day in, day out. They should be a core part of the company's induction programme. In actual fact, they should be communicated long before a new employee joins the business – through the website, on marketing communications and within the interview process itself. After all, if the business wants to maintain its culture, it needs to ensure that it always brings in new employees who share its values.

Camaraderie

The businesses with the best cultures have a tangible sense of camaraderie. 'We're all in it together and all there to support each other.' But it goes deeper than that. It's also about getting to know your colleagues and learning more about their life outside of work and what they're like outside of the work environment. This can be achieved by having regular social activity, encouraging colleagues to participate in charity events, and inviting partners and families to work social events.

Celebrations

Celebrations are another highly effective way to both celebrate success as well as create a sense of togetherness within the business. There is no better way to motivate a team or individuals than to recognize their achievements publicly within the business. It's even more effective when the recommendations come from peers and co-workers.

Businesses with great cultures also celebrate a host of non-business-related events, from new babies to weddings and from sports accomplishments to educational achievements.

Community

Brands with great cultures encourage their colleagues to give back to the community. This can be through volunteering, community service initiatives or providing support in some capacity. Anything that helps society is a good thing and acts as a source of pride, both for the business and for all those involved.

Communication

There is nothing worse than feeling out of the loop when you work for a business. The best companies have very open communications with their staff. They regularly share news about developments and make everyone feel that they're on the journey together. From town hall meetings, as they're called in the US, to company updates in the UK, giving all colleagues a regular view of the performance of the business, its direction of travel, new products and services – these are all important in ensuring colleagues feel engaged.

Caring

You might think that the bigger a business is, the harder it is to show employees that it genuinely cares about them. But size need not be a barrier to doing this well. You need to have a culture of care so that you put in place the processes that ensure recognition of events that are going on in someone's life outside of the workplace – births, deaths, marriages, birthdays and other life events.

Home Depot, one of the largest retailers in North America, provide financial support for employees who have financial emergencies. They also enable colleagues to undertake further education and help by reimbursing tuition and other related costs. Now that is what you call a caring culture (Charan, 2019).

Commitment to learning

Learning and development is one of the biggest gaps in consumer-facing organizations. We wonder why Millennials and Gen Z sometimes leave after short periods of employment. While there can be a number of reasons, one of the main factors is that they see no opportunity to learn and develop new skills. Without this, they see limited scope for career progression.

Consistency

Company culture is something that is borne out of tradition. However, it is also something that can be crafted and evolved. It's important that whatever wordsmithing or events you come up with are delivered consistently and regularly. Any one-off attempts to improve culture will come across as being disingenuous.

Back in 2018, we sold our consultancy business, Practicology, to Pattern, a global marketplace reseller and driver of ecommerce sales. They have some very commercial, but highly effective, values that are a core part of their culture (Hoeijmans, 2020). They are data fanatics, a team of doers, game changers and partner obsessed. Their sales are growing exponentially year in, year out. So, whether your cultural values are commercial or more earthly, they have to be executed consistently. This is clearly something Pattern does extremely well. It lives and breathes these every day. They also do many other things well, such as celebrating success.

Connect

Many CEOs sit in large offices on the 'executive floor' and are rather isolated and insulated (maybe that's their intent) from the rest of the business. They would rarely know the first names of anyone below the senior leadership team.

Whereby the best and most effective CEOs I've known are far more personable. They take time to get to know everyone, they try to remember everyone's first name and take an interest in their life outside of work. They often walk the floor of the office and other parts of the business to get the pulse and mood of the workforce. They also use this time to learn about what's frustrating them day-to-day – lack of tools to do their job, decisions they feel are unfair, things that are frustrating customers and so on. This feedback provides insight on how to do things better and is rarely accessible to the CEO who only breathes rarefied air on the sixth floor.

Dave Wright, the founder of Pattern, fits the mould of the curious, personable CEO, as does Mike Logue, CEO of Dreams, the leading UK bed and bedding retailer (Jones, 2018).

Chronicles

I think it's really important for everyone to know the history of the business – how it started, when, where and by whom, the ups and the downs, and ultimately how the business became sustainable and successful.

We all want to be part of a business that stands for something, that has a rich heritage or is challenging the status quo. Whichever the case, this should all be a core part of the induction programme for new employees.

What constitutes a values-led business

CASE STUDY
IKEA

With over 29 million fans on Facebook and global brand recognition, has anyone in the world not heard of IKEA? That in itself tells a story!

One of IKEA's core aims is to have a positive impact on the world. This can be evidenced from where they source their product to creating products in a way that helps their customers live more sustainably. In the world of retail, they were early to sustainability and published their strategy back in 2012.

It's safe to say that they are regarded as a world leader when it comes to sustainability. Their concept of 'democratic design' is to create beautiful, functional products that are sustainable and affordable, because 'good home furnishing is for everyone'.

On one hand, they are democratizing furniture design by making it affordable to the masses, and on the other hand, they are attempting to tackle the issue of unsustainable consumption by making products that last longer, are easier to fix, sell, share and recycle.

The cotton IKEA uses comes from sustainable sources, and they achieved their objective for 100 per cent of their wood to be sustainably sourced in 2020/21.

They also continue to produce as much renewable energy as they consume, via investment in wind turbines and solar panels. Ingka, IKEA's holding company, owns approximately 180,000 hectares of responsibly managed forests, offers home solar energy and has partnered with 58 social entrepreneurs and social businesses in 14 countries.

IKEA in Japan offers a buy-back service for furniture that's in good condition but no longer needed. Furniture is swapped for a voucher redeemable against another purchase, and the furniture itself is refurbished and sold at a reduced rate.

Ingka has a commitment to help disadvantaged people (including people with disabilities, migrants and refugees) to find work in retail. As part of this, in 2018 they ran Skills for Employment programmes in 15 countries.

IKEA's Corporate Statement: 'Our vision is to create a better everyday life for the many people – for customers, but also for our co-workers and the people who work at our suppliers.'

SOURCE IKEA (2020) and Ethical Home (2020)

Should we be surprised that a business with strong values such as IKEA is successful over a sustained period of time? These values are extolled daily by all of their people. And this ultimately manifests itself in people going the extra mile in their day-to-day roles. As consumers, you also get a strong indication of IKEA's values and what the business stands for. There is a certain level of pragmatism and straightforwardness that seems to exist in Scandinavian brands.

CASE STUDY
Nudie Jeans

Nudie Jeans is a Swedish brand launched in 2001, but they identify the moment real momentum began with their business as around 2010, when consumers started to take responsible design seriously.

Nudie Jeans' vision is to 'become the most sustainable denim company'. They promote the concept that denim improves with age and wear, and offer repair services for their products worldwide, including 'mobile repair stations' and 32 repair shops. They provide a free repair kit in regions where no repair service is available – a very interesting and transparent brand proposition and one that engenders trust. It is highly unusual for an apparel brand to seem to limit the customer lifetime value of customers by making sure their products last longer. Of course, the reality is that if they do, consumers will still look to buy new styles to add to their collection.

In 2018, 98 per cent of their garments were sustainable, and they replaced the leather back patches with a vegan paper version. They repaired 55,000 pairs of jeans in their stores in 2018. They also sell second-hand products on their website.

They release around 200 pairs in a drop, and these sell out within 48 hours. So, there's clearly significant consumer engagement with the brand's focus on sustainability. In addition, customers are incentivized to recycle their Nudie product with a 20 per cent discount off their next purchase when they donate an old pair of jeans in store. The brand estimates that their Nudie Jeans recycling programme has prevented 44,000 kilograms of denim from being thrown away. That has a significant carbon footprint benefit. This also drives a feel-good factor with consumers and how they perceive the brand.

Their 'Get the Balance Right' campaign promoted their use of organic cotton, living wages and their repair and reuse activities. They are working towards their full supply chain being carbon-neutral by 2025. That would be a fantastic achievement. Unlike other brands that are kicking the sustainability can down the road to 2030 or beyond, Nudie Jeans are walking the talk.

SOURCE Nudie Jeans (2019, 2020), Velasquez (2016) and Nuguyen (2019)

As is the case with Nudie Jeans, a business that demonstrates purpose, values and a commitment to sustainability and the environment is one that walks the talk. It isn't about ticking a box. It's about making a difference and having a clear reason or reasons to exist. This also makes it easier for consumers to engage with them, as they come across as being authentic and trustworthy – a brand that does what it says it's going to do.

Even if we aren't all measuring our carbon footprint on a day-to-day basis, or volunteering to work for a charity, there is a sense of doing the right thing and making your own little contribution to society when you buy from a brand that has an overt purpose and commitment to sustainability.

CASE STUDY
Patagonia

Patagonia's customers, or should I say their fans, love them. From being one of the most trusted brands in the US to one that lives by their purpose and principles in all that they do, they have over 1.6 million fans on Facebook and 4.5 million followers on Instagram.

Patagonia sell sustainable outdoor clothing. They were founded in 1973 and are still privately owned. Their mission statement states: 'We're in business to save our home planet.' They have been involved in environmental activism for 45 years, distributing around 500 grants a year to activist organizations, promoting sustainable supply chains and advocating for public lands. They invest in sustainable start-ups. They provide a used clothing programme called Worn Wear, which involves clothes made from other clothes. It sells second-hand Patagonia gear online and they issue store credits when customers bring in old product for recycling.

They also have an activist hub to connect customers with environmental organizations called Action Works. They have even taken the Trump administration to court over their public lands policy.

Patagonia have expanded beyond garments with Patagonia Provisions – a food marketplace selling products from like-minded farmers, fishermen, artisans, etc, offering an alternative to industrial agriculture. The vision is to establish a model for a new kind of food chain. They offer a selection of foods that address environmental issues as well as supporting local food producers.

They promote regenerative agriculture in their apparel and food products. The scale of their efforts is huge – they're working with the governments of Chile and Argentina to establish new protected lands.

Their commitment towards environmental issues extends to their hiring policy. The HR department was told by founder Yvon Chouinard, 'Whenever we have a job opening, all things being equal, hire the person who's committed to saving the planet no matter what the job is.' They only work with social influencers and brand ambassadors who are vocal environmental advocates.

Patagonia, more than almost any other brand I can think of, live and breathe their core values in *everything* that they do.

SOURCE Beer (2018), Provisions (2020) and Patagonia (2020)

The commercial impact of businesses who put purpose before profit

For some reason, as is the case with their view of customer service being a cost centre, too many businesses view being purposeful, values-led or sustainable as coming at a cost. There seems to be very little understanding of the commercial implications of not doing the right thing just as much as there is a gap in understanding of the potential upside to putting purpose before profit.

CASE STUDY
Innocent Drinks

Innocent Drinks is a B Corp certified business, which means they are a for-profit company that is certified to meet rigorous standards of social and environmental performance, accountability and transparency.

Started in 1998, Innocent Drinks state that 'we're here to make it easy for people to do themselves some good (while making it taste nice too). We want to leave things better than we find them.' Despite being 90 per cent owned by Coca-Cola (who committed to their ethical ideals when they bought the brand), they have remained true to their principles, aiming to become a truly sustainable business:

- Make sure suppliers meet international sustainability standards.
- Innovate innocently.
- Grow a green business by reducing energy and water consumption.
- Invest in innovative agriculture projects.
- Commit 10 per cent of profits to charity.
- Use recycled and plant-based plastics for bottles.
- Transform logistics to reduce road miles.
- Champion green bottling in Europe.

They've successfully used their cheeky tone of voice to build a trusted brand, particularly via social, but it's reflected in all of their materials, including their product packaging. It is consistently voted one of the best companies to work for in the UK. They hold an annual meeting where the company invites customers to come to the office (Fruit Towers) to try new recipes and share their views.

Their long-running 'Big Knit' campaign asks customers to knit and send in woolly hats that it puts on top of the bottles it sells in store. For every smoothie with a hat that is sold, it makes a donation to Age UK. They also donate 10 per cent of their profits to charity, mainly through the Innocent Foundation, supporting global projects to prevent hunger.

They are highly profitable and turnover is well in excess of £400 million – not bad for a business that was founded in 1998!

SOURCE Innocent (2020), Smale (2018) and O'Reilly (2014)

CASE STUDY
Leon

Founded in 2004 with the aim of making healthy food for everyone, Leon were the first restaurant chain to display nutritional information on their menus. They are one of the fastest growing restaurant brands in the UK and have expanded across Europe and to the US.

One of their core aims is to revolutionize fast food and demonstrate there's a better way to do business, by being kind to yourself, each other and the planet. 'Naturally fast food that's good for you and good for the planet.'

With double-digit like-for-like growth, their success has come from wanting to do the right thing. They don't just make something that will make lots of money; they like to make something that customers will love.

Leon has a strong focus on sustainability, selling seasonal, locally sourced produce. The menu is predominantly vegetarian, and over a third of their dishes are vegan. Their packaging is compostable, and plastic straws and cutlery are biodegradable.

Personalization of the menu on their website allows customers to filter by dietary needs, eg gluten free, vegan, nut allergy.

SOURCE Cotton (2019), Price (2019) and Chomka (2019)

How and why to avoid purpose greenwashing

Greenwashing is generally described as when a brand wrongly purports that its products are environmentally friendly (Kenton, 2020).

Sixty-six per cent of global consumers in a Neilson report stated that they would pay more for brands that are sustainable. The flip side of this is that consumers have heightened awareness of brands that say they're sustainable but in actual fact are not. It has created an atmosphere of suspicion with consumers, and not without foundation. According to TerraChoice Environmental Marketing, 98 per cent of green-labelled products are actually greenwashed (Faizal, 2019).

There is no question that many consumers will hold a brand to account when it comes to sustainability. But how can brands communicate their progress without appearing disingenuous or, even worse, being accused of greenwashing or purpose washing?

You need to get the balance right and prove to consumers that you take it seriously and are taking action and steps to become sustainable but avoid using technical terminology that makes it sound as though you're jumping on the sustainability bandwagon.

There are a number of common types of greenwashing:

1 While portraying that they were influenced by an eco directive, a company might try to claim the credit for an existing production method with green

credentials. Often, the real driver was to cut costs and had nothing to do with an environmental initiative. An example of this would be eliminating the use of shrink wraps for packaging.

2 Companies often use creative marketing licence to promote the eco-friendliness of a product by leveraging terminology and phrases such as 'best in class ecology' on their packaging, which uses environmental imagery of green fields and flowers when in actual fact the products are not eco-friendly nor sustainable. Brands that lie to consumers will always be found out in the end.

3 Misleading labels – companies will label products as being 'certified', '100 per cent organic' often without any additional information that proves this is the case. More often than not these are examples of where the business has 'self-certified' with no proof or justification for doing so.

4 Hidden trade-offs – this is when a business attempts to position itself as being environmentally friendly and sustainable but then does the opposite with a trade-off that is most definitely not environmentally friendly. One example would be when a fashion brand uses natural or recycled materials while their designs are being produced through exploitative conditions (Faizal, 2019).

One company that was accused of this is Volkswagen. They created and released a marketing campaign with the aim of debunking negative perceptions of diesel and portraying that the technology it used enabled them to emit fewer pollutants.

It was later suggested that Volkswagen had rigged 11 million of their diesel cars with technology designed to undertake, and pass, emissions tests. In reality their diesel cars emitted up to 40 times the permitted levels of pollutants allowed in the US (Hotten, 2015). They subsequently paid out $14.7 billion to settle allegations of cheating emissions tests and deceptive advertising; in the years since this happened, their share price has reduced by around 40 per cent (Hull, 2020).

Short-term commercial gain for long-term commercial pain

The Covid-19 pandemic saw many organizations put purpose before profit, where they repurposed their machines to make masks or gowns for health service staff on the front line. On the flipside, there were many who appeared to put profits ahead of their staff, community and customers by allowing their stores to stay open, while positioning themselves as a retailer of 'essential items'. In the early stages, this included Sports Direct, albeit they did close their stores after the initial furore and issued an apology (Sweney and Goodley, 2020). Others, including The Range, remained open. The Range is not a DIY store. They primarily retail homewares and accessories, but as they sold a small amount of food they were allowed to stay open; however, they were criticized for not maintaining social distancing (BBC, 2020).

Then we had Weatherspoons pub chain and Tottenham Hotspur, who furloughed or terminated their staff contracts while continuing to pay senior staff, including footballers' full salaries. This decision was subsequently reversed soon after the outbreak on social media (MacInnes, 2020; Pratt, 2020).

I undertook research at the time, which suggested that 72 per cent of consumers would boycott a brand that misbehaved during the pandemic. While in the following years I'm sure many will have forgotten these issues, others will not. Even if 20 per cent turned away from a brand as a result of ill-judged behaviour, who can afford to lose a significant number of customers in this day and age (Newman, 2020)?

Conclusion

Purpose is not some wishy-washy or fluffy feel-good piece of text on a company's mission statement or something that hangs on the wall in the boardroom. It is a fundamental driver of profitability for a business. It should be at the heart of the culture of the business and something that all employees want to stand behind. Moreover, it makes them want to work with the business in the first place. Your purpose will also demonstrate to customers what you stand for and whether or not they want to stand alongside you as well.

KEY TAKEAWAYS FROM CHAPTER 8

1 Purpose is a key driver of profitability. If you put profit before purpose, you'll only achieve short-term goals and will most likely impact the sustainability of your business in the long term.

2 The culture of the business is a huge driver for sustainable success. Implement the 10Cs of company culture, as this will ensure you create and

maintain a highly effective organizational culture that subsequently means your team goes the extra mile for customers.

3   Avoid purpose washing at all costs as you'll only be found out by your customers if you don't.

4   Similarly, avoid greenwashing. Consumers now are too savvy for this behaviour. You'll be found out and called out quickly. The commercial implications of this are potentially catastrophic.

References

BBC (2015) [accessed 20 July 2020] Starbucks #Racetogether campaign mocked, *BBC News* [Online] https://www.bbc.co.uk/news/blogs-trending-31932351 (archived at https://perma.cc/FG6D-M597)

BBC (2020) [accessed 27 November 2020] Coronavirus: The Range staff say social distancing 'ignored', *BBC News* [Online] https://www.bbc.co.uk/news/uk-england-devon-52413796 (archived at https://perma.cc/8T9Y-3VWB)

Beer, J (2018) [accessed 21 July 2020] Exclusive: 'Patagonia is in business to save our home planet', *Fast Company* [Online] https://www.fastcompany.com/90280950/exclusive-patagonia-is-in-business-to-save-our-home-planet (archived at https://perma.cc/H9C9-8HN9)

Charan, R (2019) [accessed 25 October 2020] Home Depot's blueprint for culture change, *Harvard Business Review* [Online] https://hbr.org/2006/04/home-depots-blueprint-for-culture-change (archived at https://perma.cc/AE6G-5CHS)

Chomka, S (2019) [accessed 21 July 2020] Plant-based dishes help drive Leon's sales growth, *bighospitality.co.uk* [Online] https://www.bighospitality.co.uk/Article/2019/05/10/Plant-based-dishes-help-drive-Leon-s-sales-growth (archived at https://perma.cc/W33G-UMG9)

Cohen, R (2017) [accessed 20 July 2020] When CVS stopped selling cigarettes, some customers quit smoking, *Reuters* [Online] https://uk.reuters.com/article/us-health-pharmacies-cigarettes/when-cvs-stopped-selling-cigarettes-some-customers-quit-smoking-idUKKBN16R2HY (archived at https://perma.cc/YET3-7BLF)

Cotton, B (2019) [accessed 21 July 2020] The rise of Leon restaurants – how they turned 'healthy eating' into a global business, *Business Leader* [Online] https://www.businessleader.co.uk/why-are-leon-restaurants-at-the-forefront-of-the-healthy-food-revolution/63504/ (archived at https://perma.cc/46BF-P49U)

Ethical Home (2020) [accessed 20 July 2020] Reviewed: how ethical and sustainable is IKEA?, *The Ethical Home Edit* [Online] https://www.theethicalhomeedit.org/brand-reviews/reviewed-how-ethical-and-sustainable-is-ikea (archived at https://perma.cc/NDP7-ALQM)

Faizal, F (2019) [accessed 21 July 2020] What is greenwashing? Types & examples, *Feedough* [Online] https://www.feedough.com/what-is-greenwashing-types-examples/ (archived at https://perma.cc/XA3B-8T4L)

Hoeijmans, N (2020) [accessed 21 November 2020] Iserve acquires global ecommerce consultancy Practicology, *Cross-Border E-commerce Magazine* [Online] https://cross-border-magazine.com/iserve-acquires-global-ecommerce-consultancy-practicology/ (archived at https://perma.cc/KA5C-LYX9)

Holson, L (2019) [accessed 20 July 2020] Dick's Sporting Goods destroyed $5 million worth of guns, *Nytimes.com* [Online] https://www.nytimes.com/2019/10/08/business/dicks-sporting-goods-destroying-guns-rifles.html (archived at https://perma.cc/C763-YGUU)

Hotten, R (2015) [accessed 21 July 2020] Volkswagen: The scandal explained, *BBC News* [Online] https://www.bbc.co.uk/news/business-34324772 (archived at https://perma.cc/T5Z7-HFSJ)

Hull, R (2020) [accessed 21 November 2020] High Court throws out Volkswagen's appeal over emissions scandal, *This Is Money* [Online] https://www.thisismoney.co.uk/money/cars/article-8611565/High-Court-throws-Volkswagens-appeal-emissions-scandal.html (archived at https://perma.cc/BM3S-YSRN)

IKEA (2020) [accessed 20 July 2020] IKEA vision and business idea, *Ikea.com* [Online] https://www.ikea.com/gb/en/this-is-ikea/about-us/vision-and-business-idea-pub9cd02291 (archived at https://perma.cc/47UX-7LFN)

Independent (2020) [accessed 9 April 2020] Burberry funds coronavirus vaccine and produces gowns and masks from Yorkshire factory, *Independent* [Online] https://www.independent.co.uk/life-style/fashion/burberry-coronavirus-masks-gowns-covid-19-donations-chanel-a9437066.html (archived at https://perma.cc/6J59-27RS)

Innocent (2020) [accessed 21 July 2020] Sustainability strategy, *Innocentdrinks.co.uk* [Online] https://www.innocentdrinks.co.uk/static/sustainability/2020SustainabilityStrategy.pdf (archived at https://perma.cc/DW5U-5ALN)

Jones, S (2018) [accessed 21 November 2020] The turnaround secret that saved Dreams Beds, *Managementtoday.co.uk* [Online] https://www.managementtoday.co.uk/turnaround-secret-saved-dreams-beds/leadership-lessons/article/1498549 (archived at https://perma.cc/DGB6-HESL)

Kantar (2020) [accessed 20 July 2020] Purpose 2020: Igniting purpose-led growth, *Consulting.kantar.com* [Online] https://consulting.kantar.com/wp-content/uploads/2019/06/Purpose-2020-PDF-Presentation.pdf (archived at https://perma.cc/W36H-2G3D)

Kenton, W (2020) [accessed 21 November 2020] What you should know about greenwashing, *Investopedia* [Online] https://www.investopedia.com/terms/g/greenwashing.asp (archived at https://perma.cc/R2ZV-F7PQ)

MacInnes, P (2020) [accessed 27 November 2020] Tottenham make U-turn on decision to furlough staff after fans' fierce criticism, *Guardian* [Online] https://www.theguardian.com/football/2020/apr/13/tottenham-make-u-turn-on-decision-to-furlough-staff-after-fans-fierce-criticism (archived at https://perma.cc/WP5R-68L8)

Newman, M (2020) [accessed 21 July 2020] CSA consumer survey 2020, *Customerserviceaction.com* [Online] https://customerserviceaction.com/read-our-consumer-survey-insights (archived at https://perma.cc/WL96-S5HG)

Nudie Jeans (2019) [accessed 21 July 2020] Nudie Jeans sustainability report 2019, *Nudiejeans.com* [Online] https://www.nudiejeans.com/sustainability/highlights (archived at https://perma.cc/2MRS-5GTU)

Nudie Jeans (2020) [accessed 21 July 2020] Re-use drop 11, *Nudiejeans.com* [Online] https://www.nudiejeans.com/selection/re-use/ (archived at https://perma.cc/N7W5-CV5E)

Nuguyen, A (2019) [accessed 21 July 2020] Sustainable & Social – S & S spotlight: Nudie Jeans, *Sustainable & Social* [Online] https://sustainableandsocial.com/2019/05/06/spotlight-nudie-jeans/ (archived at https://perma.cc/AMD5-62SQ)

O'Reilly, L (2014) [accessed 21 July 2020] 15 things hardly anyone knows about Innocent Smoothies, *Business Insider* [Online] https://www.businessinsider.com/unusual-facts-about-innocent-smoothies-2014-12?r=US&IR=T (archived at https://perma.cc/3UNN-BPEJ)

Patagonia (2020) [accessed 21 July 2020] Worn Wear – better than new, *Wornwear.patagonia.com* [Online] https://wornwear.patagonia.com/ (archived at https://perma.cc/9BXH-XWPJ)

Pratt, L (2020) [accessed 21 July 2020] Wetherspoons stops staff pay until government reimbursement, *Employee Benefits* [Online] https://employeebenefits.co.uk/wetherspoons-stops-pay-reimbursement/ (archived at https://perma.cc/Y2SE-6B35)

Price, K (2019) [accessed 15 January 2021] Leon reports record sales and fifth year of revenue growth, *The Caterer* [Online] https://www.thecaterer.com/news/restaurant/leon-reports-record-sales-and-fifth-year-of-revenue-growth (archived at https://perma.cc/E4E9-MRA6)

Provisions (2020) [accessed 21 July 2020] Rethinking our food chain, *Patagonia Provisions* [Online] https://www.patagoniaprovisions.com/ (archived at https://perma.cc/TUV7-ESRA)

Smale, W (2018) [accessed 21 July 2020] How smoothie brand Innocent became a bestseller, *BBC News* [Online] https://www.bbc.co.uk/news/business-43542605 (archived at https://perma.cc/Z5J8-VCE3)

Smith, A (2017) [accessed 20 July 2020] 'We missed the mark': Pepsi pulls ad featuring Kendall Jenner after controversy, *NBC News* [Online] https://www.nbcnews.com/news/nbcblk/pepsi-ad-kendall-jenner-echoes-black-lives-matter-sparks-anger-n742811 (archived at https://perma.cc/L637-YK3B)

Spiegelman, P (2020) [accessed 20 July 2020] 10 elements of great company culture, *Inc.com* [Online] https://www.inc.com/paul-spiegelman/great-company-culture-elements.html (archived at https://perma.cc/C5KQ-99D2)

Sweney, M and Goodley, S (2020) [accessed 21 November 2020] Sports Direct's Mike Ashley apologises for poor Covid-19 actions, *Guardian* [Online] https://www.theguardian.com/business/2020/mar/27/sports-direct-mike-ashley-apologises-for-poor-covid-19-actions (archived at https://perma.cc/MW4G-MLYC)

Velasquez, A (2016) [accessed 21 July 2020] For Nudie Jeans, repair and resale is the next major sustainable step forward, *Sourcing Journal* [Online] https://sourcingjournal.com/denim/denim-brands/nudie-jeans-repair-resale-reuse-sustainability-sandya-lang-denim-pv-184551/ (archived at https://perma.cc/9PWF-D5H3)

Verity London (2019) [accessed 20 July 2020] Developing and communicating your social purpose, *Verity London* [Online] http://content.veritylondon.co.uk/whitepaper-gated/ (archived at https://perma.cc/X8J6-KBQE)

09

Diversity and inclusion

On the outside and the inside

WHAT YOU WILL LEARN IN THIS CHAPTER

- There is a broad range of people and requirements that fall within diversity.
- There are obvious benefits of being a diverse organization.
- Brands that have embraced diversity and inclusion are more customer-centric and ultimately more successful.

There is a risk of thinking of diversity on its own. It has the potential to cause controversy, particularly if it's seen as a box-ticking exercise rather than something that changes the business fundamentally and makes it a better place to work and a brand that connects more effectively with a broader range of customers.

To be effective, the approach must be one of both diversity and inclusion. It is inclusion that leads to genuine participation. The diversity and inclusivity of the business should be something that's a cause for celebration and a core part of the culture and DNA of the brand.

The broad range of requirements that fall within diversity

Diversity as a term is often interpreted too narrowly. Many perceive it to be only about gender or ethnicity. While those are very much part of the

FIGURE 9.1 Core areas of diversity

```
              Ethnicity
              and
              religion


                              Gender
Disability    Diversity       and
                              sexuality


              Age and
              demo-
              graphics
```

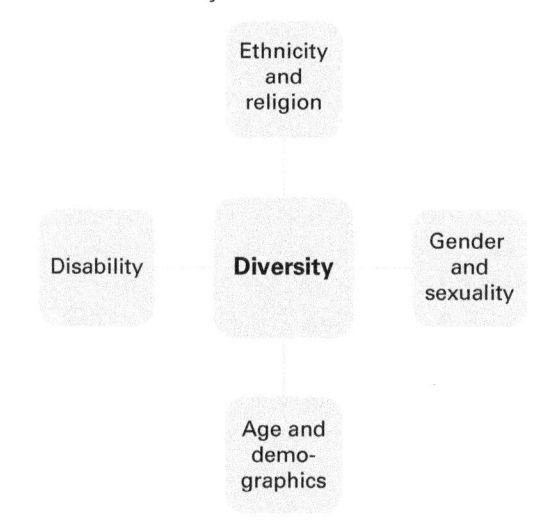

requirements for a diverse organization, it is much broader than that. It is too often approached like many other industry buzzwords, such as social responsibility, with a focus on ticking a box, proving to shareholders that it's an 'issue' that has been addressed.

The requirement to be a diverse business cannot be met by quotas. Nor can it be achieved by adding a few lines to the annual report. To be a truly diverse business, you have to start with your team. A diverse workforce should be representative of society in all areas, including gender expression, age, ethnicity, religion, disability, hidden disabilities, sexuality and demographics (Figure 9.1).

Of course, all of this also applies to customers and how it affects their experience. As mentioned in Chapter 1, there are over 2 million people with visual impairments in the UK as a whole, which is almost 3 per cent of the population, of which 360,000 people are registered as blind or partially sighted (NHS Choices, 2019). I have spoken to a number of consumers with visual impairment, and I can tell you that their experience of going into retail stores is often not a good one.

There are many things those of us who have no disabilities take for granted. For one thing, we can walk into a store unaided and easily navigate around. On the other hand, if as a result of your visual impairment you have a guide dog, you may not even be allowed to cross the threshold of a store. This is despite it being against the law for anyone to stop you from doing so. This is often down to a lack of training within the retailer's business. Staff sometimes don't know any better and assume they're doing the right thing by refusing access to a visually impaired customer and their guide dog. Imagine for a second how that would make you feel. It is so wrong on so many levels.

Even when a visually impaired customer does make it into the store with or without a guide dog, the experience can often be hugely frustrating. From the point of sale (POS) and visual merchandising being too small for a visually impaired customer to read, to there being no Braille on the POS or swing tickets, to the frustration of the difficulty in finding a staff member to help. This is tantamount to discrimination. It may not be intentional, but it's thoughtless nonetheless. It is also morally wrong. Therefore, many customers with visual impairments end up leaving empty-handed. Let's think about the commercial impact of that for a minute – more than 2 million consumers in the UK with sight loss. That's a little like turning away customers and telling them that their money isn't good enough. Not only is it disappointing, it is commercial madness. Why turn away 3 per cent of the population who want to buy from you?

Aside from those who are visually impaired, there are 11 million people who have hearing impairments. That is around 17 per cent of the population of the UK. Ask them about their experience engaging with retailers and other consumer brands and more often than not it is a deeply frustrating one (Hearing Link, 2020).

Going back in time now to the height of the pandemic, stores, restaurants and other facilities were re-opening with staff wearing face masks. What happens if you need to lip-read to know what the staff member is saying? You can't do that unless it's a see-through mask.

Do retailers, restaurants, banks, car dealers, travel companies, etc, have members of their team who can use sign language to communicate with customers? This is often/typically not the case, and less than a handful of businesses have thought through the need for this. If you knew that 17 per cent of the population woke up one day and all spoke Spanish instead of English, would our consumer-facing brands ensure their staff could speak Spanish? Of course they would.

Let's take another minute to think about this: 11 million people in the UK with full or partial hearing loss and almost no consumer-facing business with processes in place to be able to deliver effective levels of customer service and experience? This is another example of commercial madness.

Imagine sitting on a train in the UK and there being no digital signage. All the announcements around the next stop, changes to the itinerary and so on are made verbally over the public address system – not exactly helpful if you have a hearing impairment. You'd be none the wiser. You might miss your stop or end up being hugely inconvenienced. Customer experience needs to be all-encompassing and able to address the needs of all customers.

The benefits of being a diverse organization

There are a significant number of benefits of having a diverse workforce. It can lead to greater creativity and that in turn often manifests itself in better customer experience. Diverse workforces lead to having a greater variety of perspectives. This in turn aids business strategy as well as helps to ensure that certain aspects of the customer experience have been adapted to be relevant to meet the needs of different consumers.

A more diverse workforce will also be a driver for innovation. Research conducted by Josh Bersin suggests that inclusive companies are 1.7 times more likely to be innovation leaders in their market. Invariably, the beneficiaries of greater innovation in the business are going to be customers, as developments in technology, processes and systems usually focus on improving their experience (Bersin, 2019).

There is also increasing evidence that a diverse workforce leads to faster problem-solving. According to the *Harvard Business Review*, teams that are diverse can solve problems quicker than those with people who are cognitively similar (Reynolds and Lewis, 2017).

According to a white paper from Cloverpop, workplace diversity also results in better decision-making. Researchers discovered that business decisions made by diverse teams outperformed those made by individual decision-makers up to 87 per cent of the time. This is because when employees from different backgrounds work together, they generate more ideas and solutions and better processes for decision-making (Larson, 2017).

The management consultancy firm McKinsey & Company undertook research of 180 businesses across the UK, US, Germany and France. The result proved that those companies that had more diverse leadership and executive teams were also the top performers financially (McKinsey, 2018).

Research conducted by Deloitte of 1,550 employees in three large businesses in Australia operating in retail, healthcare and manufacturing found clear correlation that staff engagement is an outcome of a diverse and inclusive culture. When employees feel included, they are more engaged; when they are more engaged, they are more creative, more innovative and more productive. They also deliver better levels of service for customers (Deloitte, 2013).

A better company reputation is another outcome and benefit of workplace diversity. Consumers are increasingly critical of companies that are seen to put profit before their people. The reverse is true of those that are clearly focused on building and promoting diversity in the workplace. They are viewed as more caring, more humane and socially responsible businesses.

All of the above also means that businesses with workforce diversity have less employee churn and are able to attract better talent into the business. In addition, they are also able to reduce costs by having to invest less in recruitment and training costs.

Diversity directly impacts your attractiveness as an employer

Diversity in the workplace is a key benefit and driver for the company's employer brand. It puts the business in a better light and positions the company as a better and more caring employer. As a proof point for this, 67 per cent of job seekers in a Glassdoor survey stated that a diverse workforce is important to them when making job decisions (Zojceska, 2018).

When you consider all the benefits outlined above of having a diverse workforce, it is even more perplexing that there are so few boards of directors that are truly diverse. There are fewer than 5 per cent of the FTSE 250 biggest businesses in the UK that have a female CEO. This percentage has even declined over the past few years (Statista, 2020). How can that be? It's certainly not down to a lack of women capable of leading our biggest businesses. In addition to this, nearly 20 per cent of the UK population is from an ethnic minority (ONS, 2012) yet 50 per cent of the FTSE 100 boards are all white (Belger, 2019).

Similarly, in the US, the numbers are low. Around 47 per cent of the US workforce are women yet less than a quarter of all senior executives in large US public listed companies are female. In Standard & Poor's list of the top 500 companies, the picture is even worse and is similar to the UK with only around 5 per cent of companies having female CEOs (Holmes, 2019).

It's worth noting that nearly 80 per cent of board members in large US public companies are men, and these are the people responsible for employing the CEOs and determining what they are paid (Ding *et al*, 2013). There is a direct cause and effect here, not to mention a potential conflict of interest. The lack of board diversity suppresses the opportunities for women to become CEOs as it does the requirement for equal pay.

Despite the lack of diversity clearly being wrong in a moral sense, it is ineffective from a commercial perspective. Another factor contributing to this is the lack of correlation of the make-up of the board of a business and that of its customer base. If there is a significant disconnect, as appears to be the case with the majority of businesses, why should we expect them to have the most relevant product, services, marketing or customer service?

The majority of studies that look into workplace diversity found that for every additional 1 per cent increase in gender diversity, the revenue of the business increases by 3 per cent, and increased levels of ethnic diversity in the workforce leads to revenue increases of 15 per cent (Social Talent, 2020).

Brands that have embraced diversity and inclusion

CASE STUDY
Sodexo

Sodexo, the French food services and facilities management company, has a clear hiring strategy and approach that is centred around gender, sexual orientation and age.

They talk about 'gender balance is our business', and their mission is to make it everyone else's business too. And they are walking the talk. Women now make up 40 per cent of the workforce, which is up from 17 per cent in 2009. The construct of their board is also becoming more balanced, with 43 per cent of the board of directors being female. The commercials all add up as well. All the KPIs improve when there is an increased gender balance within one of their businesses: with employee engagement increasing by 4 per cent, they achieve an uptick in gross profit of a whopping 23 per cent and the image of the brand strengthens by 5 per cent (Globalnewswire, 2020).

CASE STUDY
Johnson & Johnson

Johnson & Johnson ensure that all of their team create an inclusive environment. Their vision for diversity and inclusion is such that it is at the heart of how they will achieve competitive advantage. So, while some other brands are simply trying to meet their gender 'quota', Johnson & Johnson see it as the core of their strategy for business success.

They have created mentoring programmes and a 'Diversity University', which is an online resource that helps their colleagues understand the benefits of working collaboratively. They have a chief diversity officer who reports directly to the CEO and chairman of Johnson & Johnson, meaning that this agenda is being driven from the very top of the organization and reflects how seriously they take diversity and inclusion.

Their focus on this has seen them attain various awards and recognition, including from the US *Veterans Magazine* as the 'Best of the Best' for the progress they've made with their efforts in diversity, in addition to being on the Working Mother 100 Best list for the past 28 years.

SOURCE Johnson & Johnson (2019)

CASE STUDY
Marriott

The global hotel chain Marriott has been named as one of the best multinational workplaces by Great Places to Work, which runs the biggest annual study of workplace excellence in the world. The commitment of Marriott International to create an inclusive guest experience includes having women-owned businesses accounting for approximately 10 per cent of Marriott's supply chain. They have committed to having 1,500 hotels owned by women and diverse partners by 2020.

Their focus on diversity and inclusion also extends to the LGBT community, achieving the 'Best Place to Work for LGBT Equality' award on the HRC Corporate Equality Index, which is also a widely recognized benchmark for diversity and inclusion.

SOURCE Social Talent (2020)

Turning to the drink industry now, one of the exemplars of diversity is Diageo.

CASE STUDY
Raise a toast to Diageo

Diageo's motto – 'Celebrating life, every day, everywhere and for everyone' – suggests that they value everyone irrespective of their background, disabilities, religion, sexuality or ethnicity. It engenders a sense of both diversity and inclusion.

Long before #blacklivesmatter became a movement, Diageo had set up support groups for employees of Asian and African heritage to support BAME (black, Asian and minority ethnic) colleagues. They also run a Rainbow Network for LGBT+ employees. They are an organization that walks the talk when it comes to diversity.

With a strong female representation of around 44 per cent of the boardroom and 40 per cent of the executive committee, it has set a similar target for female representation of 40 per cent on its global leadership team (a group of people who sit below the board and executive team) by 2025. Their efforts around diversity have also been recognized when in 2018 Diageo was named the leading FTSE 100 company for its representation of women on boards and in 2019 it was ranked second in the Thomson Reuters D&I Index. They are also a Disability Confident company; this is a government scheme designed to encourage employers to recruit and retain disabled people and those with health conditions.

In 2018, Diageo's gender pay gap sat at 5.4 per cent in favour of women, down from 8.6 per cent in favour of women in 2017.

SOURCE Cole (2020) and PRNewswire (2020)

CASE STUDY
Unilever

Similarly, at the consumer goods giant Unilever in 2018, their hourly pay figures showed that women were paid 2.5 per cent more than their male colleagues. In their UK business, women make up over 50 per cent of all of the management roles. This has been a clear strategy of Unilever's as the percentage is up from 41.8 per cent in 2010.

Unilever's board is 50 per cent female. They are listed on the 2019 Thomson Reuters Global D&I Index and the business is also a Disability Confident employer.

SOURCE Unilever (2018)

These are just a few of the examples of consumer-facing brands that are not just paying lip service to diversity and inclusion; they are taking action. My hope is that by the example they are setting, they encourage other brands to follow suit. Again, there is a clear correlation between their levels of diversity and inclusion and their commercial performance. One would hope that this also encourages more businesses to embrace it.

Defined as a process of building relationships based on trust, consistency, and accountability with marginalized individuals and/or groups of people, allyship is an opportunity to drive change within the organization. Here are some of the processes and steps that can support this:

1 Openly and proactively sponsor someone from an underrepresented or marginalized community or group within your business.
2 Share your sponsee's career goals openly with influencers in the business.
3 Speak your sponsee's name when they aren't around.
4 Put forward your sponsee for projects and assignments that help to facilitate career progression and growth of new skills.
5 Increase the visibility and awareness of your sponsee by inviting them to high-profile business meetings.
6 Endorse them openly and in public.

Underrepresented groups and communities need a voice in the business and allyship is a great opportunity to ensure their voice is heard. Allyship is also effective in helping to break down and break through any unconscious bias that might exist in the organization.

Conclusion

Humans need to see people who look, sound and have similar backgrounds to them in their leadership and organization – equally, they need to see people who do not look, sound or have similar backgrounds to them. The industry needs to embrace diversity and inclusion because no consumer industry has just one face (Atcheson, 2020).

Suffice to say, if anyone still needs convincing of the benefits of workplace diversity, you just need to know that companies with greater workplace diversity generate better profits.

KEY TAKEAWAYS FROM CHAPTER 9

1 Diversity on its own is just a tick-box exercise. It must run alongside a focus on inclusion. You can be diverse, but those who are from a minority group also need to feel and believe that they are being included. This is the difference between talking the talk and walking it, turning words into action.

2 Diversity covers a broad range of people and issues. They include the following:

- the split of the workforce that is female versus male;
- the number of senior and executive leaders who are female and their percentage of the total leadership team;
- the percentage of the board of directors that is female;
- the pay gap between men and women;
- the split in the total workforce who come from the BAME community;
- the percentage of the senior and executive leadership team who are from the BAME community;
- the number of board of directors who are from the BAME community and the percentage of the board that they constitute;
- the size of the LGBTQ+ community as a percentage of the total workforce;
- the percentage of the senior and executive leadership team that is from the LGBTQ+ community;
- the percentage of the board of directors that is from the LGBTQ+ community;
- how many of the workforce who are disabled;
- the number of people in the workforce who have hidden disabilities;
- the number of directors on the board who have a disability;
- how represented different religions and ethnicities are on your board and executive team;
- having a broad representation of class and demographics on the board and executive team;
- support groups and networks within the organization that are set up to meet the needs of all groups of people.

What can your business do today to improve the experience for diverse customers and colleagues? You don't need a board mandate to drive positive change. However, the board of your business must embrace the requirement for full and complete diversity and inclusion.

3 Diversity and inclusion are not only the right things to do from a moral and ethical perspective; they are the right thing to do from a commercial standpoint. As is the case with great customer experience, the more diverse and inclusive a company is, the more successful it is both in terms of top-line sales and profitability.

References

Atcheson, S (2020) [accessed 22 November 2020] Embracing diversity and fostering inclusion is good for your business, *Forbes* [Online] https://www.forbes.com/sites/shereeatcheson/2018/09/25/embracing-diversity-and-fostering-inclusion-is-good-for-your-business/?sh=568039d272b1 (archived at https://perma.cc/4KRZ-WRJG)

Belger, T (2019) [accessed 26 February 2021] Bosses at nearly half of top UK firms are all white, *Yahoo!* [Online] https://uk.movies.yahoo.com/ftse-boards-all-white-century-ftse-100-report-bme-representation-ethnic-diversity-racism-discrimination-102255386.html (archived at https://perma.cc/Y6HW-G4D7)

Bersin, J (2019) [accessed 21 July 2020] Why diversity and inclusion has become a business priority, *Josh Bersin* [Online] http://joshbersin.com/2015/12/why-diversity-and-inclusion-will-be-a-top-priority-for-2016/ (archived at https://perma.cc/T5HT-AHX6)

Cole, C (2020) [accessed 20 July 2020] Diversity plus inclusivity equal success at Diageo, *DiversityQ* [Online] https://diversityq.com/diversity-plus-inclusivity-equals-success-at-diageo-1509264/ (archived at https://perma.cc/DYK7-SFV9)

Deloitte (2013) [accessed 22 November 2020] Inclusion in my soup, *Deloitte* [Online] https://www2.deloitte.com/content/dam/Deloitte/au/Documents/human-capital/deloitte-au-hc-diversity-inclusion-soup-0513.pdf (archived at https://perma.cc/W8B9-L2NK)

Ding, W, Murray, F and Stuart, T (2013) [accessed 21 July 2020] From bench to board: Gender differences in university scientists' participation in corporate scientific advisory boards, *The Academy of Management Journal*, 56 (5), pp 1443–1464 [Online] www.jstor.org/stable/43589224 (archived at https://perma.cc/7RZ5-3DML)

Globalnewswire (2020) [accessed 22 November 2020] Sodexo recognized for the feminization of its board of directors by European Women on Board and Ethics & Boards, *GlobeNewswire News Room* [Online] https://www.globenewswire.com/news-release/2018/11/29/1658747/0/en/Sodexo-recognized-for-the-feminization-of-its-Board-of-Directors-by-European-Women-on-Board-and-Ethics-Boards.html (archived at https://perma.cc/M3W7-FJAP)

Hearing Link (2020) [accessed 21 July 2020] Facts about deafness & hearing loss, *Hearing Link* [Online] https://www.hearinglink.org/your-hearing/about-hearing/facts-about-deafness-hearing-loss/ (archived at https://perma.cc/599U-REKM)

Holmes, M (2019) [accessed 21 July 2020] Why are there so few women CEOs?, *The Conversation* [Online] https://theconversation.com/why-are-there-so-few-women-ceos-103212 (archived at https://perma.cc/RNG9-9Y9V)

Johnson & Johnson (2019) [accessed 22 November 2020] Advancing diversity & inclusion: 2019 health for humanity report, *Johnson & Johnson* [Online] https://healthforhumanityreport.jnj.com/responsible-business-practices/empowering-people/advancing-diversity-and-inclusion (archived at https://perma.cc/6CMD-DT6Z)

Larson, E (2017) [accessed 22 November 2020] Research shows diversity + inclusion = better decision-making at work, *Cloverpop.com* [Online] https://www.cloverpop.com/blog/research-shows-diversity-inclusion-better-decision-making-at-work (archived at https://perma.cc/6V2X-3DMT)

McKinsey (2018) [accessed 22 November 2020] Delivering through diversity, *www.mckinsey.com* [Online] https://www.mckinsey.com/business-functions/organization/our-insights/is-there-a-payoff-from-top-team-diversity (archived at https://perma.cc/F6J2-NASJ)

NHS Choices (2019) [accessed 22 November 2020] Blindness and vision loss, *NHS Choices* [Online] https://www.nhs.uk/conditions/vision-loss/ (archived at https://perma.cc/LS4A-J2ZD)

ONS (2012) [accessed 26 February 2021] Ethnicity and national identity in England and Wales: 2011, *Office for National Statistics* [Online] https://www.ons.gov.uk/peoplepopulationandcommunity/culturalidentity/ethnicity/articles/ethnicityandnationalidentityinenglandandwales/2012-12-11 (archived at https://perma.cc/SD4G-DWH5)

PRNewswire (2020) [accessed 22 November 2020] Diageo North America continues to champion inclusion and diversity every day, *Prnewswire.com* [Online] https://www.prnewswire.com/news-releases/diageo-north-america-continues-to-champion-inclusion-and-diversity-every-day-300991627.html (archived at https://perma.cc/6N4Z-V2EY)

Reynolds, A and Lewis, D (2017) [accessed 21 July 2020] Teams solve problems faster when they're more cognitively diverse, *Harvard Business Review* [Online] https://hbr.org/2017/03/teams-solve-problems-faster-when-theyre-more-cognitively-diverse (archived at https://perma.cc/Y4XM-ZN64)

Social Talent (2020) [accessed 21 July 2020] 10 companies around the world embracing diversity in a big way, *SocialTalent* [Online] https://www.socialtalent.com/blog/recruitment/10-companies-around-the-world-that-are-embracing-diversity (archived at https://perma.cc/E9UT-2V4U)

Statista (2020) [accessed 22 November 2020] Female held CEO positions in FTSE companies 2019 statistics, *Statista* [Online] https://www.statista.com/statistics/685208/number-of-female-ceo-positions-in-ftse-companies-uk/ (archived at https://perma.cc/933R-SS9M)

Unilever (2018) [accessed 20 July 2020] Gender pay gap report 2018, *Unilever.com* [Online] https://www.unilever.com/Images/sam---unilever-gender-pay-report-2018_v9-final-10-jan-2019_tcm24 4-535261_1_en.pdf (archived at https://perma.cc/5X5S-A5VP)

Zojceska, A (2018) [accessed 21 July 2020] Top 10 benefits of diversity in the workplace, *TalentLyft* [Online] https://www.talentlyft.com/en/blog/article/244/top-10-benefits-of-diversity-in-the-workplace-infographic-included (archived at https://perma.cc/9JYD-9CRJ)

10

Commercially successful disruptive business models in consumer sectors

> **WHAT YOU WILL LEARN IN THIS CHAPTER**
>
> - Even travel, one of the first sectors to be disrupted, is continually being disrupted!
> - Changing the eyewear, hygiene and fashion space.
> - How gyms are being disrupted.
> - Telecoms sector – the next to be disrupted?
> - Delivery and logistics disruption in the restaurant space.
> - The ultimate objective for any brand – when the brand becomes a verb.

Disruptors are, more often than not, entrepreneurs or outsiders as opposed to being specialists from within the market they plan to disrupt. They seek to create products or services and a way of doing things that will ultimately displace the existing market leaders, eventually replacing them as the leading brands in the sector.

Disruption by definition entails brands that have discovered how to do something better, quicker or more effectively while delivering a better experience for the customer. They have worked out how to disrupt the status quo. It's not a new concept. Businesses have been disrupted for hundreds of years. The difference now is that we live in the digital age and this has sped up the level of innovation while reducing the time to market. Therefore, disruption happens quicker and more frequently.

To be clear, these disruptive businesses did not start with the technology; they started by recognizing that there was a problem with the customer's experience and they set out to leverage technology to solve it. In all cases, the 'problem' stemmed from a lack of consumer empowerment.

Uber empower consumers to see where their taxi is, when it will arrive, how much the journey will cost, how long it will take to get there and the route taken. This is the antithesis of the more traditional taxi experience.

Monzo Bank put customers in control of their experience from start to finish – from opening an account in a few minutes to getting insight into how they can save money or budget more effectively, to being able to freeze their debit card when they can't find it to being able to unfreeze it when it turns up in the washing machine after a good night out! Again, this is pretty much the opposite to the experience you'd have with a traditional bank.

Rockar, the technology that enables automotive brands to go direct to consumers, has transparent pricing, dealer locations that are in places where customers are rather than out of town and female sales assistants to help the customer spec up their car – no pushy salespeople. It is a very different experience all round compared with traditional car buying.

Another great example of an innovative disruptor is Netflix. They began with their DVD-by-mail model, which ultimately led to the demise of the then market leader, Blockbuster. You can almost hear the conversation in their boardroom: 'Why would anyone watch DVDs? And why would they order DVDs by mail and miss out on coming to the Blockbuster store to browse our amazing collection of videos?' Netflix subsequently turned the video and DVD rental business upside down.

Timing is everything, but how many Peloton exercise bikes were sold when lockdown was announced? Their revenue jumped 172 per cent when it was announced that gyms were closed (BBC, 2020). I bought one! What a great model. Instead of going to the studio, why not work out on your bike at home? Not only did they tap into the ongoing uptick in demand for health and well-being, but they also provided the huge segment of outdoor cyclists with an alternative solution for keeping fit for when the weather doesn't allow you to venture outdoors.

In every case I can think of, disruptors have found a way to leverage technology to empower customers and give them a superior customer experience to the one they're used to with established, traditional suppliers in these respective sectors.

Women entrepreneurs lead the way in disruptive businesses

Possibly as a result of the glass ceiling that still seems to exist for women, when it comes to landing the top job in too many corporate environments, the rise of the direct-to-consumer (DTC) sector appears to be democratizing entrepreneurship. According to IAB, women make up 53 per cent of the founders/CEOs of DTC brands (IAB, 2020).

Disruption in the travel sector

Time to travel

One of the first consumer sectors to be disrupted was the travel sector. After all, easyJet was founded in 1995, the year after the World Wide Web saw its first transaction.

Its whole low-cost model was predicated on an operating model that used technology where previously airlines required people to do the job.

FIGURE 10.1 The drivers for successful disruption

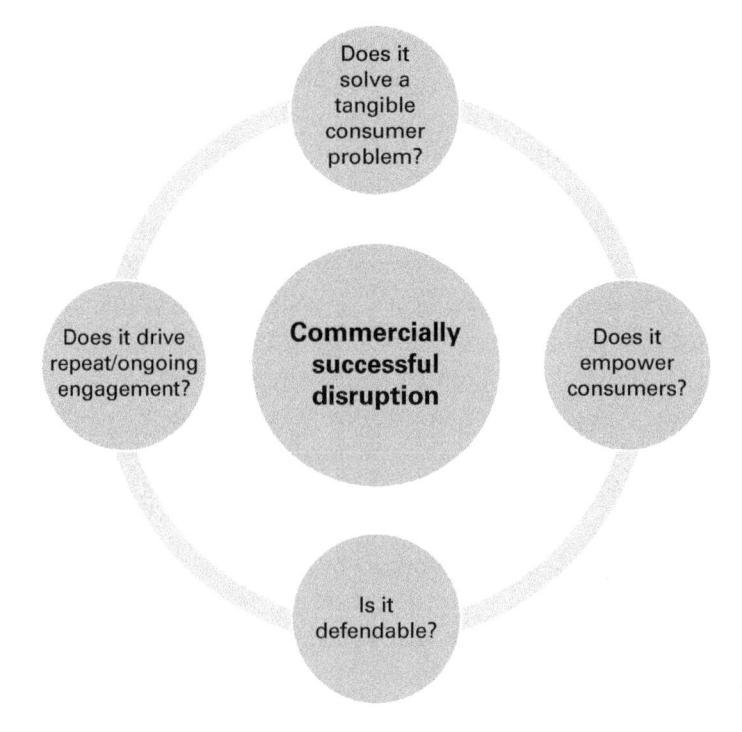

- Does it solve a tangible consumer problem?
- Does it empower consumers?
- Is it defendable?
- Does it drive repeat/ongoing engagement?

Commercially successful disruption

Whereby airlines had previously relied upon travel agents and their own call centres to push sales of their flights and packaged holidays, easyJet implemented a direct-to-consumer model, cutting out the go-between, meaning they made additional margin on sales, which meant they could pass some of this on to the consumer through lower prices.

As they moved to reduce other operating costs, including the requirement for less human intervention and a pared back service (no inflight meals, no monitors, etc), this gave them additional scope for reducing costs and positioning as a low-cost, no-frills airline.

In the years to come after the birth of ecommerce in 1994 we saw a plethora of online-only travel sites. Expedia arrived in 1996 and lastminute.com in 1998. This created a new channel of choice for consumers and led to the disruption of the travel sector whereby consumers could now book flights and accommodation separately – sometimes from different websites.

Consumer adoption of travel sites was rapid. The online players provided a quicker and more cost-effective way to book a flight or buy a holiday than traditional brick-and-mortar travel agents. Over the past 25 years we've seen the brick-and-mortar travel agents almost disappear completely from our high streets.

In recent years, new disruptors have appeared – the highest profile of which being Airbnb. Whether you're off on holiday or a business trip, Airbnb offers a viable alternative to either the pureplay travel booking engines such as Booking.com or Expedia, or the brick-and-mortar travel agents. At the same time, they offer a very strong customer value proposition (Singla, 2019).

- **range/choice:** a broader choice than any other online site;
- **price:** anyone can book accommodation on Airbnb as they have products to suit anyone's budget;
- **availability:** you'll only see what's available for when you want to travel;
- **peer credibility:** the first thing you see are experiences and accommodation viewed by your friends.

Changing the eyewear, hygiene and fashion space

Take a look at this

The retail optical market has been disrupted more than once. In the 1980s we saw the evolution of the optician chains such as Vision Express,

Specsavers and Optical Express. Previously, opticians were like doctors: they had one, maybe two places of practice.

One thing that hasn't ever really changed is the cost model. Buying spectacles is an expensive business.

CASE STUDY
Ace & Tate

Along came Ace & Tate. They deliver a great customer experience: same-day prescription glasses at a fraction of the cost, quality frames at a fair price. With their own label and cost-effective manufacturing, they have cut out the well-known brands.

You can try on for free at home and you're free to change your mind within 30 days – even after your glasses have been produced.

The eyewear industry has traditionally been characterized by high prices and inconsistent customer service. Ace & Tate are changing that. Founder Mark de Lange has an updated view on the industry, saying, 'We are focused on building a brand people love interacting with by offering the best customer experience around, thoughtful design and great shopping environments – both digital and physical.'

They are a tech-enabled brand, using digital technology to improve the customer experience. They're a true omni-channel retailer. If you have an eye test in store, your prescription is immediately stored in an online account, so if you want to go on to order more frames all the details are available. Online and offline channels are seamlessly integrated. They are a digital/online-first company, with stores supporting the in-person experience for those who want it.

Ultimately, they are a great example of what being a customer-centric business entails. If you were starting a new optician business, Ace & Tate would be your blueprint for success.

SOURCE Bungay (2017)

CASE STUDY
Keep tight with Heist

Sometimes the best ideas seem so simple. Budding entrepreneurs often have the thought of, 'why didn't I think of that?'

One such disruptive brand is within the women's lingerie sector. The CEO of Heist, Toby Darbyshire, was actively seeking a consumer sector that was in need of disruption. His view was that the women's underwear category was broken as it was focused on fashion and function and lacked innovation. He is quoted as saying, 'Underwear is worn by all women, all of the time, yet nobody's figured out how to make a pair of tights that stay up.'

With the simple premise that women's bodies are different shapes, sizes and colours and that hosiery should be designed that way, Heist conducted a two-year survey of 100,000 women with their team of data scientists developing seven shades of 'nude' tights to meet the skin swatches that had been submitted in the research.

They created their own internal innovation team, which they call Lab 12. Using big data, they looked at the issues not from a design perspective but from an engineering one and gained an understanding of why things were failing.

The brand is also applying technology to sustainability. Heist has just launched fishnet tights made from fishing nets. They are the first tights, to Darbyshire's knowledge, that use both recycled nylon and recycled elastane. The company has committed to rolling out the same eco technology in the core range by autumn/winter 2020.

Heist has seen triple-digit growth every year since it was founded – no surprise given their customer focus.

SOURCE Rea (2020) and Financial Times (2020)

Is there a snag in Heist's growth plans, or is there room for two?

Another disruptor in the lingerie space is Snag Tights. Having solved the decades-old dilemma of tights not staying up and sagging around the knees, in just a couple of years from its inception, Snag Tights has sold well over 1.5 million pairs of tights, generating tens of millions of pounds of sales in the process.

They now have 3 per cent of the UK market and are growing sales internationally around the world (Frost, 2020).

How gyms are being disrupted

Just as is the case in the travel sector, the health and leisure space has also been disrupted with new innovative entrants that have leveraged digital technology to create new operating models.

Work out at your leisure

Gyms and fitness providers have had to adapt their operating models to meet the changes in consumer behaviour as a result of Covid-19. The increase in working from home has led to the requirement and opportunity to engage digitally by offering participation in virtual classes.

Hybrid models emerged that enabled the customer to choose from a membership giving access to the physical environment versus the digital one as well as one offering the flexibility of engaging with both physical and digital.

Again, this is about customer empowerment. Flexibility puts the customer in control, not the other way around.

Automotive is electrifying

The best example of a disruptive brand in the automotive space is Tesla.

They were the first electric vehicle manufacturer of scale. They were the first car brand to disintermediate and cut out the intermediary, in this case the car dealership, and go direct to the consumer. You can only buy directly from them.

You no longer have to go out of town to an inconvenient location to look at cars. Tesla took theirs to the consumer by opening up in shopping malls. By opening in retail outlets in traditional shopping, they extended the reach of the brand, potentially pulling in new customers who may have been 'passing trade' and spontaneously decided to go into the Tesla showroom. This has made them accessible to anyone who wants to experience the brand.

Has Tesla been successful? Their market capitalization is more than Ford, GM and Honda put together.

We will see others follow the Tesla path. As mentioned above, Rockar is a company that empowers car brands including Jaguar Land Rover to go direct to the consumer by opening their own showrooms as well as opening their own digital car outlets.

As Covid-19 taught us, we can't always rely upon having access to the physical product. The visualization platform ZeroLight enables potential consumers to put on a headset and be transported into the car. The car can be examined closely, and the configurations determined by the user. ZeroLight has been integrated into Amazon Alexa whereby car buyers can explore, interact and make changes to the model being viewed by simple voice commands. This type of technology will ensure that consumers can access the brand at any time (Valich, 2020).

Delivery and logistics in the restaurant space

Delivery companies have the path to opening up the food sector. Now you can order online from any of your local takeaway food establishments without having to brave the elements or set foot outside your house and have your order delivered to your front door. From Deliveroo to Uber Eats, there are a multitude of companies now in this space.

When you're buying a coffee, often on the way to work, you're in a hurry. Starbucks continues to develop its extremely popular mobile order and pay app, with My Starbucks Barista being added to enable customers to order and pay for their food and drink just by speaking in a conversational exchange. The success of the ordering-ahead capability, which in 2017 accounted for 7 per cent of all transactions in the US, has led Starbucks to open a mobile order and pay store at its Seattle headquarters (Retail Insider, 2017). Again, this is all about customer empowerment and convenience.

Telecoms sector – the next to be disrupted?

There is a direct correlation between the cost and ease of switching from one brand to another and the opportunity for a disruptor to change the dynamics of a sector. Telecoms, and in particular mobile, feels a little like banking used to be. The cost, time and hassle to change provider meant that most consumers stayed with their current provider.

Although you can port your number relatively easily now from one network to another, most of us are tied into contracts and are induced by a 'free' upgrade to the latest iPhone in a year's time if only we hang on that little bit longer! I have a feeling we will see this sector disrupted in the years to come in a way that other consumer sectors have been.

CASE STUDY
When the brand becomes a verb

At one point Uber were the highest-value private start-up company in the world. They identified three key differentiators to appeal to customers:

1 request from anywhere;
2 ride with style and convenience;
3 hassle-free payment.

The initial concept was to make ordering a car as easy and simple as possible. Utilizing GPS to identify the user's location meant you could order a car without knowing where you are (pretty useful after a night out), and as the fare is automatically charged to your card there is no need to find cash.

It's also a global service, so you can use your Uber app like you would at home in New York, London, Amsterdam or Sydney.

Uber use behavioural science techniques to improve the customer experience:

- Cars on a real-time map reduces anxiety while customers are waiting for their car to turn up.
- Payment takes place at one psychological move on from consumption, which reduces the perceived pain of the transaction.

Despite opposition from taxi companies worldwide, restrictions on licences in key cities like New York and London, concerns about safety, being called out for a sexist culture and claims of tax avoidance, it continues to be hugely popular with users because it is easy to use, customer focused and above all cheap.

I'm sure most of us have now on multiple occasions used the phrase, 'I'm going to Uber it.'

In the world of buy now pay later (BNPL) solutions, which has found huge engagement with Gen Z and Millennials, customers are saying they're going to Clearpay it or, if they're in the US or Australia, 'I'm going to Afterpay it.'

As a brand owner, you really know you've arrived when you become a verb that's widely used by consumers!

SOURCE Uber (2020) and Blystone (2019)

Conclusion

Disruption is not only the right thing to do to improve your commercial performance, it is also a business survival strategy, as you can absolutely guarantee that someone, somewhere is plotting how to disrupt your sector. Therefore, you need to ensure that you get there first.

Many businesses have innovation labs these days. But I'm not sure they go far enough, as they are more about evolution than revolution. And you may need to do more than just innovate to ensure you stay in the game in the long run.

KEY TAKEAWAYS FROM CHAPTER 10

1 Disruptors always solve a problem that exists in the market they plan to enter. When it comes to consumer-led sectors, the problems solved are almost always around lack of customer empowerment – whether that's being empowered to have your favourite takeaway food delivered or ordering a taxi (Uber) and knowing where it is, when it'll turn up and how much it'll cost. The disruptors put the customer in control.

2 Disruptors always make customer experience the focal point. They recognize that the more barriers they remove on the customer journey, the more sticky customers will become. And the better job they can do of this, the more chance they have of becoming a verb used as a replacement for a traditional term to describe the activity being undertaken!

3 Disruptive brands tend to use data more effectively than established players. That is because they work out how to turn data into insight and how to leverage that to improve the performance of their business.

4 Disruptors have very clear value propositions that customers get instantly. There is complete clarity around their purpose, their brand and what their promise to consumers is. And invariably due to the nature of their proposition being technology-led, they deliver on their promises more consistently than established brands in the sector.

5 While disruptive brands often take some time to pay off the investment that it took to grow them in the first place, they ultimately become more profitable than the incumbents. They also enjoy significantly higher valuations as a result of the fact that the market can see their potential to become the top dogs in their sector.

References

BBC (2020) [accessed 22 November 2020] Peloton sales surge as virus boosts home workouts, *BBC News* [Online] https://www.bbc.com/news/business-54112461 (archived at https://perma.cc/2RQ4-FZPL)

Blystone, D (2019) [accessed 20 July 2020] The story of Uber, *Investopedia* [Online] https://www.investopedia.com (archived at https://perma.cc/2BAE-6QGV)

Bungay, A (2017) [accessed 20 July 2020] A closer look at Ace & Tate's Mark De Lange, *Spaces* [Online] https://www.spacesworks.com/closer-look-ace-tates-mark-de-lange/ (archived at https://perma.cc/3CC3-C9VE)

Financial Times (2020) [accessed 22 November 2020] Heist takes on the lingerie market, *www.ft.com* [Online] https://www.ft.com/content/a6ef99a6-3251-11ea-9703-eea0cae3f0de (archived at https://perma.cc/SXK9-MEZP)

Frost, M (2020) [accessed 27 November 2020] Snag is in shape to the tune of £24 million with tights for all women, *Express.co.uk* [Online] https://www.express.co.uk/finance/city/1244576/snag-hosiery-brand-finance-latest (archived at https://perma.cc/4UWE-NG5S)

IAB (2020) [accessed 22 November 2020] IAB '250 brands to watch' identifies the most disruptive U.S. direct-to-consumer brands and services, *IAB* [Online] https://www.iab.com/news/iab-250-brands-to-watch-identifies-the-most-disruptive-u-s-direct-to-consumer-brands-and-services/ (archived at https://perma.cc/VH7L-L2S8)

Rea, F (2020) [accessed 22 November 2020] Heist spent 2 years analyzing 100,000 skin tones to develop universal shades of 'nude' tights – here's how they look on 7 women, *Business Insider* [Online] https://www.businessinsider.com/heist-nude-tights-review?r=US&IR=T (archived at https://perma.cc/S87C-B8PG)

Retail Insider (2017) [accessed 29 November 2020] Digital retail innovations report, *Retail Insider* [Online] https://www.retailinsider.com/wp-content/uploads/2014/07/Digital-Retail-Innovations-2017.pdf (archived at https://perma.cc/48FF-VRWZ)

Singla, S (2019) [accessed 22 November 2020] How Airbnb works: Insights into business and revenue model, *JungleWorks* [Online] https://jungleworks.com/airbnb-business-model-revenue-insights/ (archived at https://perma.cc/Z4YE-33ST)

Uber (2020) [accessed 20 July 2020] The history of Uber – Uber's timeline, *Uber Newsroom* [Online] https://www.uber.com/en-GB/newsroom/history/ (archived at https://perma.cc/U8TY-4YHJ)

Valich, T (2020) [accessed 22 November 2020] How Zerolight VR tech changes car buying experience, *VR World* [Online] http://vrworld.com/2016/04/26/zerolight-vr-changes-car-buying-experience/ (archived at https://perma.cc/HM3D-RWBU)

11

If you were starting a retail business today, what would it look like?

> WHAT YOU WILL LEARN IN THIS CHAPTER
>
> - You'd most likely adopt a very different business model from those that went before you.
> - Independent retail is on the rise and it's here to stay. What makes independent retailers successful?
> - What is the future of the high street?
> - The last mile is the most important touchpoint on the customer's journey and still one of the least effective.
> - It's not what you sell, it's how you sell it that counts.
> - How you can tap into the move to conscious consumption.

To be relevant to consumers, retailers need a very different operating model

One of the most successful retailers in the UK is Selfridges. They have four stores and a successful online business. That is a very different approach from the other department store chains – John Lewis, M&S, Debenhams, House of Fraser, all of which have, or had, dozens of stores, if not hundreds, across the UK and other markets.

As a distribution plan or strategy, having hundreds of stores was successful for decades. However, as we have seen, you might now consider this to have been a flawed approach as online sales grew and consumers had a proliferation of choice across categories that the other department stores couldn't compete with (see Figure 11.1).

If your aim was to start a national retail chain today, that national coverage could potentially be achieved with three or four flagship stores in major cities, a significant direct-to-consumer proposition online, a presence on marketplaces such as Amazon and a social commerce play on Facebook and Instagram. You'd achieve the same coverage for a fraction of the investment, and it would be more profitable and more flexible. You might also consider opening up some local, smaller-format stores to tap into the increase in work from home and stay local, shop local.

The other fundamental differences would be the following:

- The stores would be far more experiential. That would include not only having content, technology and staff that created a fantastic in-store experience, but one that was always innovating and offering something new. This doesn't need to involve big investments in technology. It could be as simple as having your staff or external specialists come in to demonstrate products, or to enable local farmers, artists and other providers to showcase their wares in your store. Retail is meant to be about theatre. Going into a retail store used to be as much about being entertained and engaged as it was about buying something. But of course, the more engaging the experience was, the more customers were likely to make a purchase. I believe we've lost much of this across the vast majority of national retail chains, which in general terms have become homogeneous, dull and uninspiring experiences.

- You'd ensure that customers had a seamless experience end-to-end across all of your channels and touchpoints. Most retailers still operate in silos, which does not promote the joined-up and collaborative approach required to ensure customers have a seamless experience.

- You'd behave more like an independent retailer rather than a national chain, delivering a more personal and relevant experience for consumers. Retailers need to trust and empower their staff running their stores to make decisions at a local level that can have a positive impact upon the performance of their store.

- Customer service would be at the heart of what you did. At the moment, it's a deeply fragmented and frustrating experience for customers that in many cases feels very much as though we don't care about customers and we're just trying to make the 'problem go away' rather than embracing it, resolving it and learning from it so that we don't put other customers through the same unsatisfactory experiences.

- You'd have a single customer view from the get-go, where you had complete visibility of customer behaviour across all of their interactions with channels, customer service and marketing.
- You'd have a customer-centric approach to all that you did, as per the framework in the final chapter of this book. That means a lot more than just customer experience and the more obvious aspects such as service and consistency.

FIGURE 11.1 Proliferation of consumer choice

Retail 1994	Retail 2020s
Limited consumer choice	Proliferation of choice and channels
High street stores throughout the UK	Smaller number of flagship stores
Presence in retail parks and shopping malls	Presence in retail parks and shopping malls
Direct mail catalogues	DTC ecommerce
Internationalization (Stores only)	Internationalization (Stores and online)
	Omnichannel
	Social shopping
	Marketplaces

The rise of independent retail and what makes independent retailers successful

Independent retailers have always delivered good levels of service. The more local they are, the more personal the service levels tend to be. That is because they know you, they know your name, what you like, who your family members are, and are able to make personalized product recommendations. Additionally, they provide great customer service and experience. It feels like they go the extra mile for you. When was the last time you were made to feel special when you were in a national retail chain?

Often a visit to an independent retailer is a voyage of discovery, like going into an Aladdin's cave. You never know what great trinkets, fashion, furniture, antiques, food or electrical products you might get your hands on. It's a combination of this, the more personalized experience and great service that makes customers warm to their proposition.

The challenge for the smaller retailer is that they need a good online and digital proposition in order to extend their reach and capture demand from beyond the geographic boundaries of their store, but also to increase frequency and engagement with local customers. This is not an easy thing to achieve and cannot be done simply by building your own website. It would be challenging to compete with the digital marketing budgets and capability of larger brands. This is where platforms such as DownYourHighStreet.com come into play as they provide an independent retailer with the opportunity to sell not only domestically across the UK but internationally, while they do all the hard yards on the marketing front, generating consumer demand.

The future of the high street

Even before the Covid-19 pandemic, if you paid close attention to all the media hype around the high street, you'd be forgiven for thinking that it had died some time ago. Yes, there are lots of empty spaces around, and sadly more now due to the pandemic. There's no question the high street is evolving. It needs to. But it is not dead, it is not dying and, in my humble opinion, has a very bright future. It's just got a transition to go through before it gets there.

I know that the majority of consumers are bored of the largely homogeneous and generic offering you can find on most high streets. How do I know this? I know this because I ask them. I've been to Glasgow, Newcastle, Dublin, Colchester, Exeter, Manchester, Birmingham, Sydney, Melbourne, London and New York, where I interview consumers about what they like and don't like about shopping on- and offline. For the former, it's the inability to touch and feel the product, for the latter it usually comes down to the lack of store staff to serve them and the generic, somewhat homogeneous proposition from town to town. These are two of the key drivers for consumers going online in the first place. They're also indicative of the current lack of retail theatre and relatively flat and uninspiring experience you get when you're in a retail store.

Aside from the obvious impact of Covid-19 on town centres, one of the biggest reasons for the empty spaces we see on our high streets is that the national chains overexpanded their store portfolios in the first place. You can understand why. They found a formula that worked and kept on rolling it out across any conurbation that looked to have enough consumers to justify it. However, as a significant number of consumers began to shop online, many retailers were too slow to respond to the migration or channel shift of around 30 per cent or more of their customer base moving online. This is why many have had to go through CVAs (company voluntary arrangements) and similar insolvency measures.

While some of their customers still shop across online and in stores, many have changed their channel of choice. We call this 'channel shift' and 'migration' from one channel to another.

Another significant factor affecting the high street and retailers' ability to turn a healthy profit is business rates. This is because business rates are currently calculated on the rateable value of the property, when sales performance would be a better measure as it would be a barometer for the commercial success of the store. So, this has been a millstone around the necks of national retailers. Business rates need a fundamental rethink, and quickly.

To further demonstrate the issue, Lidl, which installed solar panels in seven of their stores, saw their business rates increase by 528 per cent as a result (Sunderland, 2020). Why are retailers and other organizations being penalized for implementing sustainable energy solutions?

If you believed the hype, you'd also believe that the internet had killed the high street. We're all shopping online now, aren't we? Yes, many of us are. However, the reality is that across all of retail, prior to the pandemic, 80–82 per cent of sales were still taking place in a store (ONS, 2019). After the lockdown and increase in working from home, this percentage grew significantly and levelled off at around 26–28 per cent of all retail sales being online. Therefore, around 72–74 per cent of retail sales still take place in a store (ONS, 2020).

Obviously, there will be some product categories where ecommerce has an even bigger share of consumer spend. Some big retailers, such as Next and John Lewis, generate half or more than half of their total sales online, but they are the exception rather than the rule (Statista, 2020a; Rigby, 2020).

To this end, there has been much debate about the impact online is having upon physical retail. There is conjecture that the government is considering implementing an online sales tax to create a fairer system for all retailers. The premise of an online tax fundamentally misses the point, both in relation to the cost structure of running on- and offline channels as well as how consumers shop.

Ecommerce on its own is not the full story. According to the IRMG, which along with Capgemini publish the sales and KPIs from hundreds of leading UK retailers, around 35 per cent of orders are click and collect (Capgemini, 2020). In the US, this figure is approximately 7 per cent of ecommerce sales; however, it is growing rapidly and will likely become as significant a percentage as it is in the UK (Statista, 2020b).

So, the internet is not only an additional sales channel; it is a driver of sales in store. Approximately 70 per cent of us start our journey online before deciding where to buy offline (Google, 2020). The reality is we live in a multichannel world and we choose whichever channel is the most relevant and convenient for us.

There are many other factors at play that have an impact upon the high street – for one, out-of-town retail parks and shopping centres that conspire to take consumers away from the high street. This really needs to be addressed by town planners and local authorities. If we continue to build these, we're going to make it harder for consumers to support their local high streets.

Something else we need to address is the retail infrastructure, or lack of it, around new housing developments. The leading UK national building companies such as Barratt, Persimmon and others create what is essentially a new small town, with thousands of flats and houses but with no retail proposition to speak of. Or at best, a supermarket in the middle of the development. There are rare exceptions to this. King's Cross and Battersea in London are prime examples – the former having 'Coal Drops Yard', which has a great mix of independent retail, food and charity shops, all surrounded by thousands of new flats and businesses.

Over the past 30–40 years, more and more of us have moved away from living in town centres and local high streets as new housing developments have been created elsewhere. In the years ahead, I see this trend reversing, with more developments like the one at King's Cross and Battersea taking consumers back to living next to retail and leisure.

We must also consider the impending significant change in consumer behaviour. I believe the age of consumerism, when we bought stuff just because we could, is dead. We're moving head-first into a world of conscious consumption. The outcome of this is that we will think much harder about whether or not we really need to buy that new dress, suit, car, sofa, laptop or mobile phone. It will also drive our decision of where to buy it from. As such, I also believe that it will engender a change in consumer sentiment to want to shop more locally and to support local businesses.

As I mentioned above, local independent retailers can offer many benefits and have a potential advantage over the national chains. They tend to be more focused on being employee-first, which is the most important and first building block on the road to being customer-centric and leads to better levels of service. Of course, in many cases, the person who owns the business is on the shop floor serving customers.

Hyper-localization

They are more able to develop a range of products and services that are relevant for the needs of local customers and are also more able to identify what these needs are in the first place.

Personalization

We've been talking about this for 15 years at least, and as of 2020, a small handful of national chain retailers can deliver any degree of personalized experiences. Independent retailers often know who their customers are by name. They know what they like and don't like and can therefore tailor the experience. They don't need expensive technology to deliver this.

Differentiation

Independent retailers' propositions are the opposite of a homogeneous, generic, national retail offering. Often, a trip to an independent retailer is a voyage of discovery. Boxpark, a food and retail park made from repurposed shipping containers, is a great example of where you can experience a host of unique, independent retail propositions.

Convenience

While Amazon can deliver faster than most retailers, nothing beats being able to pop down to your local shops for speed. And if you think differently, ask Amazon why they're opening Amazon Go – cashless grocery stores, Amazon 4-star curated stores and bookstores (Cheng, 2019).

This picture I'm painting is what I genuinely believe the future holds; however, there are many things that need to change along the way to facilitate this environment.

Local authorities need to make parking easier and more cost-effective. If they continue to see parking as a cash cow, more of us will simply drive to shopping centres and out-of-town retail parks where parking is free – that, and buy online.

Local authorities need to be the driving force behind what our high streets need to look like. What is required is to ensure that there is a better mix and proposition for consumers. We need more independent and artisanal retailers for the reasons I outline above. This drives variety. When combined with the right national chains, this can provide a compelling retail offer.

Consumers want the right mix of retail, food and beverage, entertainment, and health and well-being. And the retailers that exist on our high streets need to deliver better experiences in store, supported by a strong service ethos.

Consumers want better food choices, and as we increasingly improve our diets and look to eat healthier plant-based food, high streets need less fast food and more healthy options. We have a responsibility to ensure that all consumers are offered healthier choices.

As we consume more consciously, we will also increasingly look to the circular economy for our next purchase. Why buy new – when this might have a significant environmental impact – when you can procure an item of clothing that is as good as new or furniture that has been refurbished or repurposed? This very much plays both to charity shops as well as to a new breed of retailer.

Am I saying that it's the end for retailers who sell fast fashion and other new products? No. But consumer behaviour will change, and quicker than we realize.

I also believe that we need to look to create more multipurpose facilities. The space might be a retail store during the day and a venue for entertainment at night. This is another way that retailers will be able to justify the costs of having a physical presence on the high street.

We need to create high streets that connect with the local community and provide them with convenience, engagement, experiences and choice.

As a result of the continual consolidation of the retail and hospitality sectors, landlords have to completely rethink their models – 10–20-year leases are a thing of the past. A move to shorter-term leases, pop-ups and sales-related rents has to be a core focus for them. If we accept that independent retailers are a big part of the future of the high street, it goes without saying that landlords will need to offer them cheaper leases than those paid by the nationals.

Over the past few years, we've seen one or two national chains open pop-ups. An example is Primark opening a pop-up at Boxpark Shoreditch in London. While that feels like a brand elevation play by opening up in hipster land, why can't Primark, John Lewis and others open smaller-format stores on much smaller high streets? Greater flexibility from landlords would enable them to do that and, alongside a strong independent retail proposition, this would be a pull for consumers back to their local high street.

The last mile is the most important touchpoint on the customer's journey

The last mile of the customer's experience is arguably as important or possibly even more important than any other part of their journey – that's because it's the last touchpoint, but also it is their most recent experience with the brand they've bought from and therefore the last thing they'll remember. This experience on its own can have a huge impact upon whether or not a customer chooses to buy from a brand again or not. It really is that important.

To add to the challenge, in most cases, the brand is reliant upon third party logistics providers and couriers for the fulfilment of the customer's order. Historically, this has been a poor customer experience. Issues have included items not being delivered when the courier and brand insist they have been or, when the customer isn't in, their order has been thrown over a fence or even left in a wheelie bin! One of the biggest issues is that the customer isn't in control of the experience. They're not sure whether or not they'll be in when their order is delivered. What happens if they're not in? What happens if they need to return the goods? This engenders a sense of disempowerment and is, in my opinion, the single biggest reason why online conversion rates are still averaging between 2 per cent and 5 per cent across different retail categories (Saleh, 2020), when the conversion in store is much higher.

Thankfully there are many developments under way to address this. For example, DPD have an initiative called DPD Design Space – the art of co-creation. Recognizing that they have a ready-made customer focus group of around 20 million people to tap into, they leveraged this audience and their app to get feedback to help shape the future of their delivery proposition.

Consumers are able to suggest ideas and vote in polls to canvas opinion on potential initiatives and ideas that will be implemented to improve the customer experience.

There are over 50,000 people actively engaged with this, which has in turn generated nearly 4,000 ideas and has had almost 170,000 polls completed. This demonstrates the fact that consumers are very happy to engage and share their views, which is not only an opportunity for DPD to learn about how they can deliver better services, but also engenders a lot of goodwill among the customer base, because their opinions are being listened to and acted on (Fruncillo, 2020).

The following are just a few of the ideas that have been implemented to great effect:

1 *Prove yourself* – This solution makes it easier for customers to prove who they are when they're collecting a high-value parcel from a DPD site, no longer requiring utility bills as proof of address, etc.

2 *Partner rewards* – This development supports both consumers and the retail partners DPD work with. It gives consumers discounts from companies that DPD deliver for.

3 *Message the driver* – This is a good resource for consumers as it enables them to contact the driver with important and helpful information, such as how to find their house or flat.

4 *You're next* – This development alerts customers when the driver is five minutes away.

5 *In-flight* – This empowers consumers as they can now make changes to their delivery once it's already out on the road (eg request for it to be delivered to a neighbour or a DPD Pickup shop). This puts the customer in control of their delivery experience.

6 *Rate my driver* – Customers are able to provide instant feedback on the driver and the doorstep experience they've received. This in turn enables DPD to reward and recognize their highest-performing people but it also encourages others to up their game in pursuit of reward and recognition.

SOURCE Transforming Retail Awards 2020, with kind permission from DPD

It's not what you sell, it's how you sell it that counts

CASE STUDY
The John Lewis Partnership

Like all department store chains and retailers in general, John Lewis and Waitrose have been through a torrid time. From channel shift to Covid-19, they have had to continually pivot and find new ways to maintain their relevance and engagement with consumers. They have done this better than most. They have also recognized the need to offer consumers a broader, service-led proposition, as it is no longer enough just to sell products.

Their developments in the services area are many, a few of which include the following:

- Waitrose Cookery School;
- wine tasting at home;
- fashion personal styling service;
- nursery advisory service;
- home design service;
- fitted kitchen and bathroom appointments;
- personal shopping as well as famous beauty festival.

During Covid-19, the business recognized the need to very quickly find ways of engaging through digital with customers who could only access their brands remotely. They achieved this with everything from Partner-led advisory services to intimate cookery classes and mass-streamed festivals to over 5,000 paying customers. They now see virtual channels as a key part of the future of their business, allowing customers from all over the world to enjoy their services.

Operationally, the business successfully equipped over 150 of their partners and multiple brands with on-camera training, equipment and Zoom licences. Their stylists were broadcasting from the style studios in their branches and their chefs were live from the cookery schools. Some of their Partners also connected with customers from their own home, especially in wine tasting, where their specialists have set up 'mini studios' in their homes.

From virtual gin and wine tasting to cookery schools, and from beauty festivals to one-to-one personal shopping and advisory services, John Lewis and Waitrose has turned a crisis in Covid-19 into an opportunity by recognizing how it can more effectively empower consumers to engage with them as they choose. It has also helped them to extend their reach by engaging with customers around the world.

SOURCE John Lewis (2020)

How you can tap into the move to conscious consumption

The first time I became aware of a brand in the fashion sector that had begun a significant move towards the circular economy was February 2020, when Gant made it public that they were going to trial renting out clothes from two of their London stores for 20 per cent of the cost of buying the product (Whelan, 2020).

Climate change and the need for sustainable solutions is undoubtedly having an impact on consumer behaviour and it will continue to do so. A significant percentage of consumers are looking to reduce their consumption or at least ensure that they balance their purchases with a better mix of new, second-hand and repurposed products. This has big ramifications for retailers.

If you were starting a retail business today, in order to tap into these changes in behaviour and ensure your relevance to the broadest possible audience, you would create a very different product and range proposition than the normal retail model. In addition to having new products, you would consider offering customers the opportunity to rent instead of buy. You would also be wise to have a decent percentage of your range made up of second-hand, vintage or refurbished products. One of the terminologies used to describe the latter is 're-commerce', where pre-owned items are resold.

The rental economy is going to boom. This has huge implications for retailers in terms of their supply chain and operating model, as they need to be in a position to bring products back in from consumers who have rented them, refurbish, clean and get their products back to new, where they can then be rented out again. So, this is a whole new layer to add to their operations. There are providers such as Lizee, a French company, which you can outsource this to and they can pretty much run it for the brand. They provide everything from the software to manage the end-to-end rental model through to the logistics and refurbishment of items.

Retailers can still have a bright future. However, to ensure they are relevant to consumers, and that they have a profitable future, they need to adapt their operating models. National retailers need to consolidate their store portfolios, while small independent retailers might well have opportunities to expand their footprint. In all cases, the stores must become more experiential.

Digital and ecommerce will be the cornerstone for growth and needs the appropriate investment in order to deliver the personalized and seamless experience consumers demand. As the model below suggests, our needs are changing and, as such, product needs to reflect the very real move towards conscious consumption and changes in what we buy, not just how we buy it.

FIGURE 11.2   The buyerarchy of needs

```
         Buy
        Make
        Thrift
        Swap
       Borrow
    Use what you have
```

SOURCE Lazarovic (2020)

As heightened awareness of conscious consumption and our own carbon footprint grows, over time, an increasing number of consumers will adopt the behaviour outlined in Figure 11.2 in the buyerarchy of needs.

Conclusion

When thinking about the future of retail, it's easy to make the same mistake we do when we think about technology – that is, that we always overestimate the impact of technology in the short term and underestimate its impact in the long term. In terms of retail, there is so much noise around about the death of the high street. That is simply not true. It is evolving, and it had to, as it wasn't fit for purpose.

Of course, the fact that many of us are now spending more time locally is a benefit to smaller, independent retailers. It also presents an opportunity for large retailers to rethink how they engage with consumers. Retailers have a bright future, but they have to make some pretty big changes – not least to what they sell – as conscious consumption, and what, and from whom, consumers buy will impact retailers for the next 25 years.

> **KEY TAKEAWAYS FROM CHAPTER 11**
>
> 1 If you were starting a new national retail business today, it would look very different from a traditional retail business. You probably wouldn't have stores in every major town and city across the country. You'd have a mix of a

small number of larger flagship stores in big cities with some smaller-format, local stores in some important secondary areas. Ecommerce and digital would be a key focus and a driver for online sales, click and collect and store footfall.

2. National retailers need to behave like small independent retailers at the store level and provide their teams with the flexibility to localize the proposition across range, service, marketing and merchandising.

3. Independent retail has a strong future. However, smaller retailers should look to leverage online platforms such as DownYourHighStreet.com to extend their reach beyond their local area.

4. The high street is far from dead. But is has to go through a significant transformation. There are some great initiatives that look as though they might actually have a real impact, and this includes the Government's High Street Taskforce, which is proactively supporting local authorities across the UK on the transition of their high street propositions.

5. Retailers should be asking landlords to tie store leases to turnover, as that is the fairest and most equitable way to charge rent.

6. Ignore the last mile at your peril. You might have the best in-store and online experience, great products and knowledgeable and engaging staff, but if your courier lets your customers down, you will take most of the blame or at the very least your chances of encouraging customers back will be greatly diminished. Look for logistics partners that go above and beyond. It's worthwhile paying more to have better service than making this decision on price, as that will most likely lead to poor service levels, an increase in customer issues, a negative impact upon customer satisfaction and a reduction in customer lifetime value – not to mention the impact upon your brand equity, as customers tend to amplify these issues online.

7. Just selling stuff is no longer enough. All consumer-facing businesses need to become service providers. Whether that entails providing fashion, beauty or DIY advice online or helping customers by building or installing the furniture or electrical equipment they've purchased, it is this broader service-led proposition that will encourage customers to buy from you again. Services also provide the opportunity to increase the value of each customer, both in the short and long term.

8. To reflect the increasing demand for 'conscious consumption', when deciding what to sell, ensure you balance your range of products with a good mix of new, second-hand, refurbished and potentially offer rental as an alternative to buying.

References

Capgemini (2020) [accessed 20 October 2020] Smart stores rebooting the retail store through in-store automation, *Capgemini* [Online] https://www.capgemini.com/wp-content/uploads/2020/01/Report-%E2%80%93-Smart-Stores-1.pdf (archived at https://perma.cc/7N3Y-CARG)

Cheng, A (2019) [accessed 20 October 2020] Why Amazon Go may soon change the way we shop, *Forbes* [Online] https://www.forbes.com/sites/andriacheng/2019/01/13/why-amazon-go-may-soon-change-the-way-we-want-to-shop/ (archived at https://perma.cc/Z5PK-D437)

Fruncillo, L (2020) [accessed 27 November 2020] DPD bags delivery innovation of the year award, *Tamebay* [Online] https://tamebay.com/2020/09/dpd-win-delivery-innovation-year-award.html (archived at https://perma.cc/LXY3-8P2Z)

Google (2020) [accessed 20 October 2020] Search behavior has changed the path to purchase, *Think with Google* [Online] https://www.thinkwithgoogle.com/feature/path-to-purchase-search-behavior/ (archived at https://perma.cc/ES2U-XDXY)

John Lewis (2020) [accessed 22 November 2020] John Lewis launches virtual services and experiences to meet the new needs of Britain in isolation, *John Lewis Press Centre* [Online] https://www.johnlewispresscentre.com/pressrelease/details/72/Brand_10/12243 (archived at https://perma.cc/U6PU-ZGLQ)

Lazarovic, S (2020) [accessed 26 November 2020] Sarahl.com [Online] https://www.sarahl.com/ (archived at https://perma.cc/DKV2-4QXP)

ONS (2019) [accessed 27 November 2020] How our internet activity has influenced the way we shop, *Office For National Statistics* [Online] https://www.ons.gov.uk/businessindustryandtrade/retailindustry/articles/howourinternetactivityhasinfluencedthewayweshop/october2019 (archived at https://perma.cc/LUY4-HQQK)

ONS (2020) [accessed 27 October 2020] Internet sales as a percentage of total retail sales (ratio) (%), *Office for National Statistics* [Online] https://www.ons.gov.uk/businessindustryandtrade/retailindustry/timeseries/j4mc/drsi (archived at https://perma.cc/L67X-KLAV)

Rigby, C (2020) [accessed 22 November 2020] John Lewis and Boots cite the shift to online as they announce store closures putting more than 5,300 jobs at risk, *InternetRetailing* [Online] https://internetretailing.net/location/location/john-lewis-and-boots-cite-the-shift-online-as-they-announce-store-closures-putting-more-than-5300-jobs-at-risk-21684 (archived at https://perma.cc/K7E2-U44F)

Saleh, K (2020) [accessed 20 October 2020] The average website conversion rate by industry (updated by 2020), *Invesp* [Online] https://www.invespcro.com/blog/the-average-website-conversion-rate-by-industry/ (archived at https://perma.cc/JQQ2-QK7R)

Statista (2020a) [accessed 22 November 2020] Next Plc: retail and online sales 2009–2020, *Statista* [Online] https://www.statista.com/statistics/980296/retail-and-online-sales-next-plc/ (archived at https://perma.cc/PS4C-VYVM)

Statista (2020b) [accessed 22 November 2020] Click and collect: retail sales growth U.S. 2018–2022, *Statista* [Online] https://www.statista.com/statistics/1132011/click-and-collect-retail-sales-growth-us/ (archived at https://perma.cc/P6GB-G5TX)

Sunderland, R (2020) [accessed 20 October 2020] Lidl punished for going green as business rates on solar panels surge, *Mail Online* [Online] https://www.dailymail.co.uk/news/article-8063601/Lidl-punished-going-green-business-rates-solar-panels-surge-700-cent.html (archived at https://perma.cc/WVK4-GQH5)

Whelan, G (2020) [accessed 20 October 2020] Gant launches rental service, *Drapers* [Online] https://www.drapersonline.com/news/gant-launches-rental-service (archived at https://perma.cc/M9W7-PPQQ)

12

To infinity and beyond

What makes a successful bank, airline and car dealer in the 2020s?

> **WHAT YOU WILL LEARN IN THIS CHAPTER**
>
> - Traditional banks can learn from the disruptors of how to engage more effectively with their customers.
> - Fintech leads the way – new payment solutions are a key driver of engagement for younger consumers.
> - Airlines – even when you have a monopoly or operate in an oligopoly, you need to be customer-centric.
> - The need for car dealers to dramatically transform focus from sales to service.

All consumer sectors have been disrupted, and quite rightly so, as they were operating with legacy propositions that reflected how consumers used to behave as opposed to the technology-empowered world in which we now live. There is no place any more for monopolies; no brand or sector can rest on its laurels thinking it can continue to do business the way it always has done.

This chapter addresses how banking along with car dealerships and the airline sector need to evolve to meet consumer expectations, both now and in the future.

How banks can engage more effectively with their customers

Banking and payments in the 2020s

BANKING FINALLY GETS PERSONAL

For much of its existence, banking was one of those fortunate sectors that had experienced little disruption. The cost, even if only in the aggravation and time, for consumers to switch from one bank to another was high. As a result, banks retained most of their customers for life. That is no longer the case. It has become far easier for consumers to switch from one bank to another. But more importantly, banking has woken up to the requirement and the opportunity to move from a push to a pull approach.

Pushing generic financial products or services to consumers doesn't work anymore. If you can tailor products and services around the specific requirements or lifestyle of a customer, you can add far more value to them.

First Direct, which turned 30 in 2019, is an online and telephone banking service and it is the most established challenger bank, directly competing with the banking giants. Launched by Midland Bank, First Direct came to market with a more customer-centric proposition, offering a 24/7 telephone banking service when the established brands' branches were open from 9.30 am to 3.30 pm. Believe it or not, some banks still operate these hours, which are clearly there to serve the bank's purposes rather than the customers!

First Direct, now part of HSBC, having been taken over by them in 1992, launched their own internet banking service in 2000 and mobile banking in 2006. They have a loyal and engaged customer base of around 1.5 million customers (Finextra, 2019). They regularly top the *Which?* list of best banks (Cavaglieri, 2020), which is a testament to both their customer service and the customer experience they deliver.

Three of the current main protagonists for disruption in banking in the UK are the digital challenger banks – Starling, Monzo and Revolut – all formed in 2014 and 2015. To a large extent, they have forced the hand of the long-established banks to up their game and become more of a partner for our finances than merely a place to keep our cash.

The challenger banks have a very different customer value proposition from the established banks. As is the case with disruptors in other sectors, at the heart of their point of difference is consumer empowerment.

CASE STUDY
Monzo

From the beginning, unlike most other consumer-facing brands, the challenger banks recognized the need to deliver great customer service and view it as a profit centre rather than a cost centre. This can be evidenced by the fact that at Monzo Bank, customers can engage with a human being 24/7 365 days a year through the live chat function on their app. They make a virtue of the fact that they're there for customers to help when they most need it. Monzo's customers give them top marks for customer service and communication and they regularly get 5 stars in *Which?*'s survey of the best and worst banks (Cavaglieri, 2020).

The digital banks provide customers with more control over their spending and insight into their behaviour, with balances being updated instantly, and customers getting a notification of when they spend. Customers have full visibility of how much they've spent, as well as being able to set financial goals and keep track of their progress.

Direct debits and other payments can come as an unwelcome surprise to many. To this end, Monzo will show customers what upcoming payments they have the day before the money is due to leave their account. They also ensure that customers are aware of when a regular bill changes. This means that they don't get caught out by a hike in prices or a bad deal due to a contract expiring.

The digital banks enable you to pay friends or other contacts easily without requiring their bank details. The same goes for getting paid by others.

Monzo passes Mastercard's foreign currency exchange rate directly to customers, not charging a mark-up; in addition, they don't charge customers to pay with their card when they're abroad.

Even though Monzo is a digital bank, without any physical high street presence, customers can use any of the 28,000 convenience stores in the UK that enable Pay Point to pay cash into their accounts.

I love the way that Monzo engages their community by giving them a say on new features, what withdrawal limits should be when you're abroad and other initiatives. And unlike other banks, they are committed to using language that we can all understand.

Their terms and conditions are one page long and take approximately three minutes to read. I wish the same could be said for the T&Cs on all other consumer-facing brands' websites!

Monzo has over 2 million customers. You can clearly see why they, Starling and Revolut have become the go-to banks for Millennials and Gen Z consumers.

Monzo has a very compelling customer value proposition. This includes not charging any fees for day-to-day usage, for payments and cash withdrawals in the UK, and payments abroad, and a 10-minute sign-up process. What's not to like?

SOURCE Borbon (2019)

Starling Bank also has a clear and compelling customer value proposition. In addition to providing customers with the ability to set savings goals and have fee-free spending abroad, their accounts offer a wide range of features, including in-credit interest and overdrafts (Brown, 2020).

You can boil the proposition of the challenger banks down to providing customers with more control over their finances. The established banks have much to do to empower their customers and will continue to lose market share, particularly within the Gen Z and Millennial segments, unless and until they can prove that they can provide the same experience and level of empowerment as that of the challenger banks.

Fintech leads the way – new payment solutions that work for younger consumers

Fintech has had a huge impact upon different consumer sectors. From mobile payment services to 'buy now, pay later', consumers have a huge array of options when it comes to how they pay for the goods and services they procure.

Apple Pay and Google Pay have become widely adopted and, to a large extent, are replacing the need for us to pull out our credit or debit cards. We all have smartphones – well, almost all of us – and the ability to tap and pay is extremely convenient.

The buy now, pay later players such as Clearpay have tapped into the change in consumer behaviour among younger consumers, whereby Gen Z and Millennials have a far lower propensity to use credit cards. They want to either pay then or have the ability to buy now and pay later without accruing debt along the way. In this model, outside of the cost of the goods bought, the transaction fee is borne by the retailer, travel company or whoever the consumer has engaged with. There are almost 13 million Millennials in Britain, making up 20 per cent of the British population. For the reasons outlined above, over 60 per cent of them don't have credit cards (Rolfe, 2019).

The average Millennial's discretionary spend is high. They spend 40 per cent more on clothing than the Generation X age group (£116 per month).

For Millennials, the financial crash is not a period of uncertainty; it's the norm. This has led to a mistrust of banks and credit companies:

- Only a third of Millennials say they trust banks to act in their best interests.
- Only 3 in 10 Millennials trust credit companies.
- Only 20 per cent believe credit companies trust them.

SOURCE Newswire (2019)

A unique attitude to debt.

This is a great example of the requirement to understand customers and their behaviour, particularly in a segmentation sense. If you did, and younger consumers are a target audience for your business, you'd definitely want to offer buy now, pay later as a payment solution. It is also another great example of the requirement to understand how best to empower different types of customer.

Airlines – even when you have a monopoly or operate in an oligopoly, you need to be customer-centric

Airlines – fly to serve – or do they?

Airlines and the travel industry were arguably among the industries hit the hardest by the global Covid-19 pandemic. Hundreds of thousands of people lost their jobs as the airlines cut costs to ensure their survival.

During the crisis, the airlines were inundated with customers looking to get refunds for their flights, holidays, car hire and so on. One must have sympathy for the impact the pandemic had, and the challenges they faced, as they were overwhelmed with customers contacting them. However, the way many of them handled the communication and interaction with customers was really poor and among the worst of any consumer sector.

This is a by-product of a sector that has moved almost all of its sales and customer service interactions online and tried to use technology (unsuccessfully) to deliver appropriate levels of customer service.

Due to many airlines having a monopoly on specific routes, or at best, limited competition, they have historically been able to get away with poor levels of service. This is what sets airlines and other forms of transport apart from pretty much all other consumer sectors, where there is much more competition and choice for consumers.

However, there are a number of airlines that have earned their reputation as the preferred choice of consumers, particularly on long-haul flights. Emirates, Etihad, Delta, WestJet, Singapore, Royal Thai, Qantas and Virgin Atlantic all demonstrate consistency of service and the value of a good product, irrespective of where you're sitting on the plane, motivated staff and a good end-to-end customer experience.

This said, across the industry, there has been a gradual erosion of service and experience. The price disruption that took place in the airline industry back in the 1990s began this process. As the focus of consumers moved from service to cheap flights, in a way this led to consumer ambivalence when it came to service. We were prepared to accept poorer levels of service in return for cheaper flights. It was a trade-off that we could live with.

An interesting quote on Quora from a former cabin crew member of a major airline supports the premise that the airlines themselves shifted their focus away from service. The cabin crew member said that 'I try to treat everyone politely because that's something I try to do even in my daily life, but at my airline we are primarily there for passengers' safety and the service is considered a perk' (Quora, 2016).

You may not know this – I didn't – but on many airlines, cabin crew are not paid for many of the touchpoints we experience as consumers when we fly. They aren't paid for their time and input when we board or disembark the plane, when it is taxiing, or when the flight is delayed. So, rather than reward cabin crew for going above and beyond, they are disincentivized to deliver great service and this is rooted in their pay structures (Pardes and Santilli, 2020).

Clearly this has to change. It is a direct conflict with delivering good customer service. It is also a marker for how the airlines in general treat customer service as well as how many of them treat their front-line staff. This attitude and approach to service is born out of the dynamics of the sector.

Unlike many other consumer sectors, airlines have a get-out on many occasions when things go wrong: 'It was the weather'; 'It was an air traffic control strike'; 'There is congestion and a backlog of flights.' There are many genuine reasons why flights are delayed and things go wrong. However, this does not in any way, shape or form excuse airlines for the all-too-often poor communication and even poorer service and solutions offered to customers at these times.

So why is it that customers seem prepared to put up with this and continue to book flights with airlines they love to hate?

As I mentioned above, the airlines can blame many other factors for delays. The industry is monopolistic and an oligopoly, at least at route level. There are a small number of airlines that control domestic flights and a small number who control key international routes. That subsequently limits consumer choice.

The product proposition also makes us feel as consumers that if we pay less, we deserve what we paid for. That also relates to receiving sub-par service. Of course, the opposite is true if you bought a seat in business or first class.

I can't see why airline passengers shouldn't expect both low prices and good service.

The fact you're last to board or turn right when you board shouldn't mean that service levels are any less than those fortunate enough to turn the other direction. Airlines would also do well to remember that someone who is travelling in economy today could well be a business-class traveller tomorrow.

It will be interesting to see over time how the pandemic has affected the airlines' attitude to customer service.

Like most industries, airlines play the short game. They don't really take a customer lifetime value approach. Yes, they have a loyalty programme and, yes, it has good benefits. But despite all the data they have on you, you don't receive a truly personalized experience.

The exception to that is when things go wrong, and you receive a personalized experience of a different, negative type.

Few can forget the United Airlines Flight 3411, when a passenger called David Dao was dragged from his seat by security guards and removed from the plane as a result of refusing to accept $800 compensation for being bumped off the overbooked flight, breaking his nose in the process. This all happened in the first place because an algorithm had selected four passengers, of which he was one, to be bumped from the flight. He was the only one who refused to accept this (Goldstein, 2017).

Another trade secret you may not be aware of is that when airlines overbook, as they frequently do, their algorithms search for passengers with the lowest-price tickets and who have the least customer lifetime value. They are then selected as the ones to be bumped from the flight. You might argue that it makes sense for them to risk the relationship with less valuable customers. I'd argue that this shouldn't happen in the first place. It should always be offered as an option in the first instance, not dictated as a fait accompli (Cooper, 2018).

You cannot run a business by an algorithm. While they help to optimize different aspects of the business, in this sector in particular, they drive pricing. The problem with this is that when supply is limited, but demand is high, as is the case when you have an oligopoly, things work well for the airline from a margin perspective. However, during and post-Covid-19, when demand shrinks, value becomes even more important and it doesn't take much to put customers off booking. Therefore, the algorithms need to reflect this.

I wonder: when was the last time the CEOs of leading airlines walked the floor? When was the last time they had the end-to-end experience that customers go through? What happens when you want to change your flight? What happens when your flight is delayed and you're stuck in an airport in some far-flung country with nowhere to stay, no food, limited funds, etc? Or tried to call the contact centre to complain, change a flight, use your air miles, book a holiday? Have they travelled in economy recently? How was the experience? Have they travelled in business class? Was it up to scratch? Was it worth the money? And of course, how did all of this compare with competitors?

You get the gist. The exam question is, do they really care about all of this? If they have a captive audience who have little choice but to use their airline, then potentially they don't.

Of course, they should. And those who do will enjoy a much more sustainable and profitable future than those who don't. While some consumers over-index on their travel post-pandemic, others will be more cautious. Both business and leisure travellers will most likely travel less frequently for the coming years as a result of the pandemic and its impact upon how we do business and our concerns over where we go. As a result, consumers will be more discerning with regards to whom they choose to travel with.

In any case, consumers are also becoming increasingly frustrated with poor customer service and experience and far less willing to accept it.

The need for car dealers to dramatically transform focus from sales to service

It only just occurred to me now as I'm writing this that the term car dealer in itself doesn't conjure up the most positive perception of what the experience might entail. 'Dealer' makes me think of 'wheeler dealer' and an experience that's focused on price and not service.

Buying a car is an experience that has been ripe for disruption for a long time. From pushy salespeople to 'this is our best and final price', when you know it isn't, to car showrooms that are in the middle of nowhere to expensive car servicing (where they always seem to find something wrong that you need to pay for) – there is much not to like about the customer experience in the automotive sector.

To demonstrate the issue with poor customer experience in car dealers, a survey by Carwow revealed that 39.3 per cent of people have decided to buy a different car because of poor customer service in a dealership (Channon, 2020).

Something was bound to change. And it has.

Leading the disruption is a company called Rockar, who have turned the experience on its head. They partner with brands such as Jaguar Land Rover, Ford and Hyundai. They have associates who support customers rather than sell to them, they have complete transparency on pricing and they enable customers to shop how they want to – whether that's in a car store in a shopping centre or online (Gilliland, 2019). They provide the technology, processes and people that deliver what a customer experience should entail when buying a car. In addition, they deliver the multichannel experience customers have come to expect in other sectors such as retail.

One thing that has always amazed me about car dealers is their almost complete lack of interest in driving your lifetime value to their business. They, more than any other consumer-facing sector, seem only interested in selling to you in the first instance with almost no focus on customer retention.

While many of us take out three- or four-year contracts for our cars, you barely hear from the dealer during this period. Of course, you will get a reminder when your car needs servicing! It's a revenue generator, after all. And if you've purchased a high-end marque, you'll probably get a monthly or quarterly magazine through the post. But nothing is personalized. Nothing really builds the relationship with you. And by the time they do contact you towards the end of your contract, if indeed they even bother to do that, you've already made your mind up to go elsewhere – either to another dealer or to buy another make of car altogether.

This is even more frustrating when you consider that a Capgemini report indicated that there is a strong correlation between customer satisfaction and loyalty, particularly for car dealers: 87 per cent of highly satisfied customers would purchase the same brand again and 85 per cent would buy from the same dealer if the experience was good (Capgemini, 2015).

So, it pays to build the relationship and keep up the communication with customers, as it does to focus on service and experience. If you take a sales-first approach, you push a lot of potential customers away. Whereby focusing on customer service and experience engenders a sense of caring, which in turn creates trust, which in turn drives sales.

In my experience, the main reason why brands don't do this is the same as the over-arching issue with all things customer-focused: they see it as a cost and not a benefit. They only look at the cost to serve and not the impact upon customer lifetime value.

Another part of the issue here is that the salesperson you engaged with has probably moved on. There is so much churn of salespeople at car dealers. They never seem to last very long. I can't help thinking this is a direct impact of how they're paid, how they're treated, the hours they work and an overarching cultural challenge in the industry.

Customers really ought to have a 'relationship manager' – someone who checks in with you a couple of times a year. In an Auto Trader survey, 54 per cent of consumers said that they'd prioritize buying from a dealership that provides the best experience over one that offered the cheapest price. I really believe that car brands who proactively make an effort to build a relationship with customers will become first choice when it comes to buying a new car (V12, 2020).

In the digital age, I fear that we've lost sight of not only the importance of human interaction but the impact of it. Technology is not there to replace human interaction; it should be leveraged to support it.

Tesla is another disruptor that raises the bar. As I mentioned in Chapter 6, Tesla have also disrupted the entire car buying and car ownership experience. From being able to view and buy a car in a shopping centre to taking it there for its service or picking it up from your house, they have looked at how to remove the barriers that exist in the traditional end-to-end car buying and owning experience. There is a reason why they are now valued at more than a whole host of other long-established car brands put together!

To rent or to buy?

Electric cars will predominate in the future, as will driverless vehicles. To this end, it will be interesting to see what impact the rental economy might have on the automotive sector. I can quite easily see a time in the future when we request a driverless car on demand. To be fair, that is still some way off.

The car rental market has already been disrupted by the likes of Zipcar, where you can rent their cars by the minute, hour or day – none of this being tied into a minimum of a day or paying an extra day if you bring the car back after a certain time in the day. This is another great example of customer empowerment. You can rent a car where and when you want it and for exactly how long you want it for.

Conclusion

There is no future for legacy businesses. Any consumer-facing brand that hasn't already been disrupted will be soon. At best, a legacy business dies a slow death.

The old ways of working don't work anymore. Outdated operating models that reflect traditional retail, banking, automotive, travel and other consumer sectors belong where they began – five decades ago.

They don't have the power; customers do. They need a board that really understands what this means and a leader who can be at the heart of its transformation to a customer-centric business.

KEY TAKEAWAYS FROM CHAPTER 12

1 No one size fits all:

- Banking, car dealers and airlines at a sector level have been guilty of a lack of personalization.
- Not only do car dealers not communicate well after the sale; they make no effort to know more about you. If they knew you had a family, they could offer a package of cars for your whole family. Or at least they could try!
- Millennials and Gen Z in the main don't want a credit card. Let them buy now, pay later.
- Airline passengers might be in economy class today, but they could well be in business class tomorrow. And their friends and family may well already be business- and first-class travellers. Bumping them from their seat because they look as though they're the least valuable customers may well prove to be a false economy.

2   The banks, car dealers and airlines have also taken advantage of their monopoly or oligopoly. They must look beyond this to behave differently when it comes to customer service. Increasingly disruptors will force their hand to do so. They can no longer get away with the historically poor levels of customer service. The cost for customers to switch brands, whether in financial terms or time, has reduced dramatically across all sectors.

3   Like many consumer sectors, they need to shift their focus to driving customer lifetime value and be clear on what it takes to deliver that. If they don't take a customer lifetime value approach to their entire business, they will find that customer churn increases significantly. Playing the short game only and focusing on short-term results will risk the future viability of the business.

4   The CEOs of these businesses need to take the time to travel the same path as their customers. They need to experience their own organizations first-hand. That way they get a much clearer perspective of what's working and what's not and what needs to be done to improve the customer's experience. It really brings it to life when you experience things first-hand. What's it like when you miss a flight, or the flight is delayed? How effective and how customer-centric are our communications? How good is our service on board?

    o   How easy was it to change my flight or any of my details on our website?

    o   How easy was it to get through to our contact centre and were they empowered to make any decisions for me?

    o   Do our car service colleagues come across as a customer care team or a sales team?

    o   What was the process like when I was being sold to? Did our sales colleagues have the appropriate level of knowledge? Could they answer all of my questions?

    o   What barriers did we put in the way of the customer?

    I appreciate they'll have to go undercover and with a disguise to do this. But it will be worth the effort!

5   Brands need to empower customers. Whether in the case of a bank by providing insight based on your spending patterns or a car dealer that enables you to choose how often you want to hear from them and about what, or an airline that actually allows you to change a flight without

charging you to do so, customer empowerment is one of the key determinants of whether a customer will buy from you again or not. It determines how smooth or how difficult and how good or bad the experience of dealing with your business is. Friction and barriers to progress on the customer journey will only lead to lost demand.

6 Don't forget the human touch. Technology is an enabler, but it can never fully replace human interaction. At least not in my lifetime! A prime example is in the airline industry. As more and more of their operation has moved online, airlines have really lost their connection with customers. It is another reason why a number of airlines are perceived to have poor levels of service. A chat bot cannot resolve complicated personal requirements around travel.

References

Borbon, B (2019) [accessed 22 October 2020] 11 reasons you should definitely get Monzo, *Monzo.com* [Online] https://monzo.com/blog/2019/05/10/should-i-get-monzo/ (archived at https://perma.cc/E546-FSQP)

Brown, L (2020) [accessed 25 October 2020] Best app-based and online bank accounts, *Save the Student* [Online] https://www.savethestudent.org/money/best-digital-app-banks.html (archived at https://perma.cc/4AKA-UGKS)

Capgemini (2015) [accessed 22 October 2020] Capgemini cars online 2015 report highlights growing consumer demand for a more personalized car-buying experience, *Capgemini Worldwide* [Online] https://www.capgemini.com/news/capgemini-cars-online-2015-report-highlights-growing-consumer-demand-for-a-more-personalized/ (archived at https://perma.cc/6YC4-YD98)

Cavaglieri, C (2020) [accessed 21 October 2020] Best and worst banks, *Which? Money* [Online] https://www.which.co.uk/money/banking/bank-accounts/best-and-worst-banks-a3q5d8c6dj7y (archived at https://perma.cc/KZ22-3WJA)

Channon, C (2020) [accessed 22 October 2020] Bad customer service puts off nearly half of new-car buyers, *Car Dealer Magazine* [Online] https://cardealermagazine.co.uk/publish/bad-customer-service-puts-off-nearly-half-of-new-car-buyers/93803 (archived at https://perma.cc/4UNV-U5L2)

Cooper, K (2018) [accessed 22 October 2020] Here's why airlines don't care about customer service, *CCW Digital* [Online] https://www.customercontactweekdigital.com/customer-experience/articles/airlines-bad-customer-service (archived at https://perma.cc/G9WL-UB5Y)

Finextra (2019) [accessed 21 October 2020] Original challenger bank First Direct turns 30, *Finextra Research* [Online] https://www.finextra.com/newsarticle/34510/uks-original-challenger-bank-first-direct-turns-30 (archived at https://perma.cc/GKQ5-QT69)

Gilliland, N (2019) [accessed 27 November 2020] How digital is changing the automotive customer experience, *Phvntom Inc* [Online] https://phvntom.com/how-digital-is-changing-the-automotive-customer-experience/ (archived at https://perma.cc/68NA-7HNC)

Goldstein, M (2017) [accessed 22 November 2020] Biggest travel story of 2017: the bumping and beating of Dr. David Dao, *Forbes* [Online] https://www.forbes.com/sites/michaelgoldstein/2017/12/20/biggest-travel-story-of-2017-the-bumping-and-beating-of-doctor-david-dao/?sh=40739f97f61f (archived at https://perma.cc/RS64-D8LX)

Newswire (2019) [accessed 27 November 2020] Clearpay to launch 'buy now pay later' app for UK, *eSellerCafe* [Online] https://esellercafe.com/clearpay-to-launch-buy-now-pay-later-app-for-uk/ (archived at https://perma.cc/LU4Y-ZLL5)

Pardes, A and Santilli, M (2020) [accessed 22 November 2020] Flight attendants share what it's really like to do their job right now, *Cosmopolitan* [Online] https://www.cosmopolitan.com/career/a52657/flight-attendant-things-i-wish-i-knew/ (archived at https://perma.cc/5UM2-JR9R)

Quora (2016) [accessed 22 October 2020] What effect does poor customer service have on airline revenues?, *Quora* [Online] https://www.quora.com/What-effect-does-poor-customer-service-have-on-airline-revenues?ch=10&share=e4866aba&srid=zj4L (archived at https://perma.cc/S996-45V6)

Rolfe, A (2019) [accessed 22 October 2020] Millennials pushing shift from credit to debit and digital wallets, *Payments Cards & Mobile* [Online] https://www.paymentscardsandmobile.com/millennials-pushing-shift-from-credit-to-debit-and-digital-wallets/ (archived at https://perma.cc/PF9Z-57RQ)

V12 (2020) [accessed 22 October 2020] Automotive marketing: marketing trends overview, *V12data.com* [Online] https://v12data.com/blog/automotive-marketing-overview-current-marketing-trends-statistics-and-strategies/ (archived at https://perma.cc/65JN-7GMP)

13

We all gravitate towards social people

The same can be said of brands

> **WHAT YOU WILL LEARN IN THIS CHAPTER**
> - That you don't need to invest large sums of money in marketing or paid social media activity to generate brand awareness and engagement.
> - It pays to be social – there is a direct correlation between brands that are social and engage well with customers and their commercial performance.
> - Listening to customers is a cornerstone of building a relationship.
> - Social media is not only a key driver for engagement, but also for sales and customer service.

Social media as a term conjures up an image of lots of people socializing. And while that is of course a core aspect of it, consumers are using social media for much more than that. It has become a primary channel for customer service.

Unfortunately, when the customer's experience of engaging with a brand is not good, all too often social media is leveraged in order to shout about what went wrong. Sometimes this is simply taken as an opportunity to vent their frustration; other times it is an attempt to instigate a resolution and action from the brand.

It should be remembered that the customer's experience also relates to how a brand reacts to them and how they're communicated with on social media.

Social media has also become a key driver for sales. Social shopping is a term that has been doing the rounds for around a decade but has now come into its own as a key driver of sales – whether that relates to consumers buying off the page on Instagram or Facebook or being driven to a brand's website. The influence social media is having on sales is clear to see.

For many people, social media is often the first time they discover your brand, which is another reason why it's so important to communicate effectively – from a brand, product and customer service perspective.

Generating brand awareness and engagement

FIGURE 13.1 The social media operating model

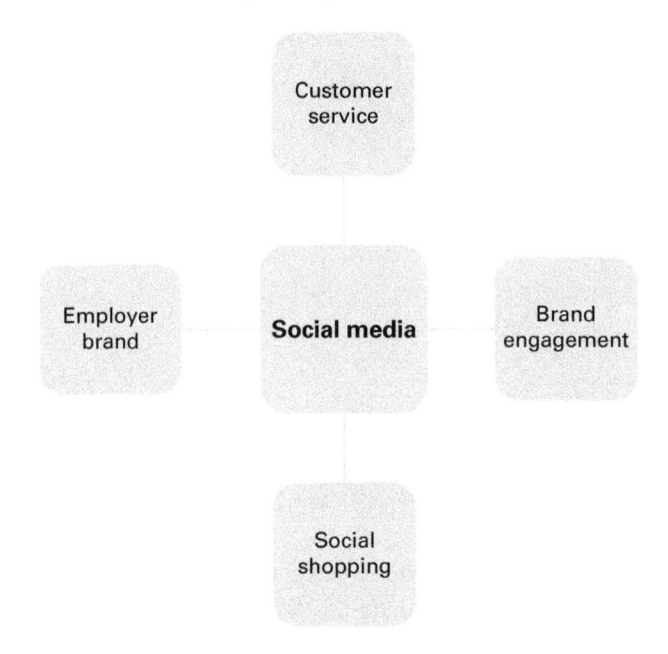

It pays to have an ego!

If I told you that a five-person barber shop in Cockfosters, North London, had a following of nearly a quarter of a million people on Instagram, would you believe me?

What about if I also told you that the same barbers now deliver training around the world in Brazil, the USA, Asia and Europe, would you believe me?

Did they have to invest large sums of money to achieve this? No. They cut hair well and they post the videos of great haircuts and of themselves on Instagram. Yes. Simple as that. This is how they've created a global brand.

The opportunity now exists for them to create their own products. Wax, hair gel, brushes and all. Why not? When they go on stage in Brazil and other countries, they're treated like rock stars adored by their loving fans. I kid you not. That is how deeply their brand has resonated.

Being social doesn't just mean leveraging social media channels. It also means being personal.

The Scandinavians know how to get to the point

I bought some underwear and t-shirts from a Scandinavian brand, CDLP. When my order was delivered it came with a handwritten note with a code to get 10 per cent off another purchase. Not hard to do. No need for a big expensive CRM solution.

Nor did they require this when they followed up with an email asking for my feedback on the product. Not from a ratings perspective. Just so that they could get feedback on how to improve their products. I love this as I do their products and all of their communication. It's completely personalized and relevant.

I'm sure that both the promotional offer as well as asking for feedback on product have an impact on driving incremental sales from customers as well as increasing their loyalty.

Covid showed us the best side and worst side of different brands

From a consumer survey I ran in 2020 during the pandemic, 72 per cent of consumers said that they'd boycott a brand that behaved badly (Newman, 2020). However, I'd instead like to focus on great examples of purposeful brands that did the right thing by their staff, customers and suppliers.

There are some really nice examples from the grocery sector of brands that led with values and purpose. One of those is the Co-op.

CASE STUDY
Co-op

The Co-op helped mourners to say their last farewell during Covid-19. They introduced cortege services that passed by a loved one's favourite place or passed by the family home, therefore enabling anyone isolating or unable to attend funerals due to restrictions to be able to pay their last respects (Mathers, 2020).

In another initiative, and in order to support consumers who were unable to get to their stores, they partnered with Deliveroo to offer home deliveries from 400 stores (Coker, 2020).

CASE STUDY
Morrisons

There are a number of examples of how Morrisons demonstrated they are a caring and purposeful business, from giving £10 million to a food bank to paying suppliers immediately and in doing so ensuring their survival, to staff dancing to keep queuing shoppers entertained. The culture of Morrisons shone through (BBC, 2020).

CASE STUDY
Toms shoes

There are various players in the buy one give one space that donate a product to people in need every time a customer buys from them. It's fair to say you'd class these brands as social brands. The brand that started this model was Toms Shoes.

However, it has evolved to the point now where customers can still give a pair of shoes to someone in need, but they also have the choice of selecting a cause they want to support, such as women's rights or ending gun violence, and instead of donating products Toms will support a non-profit organization working on the specific cause with a grant.

It has a whole department that is focused on impact evaluation, so Toms goes way beyond just being a social brand. With 4.2 million fans on Facebook and around 1 million on Instagram, it's fair to say they resonate with a substantial number of consumers.

Like most brands, however, their path has had bumps in the road. They were taken over by creditors in 2019. Toms needs to focus more on product to give its customers more reasons to continue to buy from them. Being social on its own is not enough (Peters, 2019).

Commercial performance and social engagement have a direct correlation

CASE STUDY
Glossier

The product category that has arguably used social media to the best effect is beauty.

One such example is Glossier. What started out as a beauty blog in 2010 now has over 2.8 million fans on Instagram (Danziger, 2018) and a 2019 market value of more than $1.2 billion (March, 2019).

Glossier have tapped into pent-up demand from a huge and very engaged community online. They have also made their customer base a core part of their product development focus by encouraging customer feedback to help design even more relevant products as well as create excitement and anticipation around this.

They have waiting lists for new products of up to 10,000 consumers. Their community is hugely loyal and passionate about the brand. Their social profile is heavily weighted towards Instagram with a predominantly Millennial and Gen Z customer base.

Compared with most beauty brands, Glossier has a small number of SKUs (stock keeping units/products). To give you an idea of consumer demand, according to Glossier, in 2019 they sold one tube of its $16 eyebrow pomade Boy Brow every 32 seconds.

The business model is direct to consumer (DTC) and mostly online (they have two stores and use pop-ups), affordable product and minimalist, Millennial-friendly packaging. Marketing is almost exclusively social, via Instagram.

Founder Emily Weiss is quoted as saying: 'We are building an entirely new kind of beauty company: one that owns the distribution channel and makes customers our stakeholders.'

There has been talk recently of the term retail disappearing and being replaced by consumer-led commerce, where consumers define and shape what they want to buy and from where. It would be hard to argue that Glossier wasn't already practising consumer-led commerce over five years ago. They are a business that clearly understands what it means to put the customer at the heart of all they do.

SOURCE Berger (2019), Canal (2020) and Carville (2019)

Social media as a service

There are many ways you can think of how you might become more of a service provider to your customers. Social media presents a brand with a great opportunity to up their game and be truly customer-centric.

CASE STUDY
KLM

One of the best proponents of this is KLM. They use social media channels very effectively, both from customer service and marketing perspectives.

Their focus on social media as a strategic driver for their business came about by chance. In 2010, their contact centre team were hit by a deluge of calls and emails from customers whose travel had been disrupted by the eruption of the Eyjafjallajökull volcano in Iceland and the subsequent ash cloud that persisted for some time that conspired to cause huge disruption to air traffic around the world.

As a result of this, KLM created a new customer service team that would engage with customers through social media channels. Their purpose is to be where customers are.

A great example of this in real-life terms is when a friend of mine was flying from Venice to Amsterdam and her flight was delayed by five hours. In her frustration, she tweeted the brand. She was almost immediately called to the KLM desk in the airport, at which point they were able to get her onto an earlier flight.

One gets the impression that KLM is a business that understands how their customers want to use technology to engage more effectively with them. Another example is that they don't force customers to download their app. Managing your booking, getting your boarding pass, checking on flight status and so on, can all be managed through direct messages. After all, you might not be a frequent flyer with KLM. And even if you are, how many apps does anyone want to have clogging up their phone? KLM sends well over 10,000 direct messages every day to customers, keeping them informed and empowering them to engage however they choose to with the brand.

With over 14 million followers and fans on Facebook and 1.3 million on Instagram, they clearly have significant customer engagement on social media. While their share price is volatile, as many airlines are, it increased by 500 per cent from $2 in 2015 to $10 in 2019.

SOURCE WARC (2018) and MarketWatch (2019)

Right time, right place

If you want to build relationships with customers, you need to be in the same places they are, as well as where they would expect to find you.

Of course, the key channels to build relationships are going to be social media. Two-thirds of UK consumers are actively involved on social media daily, and every second, 11 new people use social media channels for the first time. This adds up to 1 million new users on social media every day around the world (Johnson, 2020). Of even more importance is the fact that 67 per cent of UK consumers prefer brands to contact them via social media channels such as Facebook, Instagram, etc; to stay relevant, brands must be on these channels and actively engaging with consumers (Sabanoglu, 2020).

However, when it comes to building a relationship with customers, there is the obvious challenge of how to cut through the noise of all the content and posts that consumers are exposed to. Social listening is a good starting point.

In order to know what content your customers are likely to react positively to, you need to listen to them on a daily basis and regularly throughout the day. Getting involved in conversations around your brand will help you to understand what customers like and don't like and what they want to see and hear from you.

Even negative comments or when there's been a customer service issue are opportunities for you to learn not only how to improve but also to build trust by embracing and resolving issues that customers have. It's also helpful to know what they're saying about your competitors and how often they talk about them and talk about your brand.

You need to be listening to the conversations customers are having with their communities. You're not only listening out for service or product issues that relate directly to your brand; you want to be listening out for cultural trends, and to learn how customers and influencers are referencing your product. This also involves monitoring brand mentions and hashtags and what they're saying about others in your space.

Make sure to set up Google alerts in order to know what customers are saying about your business. You can also use sites such as Reddit to monitor what consumers are saying about your brand, and Netbase is a tool that can help you find online conversations that are relevant to your business. It uses NLP, natural language processing, to discover these conversations.

It's important to make a distinction between social media monitoring and social listening, as the former is more about the past and the latter is leveraged to help you shape a better future outcome.

Trust and transparency are two of the key drivers for building relationships with customers and therefore listening to customers in the first place on social media will result in more positive comments being posted about your brand.

Listening is only the start. You need to respond as well. A sizeable 84 per cent of consumers who have contacted a brand on social media expect a response within 24 hours, and for Twitter the expectations are an hour (Hutchinson, 2017).

The expectations consumers have around response times are only going to increase. I'd go as far as saying that most customers expect instant feedback through social media channels. Expectations heighten if a customer has bought from you online. But even if they purchased goods or services from you in the brick-and-mortar environment, through your stores or ate in your restaurant, they increasingly expect to get an immediate response from your customer service team on Facebook or Twitter (Ennis, 2017).

Speedy responses also result in tangible commercial benefits. A Twitter report found that airlines that responded to customer tweets in less than six minutes acquired customers who would be willing to pay £15 more per fare – so a direct cause and effect between customer response times, average selling price and margins (Huang, 2015). The reason is that a speedy response builds trust and belief that your business can be relied upon when issues arise and therefore many customers are willing to pay more for this level of reassurance.

Make the conversation personal

The expectations around communication for any of your customers or followers on social media channels has to a large extent already been determined by the nature of their engagement with friends and family on social media. After all, social media is where they share deeply personal stories, experiences and photos. Therefore, their expectations are that their communication with brands should be just as authentic as any direct message to a friend or somebody they're close to.

Here are some tips to ensure that you create a deeper connection with your customers:

- Use their first name when possible.
- Avoid jargon and business parlance and communicate with customers using language that is both easy to understand and friendly and engaging in its tone.
- Make it personal from you and sign off on comments with your team name or first name, eg 'The Brand customer service team' or 'Best wishes, Martin'.
- Reaffirm that you are listening to them, that you hear them and that you're there to help them in any way possible.

SOURCE Clearpay (2020)

Guidelines and checklist for social media

Your customer service team and all who interact with customers on social media channels will benefit from clear guidelines and a checklist for engagement. This should be a core part of your customer service approach and aligned with your brand values.

Consider the following:

- tone of voice;
- the response time and service levels for each social media channel;

- have responses ready and answers for frequently asked questions, as this will help to speed up the response times as well as improve first-time resolution levels;
- implement a clear escalation procedure and put processes in place in the event your team has been unable to resolve issues. However, ideally you'd empower your front line of customer service to be able to make decisions without going up the chain of command.

Authenticity is key

Empower all of your customer service team to respond to customers in a meaningful and authentic way. Customers can tell the difference between their interaction with a human being versus a bot! And their expectation for customer service issues is for them to be taken seriously and therefore human interaction lends itself best to this.

If it fits with your brand, you can use emojis. You can also join in conversations with your followers if it's genuinely interesting and relevant to do so.

Encouraging social media recommendations

The following are examples of how you might start to encourage recommendations and drive social media engagement:

- Although ratings and reviews are increasingly being viewed with scepticism by consumers in relation to their authenticity, they are still a driver for many customers as they provide social proof and reassurance. Ensure your customers are able to rate your products with ease.
- Offer incentives for customers to promote your brand and products on social media channels.
- Leverage hashtags to drive more engagement with social media posts. This helps make relevant content to your brand more discoverable.
- Publish and promote testimonials from existing customers in your social media content.

Contests and competitions

Lots of consumers engage with competitions and these can help to significantly increase your reach and number of followers. You can also leverage competitions to encourage an increase in app downloads. Competitions and giveaways are great ways of creating buzz around your brand and leveraging your customer base to amplify the message for you on social media channels.

Ads can be social

Paid-for social ads provide brands with the ability to personalize ads and target and measure their campaigns in a way they've probably never been able to do through any other marketing channel. Not only that, but paid ads provide the opportunity to engage both with prospective customers and lapsed customers. They can also act to increase the frequency of purchases and engagement from existing customers.

In general terms, the ROI from paid social media is likely to be higher than other activity and should be one of the first lines in your marketing budget.

Content drives engagement

Consumers are not daft. They know that the underlying objective for brands on social media is to use these channels to drive engagement and to ultimately sell products and services to them. However, nobody ever wants to feel like they're being 'sold to' on their feed. Social media channels like Facebook, Instagram and Twitter are used for more than selling, as most people are still there to discover content (and share it) and socialize.

It is therefore effective to leverage content that makes you memorable and makes customers want to become loyal. You're really looking to turn customers into fans. The example of Ego Barbers, which I talked about earlier in this chapter, is a great case study for anyone looking to build awareness and engagement through social media.

Some considerations relating to content include:

- Consumers are very influenced by what other people like them buy or like. Therefore, look to post screen grabs of people mentioning your product or brand in a way that made you yourself smile or share that piece of content.
- Images that are authentic and borne out of real-life situations or conversations will drive more engagement.
- The inclusion of tips and tricks for using and maximizing your products will also drive more engagement, as well as encourage customers to share these and amplify your content and messaging.

- It's also highly effective to share images of people engaging with your products. This is the best form of advocacy and endorsement that you could ask for.

Everyone loves a good story

Due to our mobile usage and our alleged shorter attention spans, we continue to engage in increasing numbers with 'stories', which are at the heart of the rise in ephemeral content.

With more than 1 billion stories posted every day, stories will soon overtake the consumption of original news on Facebook and will become the default for content consumption among most users. As a result, brands will be posting more in-the-moment content as opposed to highly stylized content (Reed, 2018).

Here are some tips on how your business can leverage stories to increase awareness and amplification about your purpose and help to drive the acquisition of new customers:

- Put your people front and centre, by interviewing those responsible for different parts of your business and feature them on stories: using your app or product and 'live' reviewing your offerings.
- Consider how you can lift the bonnet and welcome customers into your world with a compelling narrative, images, creative and copy that draws them in.
- Test and learn and experiment! Ephemeral content only lasts for 24 hours. Create, innovate and constantly try new things, until you land on the type of stories that really resonate with your customers and drive the most engagement.

Shopping is a social thing

The following list includes some of the more obvious steps to ensure you optimize the take-up of, and impact from, social shopping:

- Ensure that your calls to action are clear.
- Make it easier for your customers and followers to directly link to and shop or browse products that they've seen on your feed and in your stories.
- Always ensure that your links are working. Test them every day. If your links fail, you not only lose sales; you might lose customers for good.

- Make sure that your product-related posts read as though they've been written by a fellow human being as opposed to a bot!
- Ensure that you surface the personality of your brand across all of your posts, even when you're encouraging customers to shop.

People who have influence, do influence others!

According to Expertcity, 82 per cent of consumers are highly likely to make a purchase based on the product recommendation of an influencer. This is why it's so important to work with influencers who are a good fit with your brand. Influencer marketing is a driver for credibility and trust and has a huge role in turning followers into loyal customers (Berger, 2016).

Despite their well-publicized issues around their supply chain (Financial Times, 2020), Boohoo Group (which includes Boohoo, PrettyLittleThing and Nasty Gal) leverages influencers and their endorsements to great effect. They engage with a young audience on Instagram in particular (where they have over 6.6 million followers). Boohoo reportedly spent £80 million on influencer marketing in 2018; they have continued with that strategy ever since (Gilliland, 2020).

Do consumers want to be seen with you?

Who you engage with on social media says a lot about who you are. Therefore, brand fit is key. How does a consumer feel about being seen to engage or even 'hang out with you'?

One relatively new brand that have made themselves a destination for Gen Z is Depop. It has been described as part Instagram, part eBay. It is, at its core, a social selling app that has become hugely successful as a result of generating incredible levels of engagement with its community of some 15 million Gen Z fashion fans. This audience view Depop the way they do Snapchat and TikTok, as not only a place to buy and sell fashion but somewhere to hang out with friends and other like-minded Gen Z consumers (Valentine, 2019).

Conclusion

From sales to service and from product development to brand engagement, social media should be at the very heart of your approach to customer experience, customer engagement and driving customer-centricity. This is where most of your customers will look to engage with you and therefore you need to resource this effectively in order to deliver the customer experience expected. Social media is a key strategic driver for your entire business.

> KEY TAKEAWAYS FROM CHAPTER 13
>
> 1 Resource social media effectively. There's still a tendency to under-resource it, primarily because the business hasn't yet understood the strategic nature of it. Focus on maximizing its value as a sales and customer service driver.
>
> 2 Social media must be at the heart of your consumer engagement strategy. It should also be the first line on your marketing budget and a key driver for customer service. Social media is not only a fantastic opportunity to drive more targeted customer acquisition, but also to increase customer retention and lifetime value.
>
> 3 As more and more consumers use social media to get a response from a brand, it must be treated as a core part of the front line of customer service. It's bad enough having customers calling you out for bad service on social platforms; it's even worse if you fail to respond to them or within an appropriate period of time, as this just acts to amplify the issue to many other customers.
>
> 4 To this end, it is not acceptable for customers to wait 24 hours or longer to receive a response to their message to you. It really has to be instantaneous, even if only to recognize the customer and buy time to get to the bottom of what the issue is.
>
> 5 As I've discussed previously, one of the key drivers for effective customer service is to empower your people to make decisions. The same can be said of the social media team, specifically those whose responsibility it is to respond to customers on Twitter, Instagram or Facebook. In order to meet customer expectations, and to deliver more effective levels of service, they should have the authority to make decisions around refunds, compensation or whatever is required to resolve an issue.
>
> 6 I'm also in favour of empowering teams in your stores, branches or dealerships to engage with customers locally through social media. However, you need to also ensure that clear guidelines have been communicated in terms of what's acceptable and what's not when it comes to what you promote and how you communicate.

7   You need to listen to what customers are saying about your brand. Despite what I said above about customers calling you out, not all of it will be said to your face! Only by listening in their communities can you learn what they really think of you, your products and services. Social listening is an incredibly powerful tool to help you learn about what is and isn't working in your business.

8   Social shopping should be a core part of your channel strategy. Think of it as an extension to your direct-to-consumer proposition. It really has come of age. If I were you, I'd even think about having a team dedicated to driving social shopping sales – how to maximize the opportunity on Facebook, Instagram and Pinterest.

9   Content is king… and queen! The stories you tell and content you share will be the key determinant of consumer engagement. Engagement drives loyalty and loyalty drives sales and customer lifetime value. Again, you need to resource this effectively and ensure that what you share is going to resonate.

10 Always be authentic. Consumers can see right through you when you're not. Authenticity drives trust and trust drives sales. Being able to trust a brand is at the heart of a Gen Zer's belief system. You will only ever engender a sense of trust if you prove you have purpose and are authentic.

11 You don't have to be a big business or have deep pockets to be successful in social media. If a five-man barber shop in Cockfosters in North London can generate an Instagram fan base of 240,000 and become a global training brand for cutting hair, you can have a similar impact in your respective sector.

12 Last but not least, social media is also key to building your employer brand. Anyone thinking of working with you is going to look at how you communicate and engage on social channels. It'll be part of their interview research!

References

BBC (2020) [accessed 22 October 2020] Morrisons, *BBC News* [Online] https://www.bbc.co.uk/news/topics/c207p54m4det/morrisons (archived at https://perma.cc/372K-93BH)

Berger, J (2016) [accessed 23 October 2020] The power of influencers: quantified, *Expert Voice* [Online] https://www.expertvoice.com/wp-content/uploads/2016/12/Power-of-Influence-Quantified.pdf (archived at https://perma.cc/V5VN-DQCB)

Berger, S (2019) [accessed 23 October 2020] Glossier: how this 33-year-old turned her beauty blog to a $1 billion brand, *CNBC* [Online] https://www.cnbc.com/2019/03/20/how-emily-weiss-took-glossier-from-beauty-blog-to-1-billion-brand.html (archived at https://perma.cc/BH9H-J7CC)

Canal, E (2020) [accessed 23 November 2020] Fresh off its $1.2 billion valuation, Glossier proves it's more than just a buzzy beauty brand, *Inc.com* [Online] https://www.inc.com/emily-canal/glossier-makeup-skincare-emily-weiss-unicorn-valuation.html (archived at https://perma.cc/WYQ4-9QQL)

Carville, O (2019) [accessed 23 October 2020] Glossier is NYC's newest unicorn with $1.2 billion valuation, *Bloomberg.com* [Online] https://www.bloomberg.com/news/articles/2019-03-19/glossier-is-nyc-s-newest-unicorn-with-1-2-billion-valuation (archived at https://perma.cc/6FWT-9X7F)

Clearpay (2020) [accessed 23 October 2020] How to connect meaningfully with customers on social media, *Clearpay* [Online] https://www.blog.clearpay.co.uk/blog/how-to-connect-meaningfully-with-customers-on-social-media (archived at https://perma.cc/ZW8Y-53RD)

Coker, J (2020) [accessed 23 November 2020] Co-op's rapid delivery partnership with Deliveroo reaches 400 stores, *Essential Retail* [Online] https://www.essentialretail.com/news/coops-partnership-deliveroo-400/ (archived at https://perma.cc/8C2G-RAEM)

Danziger, P (2018) [accessed 22 October 2020] 5 reasons that Glossier is so successful, *Forbes* [Online] https://www.forbes.com/sites/pamdanziger/2018/11/07/5-keys-to-beauty-brand-glossiers-success/#4d65ecd5417d (archived at https://perma.cc/D27R-LAKJ)

Ennis, G (2017) [accessed 23 October 2020] Quicker response times on social media – small businesses, *NSDesign* [Online] https://www.nsdesign.co.uk/need-quicker-response-times-social-media/#:~:text=You%20need%20quicker%20response%20times%20on%20social%20media%20because%20that's,hours%20should%20be%20enough%20time (archived at https://perma.cc/9XSG-B957)

Financial Times (2020) [accessed 23 November 2020] Boohoo has 'significant issues' in its supply chain, review finds, *Ft.com* [Online] https://www.ft.com/content/3cc4acc9-3f8a-4fb8-90e5-9a70116df7d4 (archived at https://perma.cc/GL5L-24E5)

Gilliland, N (2020) [accessed 23 October 2020] 30 brands with excellent social media strategies, *Econsultancy* [Online] https://econsultancy.com/30-brands-with-excellent-social-media-strategies/ (archived at https://perma.cc/T66A-D9G4)

Huang, W (2015) [accessed 23 October 2020] Consumers spend after positive customer service interaction on Twitter, *Blog.twitter.com* [Online] https://blog.twitter.com/en_us/topics/insights/2015/Consumers-spend-after-positive-customer-service-interaction-on-Twitter.html (archived at https://perma.cc/F8BD-X7Z7)

Hutchinson, A (2017) [accessed 27 November 2020] Consumer expectations rising on social customer care, *Social Media Today* [Online] https://www.socialmediatoday.com/social-business/consumer-expectations-rising-social-customer-care-report (archived at https://perma.cc/BRX5-Z7HD)

Johnson, J (2020) [accessed 23 October 2020] UK: social media usage 2019, *Statista* [Online] https://www.statista.com/statistics/507405/uk-active-social-media-and-mobile-social-media-users/ (archived at https://perma.cc/7WVU-XU85)

March, B (2019) [accessed 23 October 2020] Glossier is now valued at more than $1.2 billion, *Harper's Bazaar* [Online] https://www.harpersbazaar.com/uk/beauty/make-up-nails/a26881951/glossier-valuation-unicorn/ (archived at https://perma.cc/HV6E-K3V9)

MarketWatch (2019) [accessed 12 April 2020] KLM, *MarketWatch* [Online] https://www.marketwatch.com/investing/stock/klmr (archived at https://perma.cc/69H5-PEN9)

Mathers, M (2020) [accessed 22 October 2020] Co-op introduces new services to help mourners unable to attend funerals, *Independent* [Online] https://www.independent.co.uk/life-style/coronavirus-funeral-service-co-op-lockdown-a9504231.html (archived at https://perma.cc/V7CH-9UAP)

Newman, M (2020) [accessed 22 October 2020] Read our consumer survey insights!, *Martin Newman* [Online] https://martinnewman.co.uk/read-our-consumer-survey-insights/ (archived at https://perma.cc/E35G-9X67)

Peters, A (2019) [accessed 22 October 2020] Toms made buy-one, give-one famous. Now it's updating the model, *Fast Company* [Online] https://www.fastcompany.com/90344987/toms-made-buy-one-give-one-famous-now-its-updating-the-model (archived at https://perma.cc/C73X-2KE5)

Reed, A (2018) [accessed 27 November 2020] Life after the news feed: Why Facebook is shifting to stories (and why your business should too), *Buffer Resources* [Online] https://buffer.com/resources/life-after-the-news-feed/ (archived at https://perma.cc/NR94-Y5H7)

Sabanoglu, T (2020) [accessed 23 October 2020] UK consumers: Preferred social channels for hearing from brands 2019, *Statista* [Online] https://www.statista.com/statistics/1042622/preferred-consumer-channels-for-hearing-from-brands-uk/ (archived at https://perma.cc/EHZ2-5GTN)

Valentine, M (2019) [accessed 23 October 2020] Social selling site Depop on why quantity is the key to quality, *Marketing Week* [Online] https://www.marketingweek.com/depop-content-quality-quantity/ (archived at https://perma.cc/DM65-S645)

WARC (2018) [accessed 12 January 2021] How social became strategic at KLM, *Warc.com* [Online] https://www.warc.com/newsandopinion/news/how_social_became_strategic_at_klm/41208 (archived at https://perma.cc/QUJ4-SH73)

14

Generation Z will show us the way

> **WHAT YOU WILL LEARN IN THIS CHAPTER**
>
> - Generation Z are a mercurial lot – how do you get to understand them better?
> - If you want to know the future, look to the past.
> - Gen Z will tell you where you're going wrong.
> - How to engage with Gen Z.
> - How Gen Z will reshape all consumer sectors for the next 50 years.
> - The marketing mix for Gen Z.

Who are Generation Z?

Generation Z (Gen Z) is defined as having been born between 1995 and 2012. While they are still young, they are already having more influence than Millennials and all other age segments. If you need any additional proof, just look to Greta Thunberg! I think it's fair to say that her impact has changed the world. Literally. The movement of Gen Z, Millennials and others to reverse climate change has been hugely significant and she has been a key architect of this.

Gen Z are the change agents. They won't just sit there and take it; they won't accept anything that flies in the face of their belief system. Why should they? They are activists. They walk the talk. If they're not happy about something and don't believe it's in their best interests, their communities or the greater world at large, they'll take to the streets, they'll start a petition online, they'll take whatever action is required to right the wrong.

Don't be fooled into thinking that Gen Z are just an extension of Millennials or that they share similar behaviour. You need to remember that, for a start, the oldest Millennials turned 40 years of age in 2021. Increasingly they are at an age when they have their own families, they have high-powered jobs and lots of responsibility. Gen Zers, on the other hand, are still mainly teens and young adults who definitely do not behave the same way nor do they identify with Millennials. They see themselves as distinctly different (Germano, 2020).

Despite their tender years, they are the ones we will pay attention to as they teach us how to behave better and what needs to happen to improve the world we live in.

In this chapter, I'll explore what makes them tick, what the core drivers are for meeting their expectations around customer experience and what you need to do to be customer-centric as far as this segment is concerned. How do you get inside the mind of a Gen Z and, more importantly, can you build a relationship with them and, if so, how? It is undoubtedly in your interests to do so, as Gen Z lead the way in terms of their spend across a number of sectors including retail and hospitality (Bedgood, 2019).

At this juncture, I should probably qualify my credentials for talking about Gen Z. After all, I'm a man in my mid-50s! Believe me, I am qualified to discuss Gen Z as I have two of them at home! So, I have a pretty good handle on their behaviour and their drivers and what they like and don't like. I have to say that my daughters very much fit the profile I'm about to describe in this chapter.

If you want to know the future, look to the past

The following comes from a blog I wrote for Clearpay in 2020 and is reproduced with kind permission.

> The shape of the world over the next 50 years will be defined by Gen Z. And it will be influenced to a level never seen before.
>
> As Einstein is attributed as having said, if you want to know the future, look at the past (QuoteTab, 2020). In the 1960s and 70s, the baby boomers fought for women's rights, gay rights, civil rights and for social equality. They also played a big role in shaping popular culture and retail.
>
> Therefore, just like baby boomers before them, if you want to know what you need to do to be relevant now, and in the future, Gen Z will provide all the answers.

It is not individuals who will define the future. It is the power of the community. That community is Gen Z. As a result of this and their focus on the environment, sustainability, the circular economy, community driven labels, financial wellness, happiness and trust, they will define the future.

Retailers and other consumer-facing brands who tap into this insight can get ahead, and stay ahead, of competitors and maintain their relevance for years to come.

While Gen Z will have a significant impact upon retail the way baby boomers did, their behaviour is pretty much polar opposite. When it comes to money, they don't want debt, therefore they don't use credit cards the way earlier generations did. They want to pay cash. That means debit cards or even better, having the flexibility to buy now but pay back later. This helps them to budget and empowers them with more control over their finances as opposed to entrapping them the way credit card debt would do (Nathanson and Stelljes, 2020).

They aren't influenced by traditional aspirational advertising that uses models and celebrities to promote their wares. They engage with brands who are empathetic and authentic and use real people in marketing that they can relate to.

They are emotional and passionate and look to engage with brands who want to have a deeper relationship with them. Trust will be at the heart of any relationship they have. However, they will often start from a position of distrust. And it will be down to a brand to prove that it can be trusted. This is hugely important. It will also require a more personalized experience with relevant content, messaging, marketing and products. This way they can see that a brand is taking them seriously and not treating them just as a number.

They are the changemakers. From planet to purpose, from inclusion and diversity to community, Gen Z will lead the way to a better world for all of us. I truly believe that to be the case.

They will force us all to take sustainability seriously, to measure our own carbon footprint. They will ensure brands have a genuine purpose and look after the planet, their people and their customers. They will drive us to care about the community and think more about others and less about ourselves. They will even reshape what retailers sell us. As we move more towards the circular economy and re-purposed products, we will find more and more retailers selling a range of products that includes both the old and the new.

Don't make the mistake of thinking that Gen Z is not your core customer and therefore you don't need to worry about any of this for the time being as their influence goes way beyond their own brand preferences. They have a bigger influence on other generations than any previous generation did. They are the activists. They are the beacons and the path-makers. And we will all look to them for what comes next.

SOURCE Newman (2020)

Gen Z will tell you where you're going wrong

CASE STUDY
Gucci

Led by CEO Marco Bizzarri, who took over in 2015, Gucci is a brand that has transformed itself and its commercial performance over recent years. Gucci has become a truly customer-centric brand. His colleagues have been at the heart of driving customer-centricity. But he has been the facilitator and agent of change.

Bizzarri's goal, as he described it, has been to create an environment where new ideas and suggestions for how processes might be improved are encouraged. Everyone is made to feel that they can make suggestions without fear of recrimination. This is a culture of encouragement as opposed to a culture of fear, which I'm sure we've all experienced at some point in our careers.

As is fairly obvious, the culture of encouragement and openness drives so many better ideas, more engaged staff and better levels of customer service and experience, all of which add up to a better commercial performance – more sales, more profit and better long-term prospects.

This is part of Bizzarri's bottom–up approach, which enables anyone to feed back to top executives. Just think of that for a minute. With the layers of management and bureaucracy in most business, most people in the lower echelons of the business never get to utter a word to anyone on the board, never mind getting to feed back on how the business might be improved!

In addition to this, and in order to better understand how to engage more effectively with Gen Z and Millennials, Bizzarri created a 'shadow committee' of Millennials and Gen Z, which helps to give him and the board more relevant insight and perspectives than the usual team of senior leaders. This shadow board are all under 30 years of age. Therefore, the advice and feedback that comes from the shadow committee is completely aligned with what many of Gucci's core customers will be thinking.

This is such a great example of how to overcome the challenge of the board in a business not reflecting the customer base and, more importantly, the valuable insight that it drives and how they're able to leverage that to continually improve product, service and customer experience.

They are empowered to tell the CEO what's not working. One example of something that wasn't working efficiently that they were able to surface was in relation to how Gucci was cutting leather for its bags. They were generating a lot of unnecessary waste. So, the Millennial and Gen Z shadow board came up with the idea of a new process that successfully led to a significant reduction in excess leather and waste, therefore saving money and improving Gucci's sustainability credentials.

SOURCE Bain (2017)

How to engage with Gen Z

In order to understand the mindset of younger consumers you need to know what motivates them and the values they care about most.

It's fair to say that the majority of brands underestimate the importance to Gen Z of social responsibility. In a 2019 report, 60 per cent of Gen Z shoppers stated a clear preference to buy from brands that were able to demonstrate socially responsible values throughout their business (Petro, 2020).

One of the other key factors to consider – and one of the biggest differences between how Gen Z interact and engage with marketing content compared with Millennials and older generations – is that they respond far better to authentic content and real people as opposed to the more traditional airbrushed and aspirational advertising.

To this end, how do you set about creating more authentic marketing in order to engage more effectively with Gen Z?

Create and share content that actually matters

Research conducted by Future Labs demonstrates that Gen Z tend to connect with brands that demonstrate that they share their values on important issues such as improving the environment, society, race, gender diversity and culture (Afterpay and the Future Laboratory, 2020).

In an article published by *Forbes*, a study conducted by 3BL Media showed that 90 per cent of Gen Zers would purchase from companies that are authentically addressing social and/or environmental issues (Olenski, 2018). None of this kicking the can down the road on corporate social responsibility (CSR). An even larger number, 94 per cent, of Gen Z consumers are of the belief that businesses have a responsibility to tackle critical issues. They're not accepting of them passing the buck (Novelli, 2020).

Gen Z were also concerned by some key issues during the Covid-19 pandemic when it came to retail. They wanted to ensure that fashion businesses were paying their staff fairly and providing them with good working conditions. Not surprisingly, sustainability was top of mind, as was the safe reopening of stores during the pandemic. They're not interested in brands paying lip service to any of this; they want to know what they're actually doing about it.

Put your people first

You won't be surprised to know that the impact of Covid-19 left many Gen Zers feeling isolated, concerned and worried about their future. After all, they've never had such a seismic event disrupt their life. Therefore, no one should be surprised that they reacted badly to any brand or influencer that was seen to be promoting an unobtainable lifestyle or profiteering during the pandemic.

An article in *Vogue Business* that relates to a survey undertaken by DoSomething in mid-March 2020 highlighted that three-quarters of the Gen Zers who responded stated that the most important action they wanted to see brands take was the assurance that employee and consumer safety was the primary focus. Of almost equal importance was that brands were doing all they could to protect their employees financially. The brands that understood this created content such as behind-the-scenes videos and interviews with team members on social media channels. In doing so, they showed real employees and the faces behind their brand while at the same time building trust with these younger consumers who could see for themselves that the business was undertaking safe and employee-first business practices during the pandemic (Maguire, 2020).

Authenticity means realistic people and looks as opposed to airbrushing

In a UNiDAYS survey in the UK, 63 per cent of Gen Z consumers stated that when they consume advertising, they want to see real people. This is in contrast to Millennials, where only 37 per cent share this view (Clay, 2020).

Kate Moss is undoubtedly an icon for Millennials; however, Gen Z are more interested in advertising that involves people who aren't models, who are everyday people who are imperfect and relatable (Germano, 2020).

In a research report conducted by Future Labs for Afterpay, Gen Z consumers made it clear that it's no longer cool to airbrush and colour correct. It's quite the opposite, in fact, as they now celebrate freckles as a beauty trend where once they were viewed as a flaw.

To further demonstrate this pretty seismic shift in the perception of beauty, a significant number of fashion brands are being far more diverse with the models they engage in terms of their shape and size. They are definitely moving away from featuring their clothes adorning the traditional rake-thin body type that has traditionally been used to sell clothes to women (Afterpay and the Future Laboratory, 2020).

Engage with authentic influencers

Brands that are most attuned to these changes in attitude are engaging with real people and micro-influencers. The key difference is that influencers often have a following in the millions whereby micro-influencers' followers can be counted in the range of 1,000 to 100,000. Their followers are also typically very engaged and extremely loyal.

Authenticity, trust and honesty are the new drivers and therefore brands should be looking to engage with micro-influencers who can demonstrate that they fit this profile. Aligned with that is ensuring that they have a track record of demonstrating empathy and sensitivity, both in their communications as well as in how they've previously partnered with brands. This lends itself to less shallow and far deeper and lasting relationships between brands and their customers (Anderson, 2019).

Keep it real

In order to get Gen Z to engage with you on social media, you need to understand what type of content they're interested in. They react far more favourably to real stories about real people and real events. For example, 'a day in the life' type videos, 'how to' content that provides step-by-step guides on how to create and make things, and behind-the-scenes videos that help Gen Z to see what really goes on in a business.

Yes, they like to be entertained. However, they also want to learn. Social media provides the content to enable them to enrich their knowledge, feed personal interests and gain a better understanding of the world. Too many brands spend too much time talking at Gen Zers through advertising campaigns and not enough time creating meaningful content that truly engages them. If you want to build a relationship with customers, you need to create a dialogue and have a narrative that Gen Z can relate to (Olenski, 2018).

How Gen Z will reshape all consumer sectors for the next 50 years

Gen Z will define and shape what we sell and what we buy. As we move increasingly towards the circular economy, Gen Zers want to consume more consciously and more sustainably. From vegan cosmetics to upcycled jeans, an increasing number of brands are taking action to enable them to meet their expectations.

You can see the evidence of the changes in real terms by looking at the growth in sustainable categories such as vegan make-up. In a move to have a positive impact upon sustainability, a staggering 56 per cent of women in the UK buy vegan make-up, either all the time or more than they used to. By 2025, this in turn will make a $20.8 billion contribution to the global vegan cosmetics market (Starostinetskaya, 2020).

Of course, concerns over the environment and the impact of fashion on sustainability has also had a big impact on the shopping patterns and behaviour of Gen Z. While not that long ago it was all about fast fashion and single-use, throwaway items, younger influencers are demonstrating how you can get far more usage out of an item of clothing or an outfit and, in doing so, gaining credibility among their peers while also encouraging their followers and fans to do the same thing.

This plays into the whole move towards the circular economy, which in turn has given rise to a plethora of fashion rental and resale propositions such as Depop and By Rotation. These new sites enable younger consumers to have fun and continue to enjoy fashion but in a more sustainable way.

To follow are some of the key initiatives brands can take that will ensure they remain relevant to the hugely important Gen Z consumer.

Price still matters to many

There are two sides to Gen Z. There are those consumers who don't ever want to be seen in the same outfit twice on Instagram. For them, price matters, as it gives them accessibility to throwaway fashion. I believe this segment will reduce over time as we move from early adopters to the majority of consumers shopping with conscious consumption as their key driver and their own impact upon the environment becoming increasingly important.

There is another sizable segment who are already there, where sustainability, ethics and integrity are a core part of their belief system. They are most likely in the minority but will undoubtedly become the majority. And it won't take long for that change to happen.

Promote conscious and more responsible consumption

For anyone who buys consumer goods, it is obvious that brands are underutilizing compostable packaging, and a report from Inside Packaging suggests that a third of Gen Z consumers agree (Tyndall, 2020). Moreover, they would like to see brands making more effort here and moving away from single-use plastics and excessive packaging. Retailers and brands should follow the example of JD in China, which is encouraging consumers to return their boxes and packaging so that they can be reused or recycled. They don't stop there. JD has converted over 5,000 of their delivery vehicles to use renewable energy. They are working with their partners to convert hundreds of thousands more (Lu Yong, 2019).

Waste not want not

In order to play their part to help the environment and counter the huge amount of waste that is thrown away every year, Gen Zers increasingly look to engage with brands that demonstrate that they are actively doing something to combat and reduce waste and pollution. In fact, 59 per cent of Gen Zers regularly buy products that have been upcycled (Petro, 2020).

If you're a retailer, simply selling new products the way you have done so previously isn't going to cut it for Gen Z – nor for Millennials nor any other consumers who are consuming more consciously.

A great example of a brand that does this well is Ragyard. They say that they put creativity and people before profit (Ragyard, 2020). More importantly, their actions also show this. They upcycle unwanted fabric and vintage pieces that they use to create new designs.

In order to drive more uptake and engagement with consumers for upcycling, retailers should create incentives for customers to exchange unwanted clothing, fabric and materials in return for vouchers or discounts that they can use online or in store. They could be even more proactive and organize the collection of unwanted clothing from consumers that they collect on behalf of local charities and non-profit organizations. This would be a great way of creating momentum behind this initiative.

Second-hand doesn't mean second best

As I touched on earlier in Chapter 11, when I was talking about what a retailer might look like if you launched a new retail business today, you'd want to offer customers pre-loved/second-hand merchandise. In the trade, it's known as a resale consignment model. It's gaining momentum and definitely resonating with Millennials and Gen Z, with the former (48 per cent) and the latter (46 per cent) both engaging with this market (Petro, 2020).

Some of the players in this space include The RealReal and Tradesy. However, this is not only about online retailers. Another brand is ThreadUp, and they have been supplying department stores and retailers such as Macy's and Madewell with used clothes.

In the not-too-distant future, you will walk into a retailer's store and have your choice of new products, second-hand items, upcycled products as well as items you can rent.

Help customers to easily recognize ethical products

From a customer journey and conversion perspective, for Gen Z, the ethical viability of a product is at the top of their criteria. Therefore, they fully expect a brand to make it as easy as possible for them to ascertain whether or not a product meets their expectations in terms of how ethical it is from manufacture to the shop floor.

A good example of how to do this well and empower consumers to find ethical products is on the Well Made Clothes website (wellmadeclothes.com). You can search for products by a host of relevant terms, values and criteria including whether the items are handmade, vegan, or manufactured locally. You're then taken to pages on the website that are strongly aligned with your beliefs.

The retailer Rêve En Vert uses simple icons to denote details such as handmade, organic and natural dyes on their website descriptions (reve-en-vert.com).

Influenced by friends more than celebrities

In the evolution of the peer-to-peer space (p2p), we're still quite early when it comes to Gen Z and Millennials engaging with clothing swaps and peer-to-peer marketplaces. In 2020, 24 per cent of Millennials and 29 per cent of Gen Z were buying and selling on these platforms (Petro, 2020).

However, they are only going to become more prevalent over time, particularly as consumers move increasingly towards conscious consumption. Even Instagram are getting involved with the launch of p2p transactions (InkProtocol, 2020).

At the heart of the peer-to-peer revolution is the fact that we are heavily influenced by what other people like us do, like or buy. This has been the core driver for ratings and reviews.

Storr is a marketplace for individuals to set up their own outlet. Research they conducted found that 92 per cent of all product recommendations were coming from consumers' friends and family. Recommendations from peers had led to around 21 per cent of US shoppers making a purchase, whereas when it was a celebrity recommendation, the number dropped to only 14 per cent (Whaling, 2020).

Never over-promise!

There's nothing a Gen Zer will dislike more than a brand communicating how ethical and socially responsible they are if it turns out to be fake news. Gen Zers place an enormous level of trust in the brands they love and engage with; therefore, it's vital to communicate to this audience with the utmost integrity, clarity, honesty and transparency. There's no harm in being honest about the fact you're on a journey to become more environmentally friendly and socially responsible, even if you're not quite there yet. As long as you're honest and transparent, Gen Zers will respect you for that. They will also hold you to account to complete the journey.

The marketing mix for Gen Z

Many of will you know about the four Ps – or the marketing mix, as it's more commonly known: product, price, place and promotion (Borden, 1984).

There are another three Ps to be added for Gen Z in order to be relevant for their needs: one is packaging, the next is participation and the third is purpose.

Such is the focus on sustainability that Gen Z have a heightened awareness of packaging, whether or not it's compostable, made from recycled materials and not throwaway.

In terms of participation, Gen Z want to be part of your story; they want to get involved in your brand. They also love nothing better than discovering you in the first place.

If you don't stand for something, can you expect Gen Z to stand with you? Purpose and your place in the world are increasingly important to Gen Zers as they look to align themselves with brands that can demonstrate shared values.

So, what might the marketing mix look like for Gen Z?

- *Product* – Is it authentic? Is it ethical? Is it on trend? Is it one of a kind or unique?
- *Price* – Does your price architecture exude value?
- *Place* – Is it available whenever and wherever they want to buy it, with a particular emphasis on social and mobile? You need to be where your customers are.
- *Promotion* – Are you discoverable on trusted platforms and environments, eg Snapchat, Instagram, etc?
- *Participation* – What can you do to get Gen Zers involved and actively participating with your brand?
- *Packaging* – How do you prove to Gen Zers that you are effectively addressing waste and packaging that isn't environmentally friendly?
- *Purpose* – Last but definitely not least is purpose. Brands with purpose really resonate with Gen Zers. So, what do you stand for, as they'd like to know?

Conclusion

Gen Zers can be your best friend and your biggest and strongest ally, or your worst enemy, as they don't take bad news lying down. Given their importance to the future of any consumer business, you need to do everything you can to engage with them, on their terms, in their language and with true purpose and authenticity. If you do that, you have a chance of building a long-lasting relationship and the customer lifetime value that comes with it.

Let's not forget that Gen Zers are the mums and dads of tomorrow. Student loans get replaced by good levels of disposable income.

KEY TAKEAWAYS FROM CHAPTER 14

1 Balance price with the need to cater for an increasing demand for socially responsible and ethical products. Yes, some younger consumers will still buy the throwaway dress so as not to be seen wearing the same thing twice on social. But that will definitely change as conscious consumption picks up pace. What can you do to encourage customers to bring that throwaway dress back so that it can be upcycled?

2 Gen Z more than any other generation in our history will shape the future. But they can also be your most important asset when it comes to telling you what is and isn't working in your business. The example I used of Gucci shows you the power and opportunity of giving younger people in your business a voice. They can make a real difference to your commercial performance. Make sure to remove the barriers to empower them to speak their mind. It's a cultural thing and culture comes from the top. So, over to you CEO.

3 If you want to truly connect with Gen Zers, you must engender trust and, to do that, you need to be open, transparent, authentic and honest. You need to do this consistently across all of your channels and touchpoints and ensure that you communicate in this way with everything you do.

4 Don't talk at Gen Z. By that I mean, traditional advertising doesn't work. Great looking models and airbrushed or photoshopped photography won't cut it. They want to see genuine people doing real-life things in a real-world environment. If you stick to the old ways, they will simply not respond or connect with your brand.

5 The same goes for influencers. Yes, you can use them. But best to work with real people, not perfect-looking human beings. After all, freckles are cool now!

6 The biggest influence on Gen Z and Millennials is family and friends, not celebrities – and not celebrity influencers. Therefore, how do you tap into this?

7 You need to cater for the increasing need of Gen Z to buy ethically sourced and manufactured products. The environment and sustainability are top of their agenda. This means that you also have to prove to Gen Z that your whole supply chain and ecosystem is socially responsible.

8 That also means offering them more than just new products. Can you offer them an upcycled, rental or second-hand/resale proposition? Increasingly this is what they'll be looking for. They want to play their part – and it's a big part – when it comes to leading the way towards environmental change and sustainability. You need to empower Gen Z to achieve their objectives here.

9 Peer-to-peer commerce is going to be big among this generation. You need to start planning for that now in terms of the potential implications for your business in the long run.

10 Ignore Gen Z at your peril. They lead the generational spending and spend more than any other generation across numerous categories, including retail and hospitality. They should be the most important segment because, even if they're not ready or old enough to buy your products today, they will be shortly. Also, they already have significant influence on what older generations buy.

11 You require a different marketing mix for Gen Z. Think the seven Ps as opposed to the four Ps. The additional ones are of primary importance. As your purpose drives connection and engagement, participation drives involvement and sustainable packaging makes Gen Zers feel good about having bought from you in the first place.

References

Afterpay and the Future Laboratory (2020) [accessed 24 October 2020] Afterpay Access, *Afterpay* [Online] https://access.afterpay.com/articles/afterpay-global-gen-z-report#:~:text=The%20Afterpay%20Global%20Gen%20Z%20Report%3A%20Financial%20Feels&text=Like%20Millennial%20customers%20who%20quickly,Gen%20Z%20post%20Covid%2D19 (archived at https://perma.cc/WH2W-6ZLV)

Anderson, M (2019) [accessed 24 October 2020] What are micro-influencers & why are they so effective?, *Impactplus.com* [Online] https://www.impactplus.com/blog/power-of-micro-influencers (archived at https://perma.cc/K4DP-S7NY)

Bain, M (2017) [accessed 24 October 2020] Gucci has a 'shadow committee' of Millennial advisors, *Quartz* [Online] https://qz.com/1111798/gucci-has-a-shadow-committee-of-millennial-advisors/ (archived at https://perma.cc/6FJ6-2F9Z)

Bedgood, L (2019) [accessed 24 October 2020] Consumer shopping trends and statistics by the generation: Gen Z, Millennials, Gen X, Boomers and the Silents, *Business 2 Community* [Online] https://www.business2community.com/trends-news/consumer-shopping-trends-and-statistics-by-the-generation-gen-z-millennials-gen-x-boomers-and-the-silents-02220370 (archived at https://perma.cc/CG5T-MCEQ)

Borden, N (1984) The concept of the marketing mix, *Harvard Business School Journal*, 2, pp 7–12

Clay, L (2020) [accessed 24 October 2020] Generation Z vs Millennials, *Dana Communications* [Online] https://www.danacommunications.com/generation-z-vs-millennials/ (archived at https://perma.cc/T5D2-N4TM)

Germano, C (2020) [accessed 24 October 2020] It's time to re-think your Gen Z marketing strategy, *Genzinsights.com* [Online] https://www.genzinsights.com/its-time-to-re-think-your-gen-z-marketing-strategy (archived at https://perma.cc/MZ53-28FJ)

InkProtocol (2020) [accessed 24 October 2020] Instagram will be the next great peer-to-peer marketplace, *Medium* [Online] https://medium.com/ink-protocol/instagram-will-be-the-next-great-peer-to-peer-marketplace-b93aacc71993 (archived at https://perma.cc/9CG9-YYFP)

Lu Yong, R (2019) [accessed 24 October 2020] A guide to sustainable e-commerce – by China's biggest retailer, *World Economic Forum* [Online] https://www.weforum.org/agenda/2019/01/a-guide-to-sustainability-for-online-retailers-by-one-of-the-biggest (archived at https://perma.cc/F7X8-FXPM)

Maguire, L (2020) [accessed 24 October 2020] Marketing to Gen Z during Covid-19, *Vogue Business* [Online] https://www.voguebusiness.com/consumers/marketing-to-gen-z-during-covid-19 (archived at https://perma.cc/94LN-XCSM)

Nathanson, M and Stelljes, L (2020) [accessed 24 October 2020] Gen Z is starting to make their own money – so pay attention to how they're spending and investing it, *MarketWatch* [Online] https://www.marketwatch.com/story/gen-z-is-starting-to-make-their-own-money-so-pay-attention-to-how-theyre-spending-and-investing-it-2020-08-24 (archived at https://perma.cc/HXA9-7ZL7)

Newman, M (2020) [accessed 24 November 2020] How to be relevant now, and in the future, with Gen Z, *Clearpay* [Online] https://www.blog.clearpay.co.uk/blog/how-to-be-relevant-now-and-in-the-future-with-gen-z (archived at https://perma.cc/5AHY-B858)

Novelli, P (2020) [accessed 24 October 2020] Gen Z: The next conscious group of consumers, *3blmedia.com* [Online] https://www.3blmedia.com/News/Gen-Z-Next-Conscious-Group-Consumers (archived at https://perma.cc/35CC-TEEM)

Olenski, S (2018) [accessed 24 October 2020] 5 ways brands can engage Gen Z on social media, *Forbes* [Online] https://www.forbes.com/sites/steveolenski/2018/07/28/5-ways-brands-can-engage-gen-z-on-social-media/#7d8aff8d6129 (archived at https://perma.cc/E8DG-GRFH)

Petro, G (2020) [accessed 24 October 2020] Sustainable retail: How Gen Z is leading the pack, *Forbes* [Online] https://www.forbes.com/sites/gregpetro/2020/01/31/sustainable-retail-how-gen-z-is-leading-the-pack/#2ca150d82ca3 (archived at https://perma.cc/D7J4-Q97E)

QuoteTab (2020) [accessed 27 November 2020] If you want to know the future, look at the past, *QuoteTab* [Online] https://www.quotetab.com/quote/by-albert-einstein/if-you-want-to-know-the-future-look-at-the-past#:~:text=Albert%20Einstein%3A%20If%20you%20want,QuoteTab (archived at https://perma.cc/DF8K-7F5P)

Ragyard (2020) [accessed 24 November 2020] About us: Vintage clothing London, *Ragyard* [Online] https://ragyard.com/pages/about-us (archived at https://perma.cc/ER5S-PZA2)

Starostinetskaya, A (2020) [accessed 24 October 2020] 56 percent of British women buy vegan makeup, *VegNews.com* [Online] https://vegnews.com/2019/6/56-percent-of-british-women-buy-vegan-makeup (archived at https://perma.cc/6P2E-MP3E)

Tyndall, C (2020) [accessed 24 November 2020] Youth gone wild: How young consumers are transforming brands, *Inside Packaging* [Online] https://inside-packaging.nridigital.com/packaging_sep19/youth_gone_wild_how_young_consumers_are_transforming_brands (archived at https://perma.cc/6DWW-QYVP)

Whaling, P (2020) [accessed 24 October 2020] Interview: How a peer-to-peer mobile marketplace lets anyone open a virtual store, *PSFK* [Online] https://www.psfk.com/2019/05/interview-storr-peer-to-peer-virtual-marketplace.html (archived at https://perma.cc/HZ4W-HW3S)

15

The road map to customer-centricity

> **WHAT YOU WILL LEARN IN THIS CHAPTER**
> - The 10 building blocks and framework for driving customer-centricity.
> - Doing the right thing doesn't have to be rocket science.
> - The traditional return to shareholder focus is a broken model and has to change if we're to secure the long-term future of our businesses.
> - The board needs a makeover in order to be more representative of the customer base.

This final chapter in the book provides everything you need to begin the transformation of your business to one that is truly customer-centric. It includes my highly effective framework that will help you on that journey.

So, how do we become truly customer-centric? Well, the first thing we need to do is start at the end of the funnel.

Historically, almost every business I know focuses on the top of the funnel – on customer acquisition and return on advertising spend (ROAS). This comes almost to the exclusion of any tangible efforts around retaining customers and building their lifetime value.

This is such a flawed approach. Who cares whether or not the ROAS (return on ad spend) is 10 to 1? If that customer doesn't come back as a result of us not bothering to deliver the right experience across all of our touchpoints or offer appropriate customer service or make some attempt at driving customer loyalty, we will have wasted our time acquiring them in the first place. Our focus has to be on the lifetime value of the customer.

We might have generated a sale of £100, but by the time you strip out the acquisition costs, cost to serve and product cost, we might be left with £20 if we're lucky. If only we'd focused on customer lifetime value and maximizing the value of the customer, they may well have been worth thousands of pounds to our business. And if we had some decent levels of engagement with them, we could go and find more customers who were just like them and end up with a cohort of extremely profitable customers.

The *Harvard Business Review* estimates that a 5 per cent increase in customer retention can lead to an increase in profits of anywhere between 25 per cent and 95 per cent (depending upon the category) (Reichheld and Schefter, 2020). So, there you have it, it is so obviously more profitable to focus on customer retention, on keeping the customers we already have than only trying to add more to the top of the funnel.

Think about it from your own experience as a consumer. How many brands can you think of that make any tangible or obvious attempt to build a relationship with you?

Just to be clear. I am most definitely not suggesting that we all stop acquisition marketing. Moreover, I'm recommending that we rebalance our efforts and put far more thought, effort and investment into retaining existing customers.

Add to this that those brands that deliver poor levels of customer service and experience are actually doing a pretty good job on behalf of competitors of inadvertently improving their levels of acquisition and customer recruitment!

My recommendation is to start with customer lifetime value and work back from there. What would it take to make different cohorts of customers more loyal? What might the value of that look like?

To follow are what I see as the main building blocks to achieving this.

The 10 building blocks for customer-centricity

Employee-first

As I brought to life in great detail in Chapter 7, you'll never be a customer-centric business if you don't start by ensuring that you are a people/employee-first organization. What does that actually entail? Well, it starts with creating a culture that encourages your colleagues to go the extra mile – one that doesn't penalize failure but actually encourages new ideas and failing fast.

FIGURE 15.1　The 10 building blocks of customer-centricity

1	Employee-first
2	Understand customer wants and needs (turn data into insight)
3	Technology that empowers consumers
4	Be where your customers are
5	Purpose, values and social responsibility
6	Diversity and inclusion
7	Personalization
8	Hyper-localization
9	Aligning everyone with the direction of travel
10	Measure what really matters

Incentivizing our colleagues to come up with new ideas, to try new things and celebrating both the successes and the failures are crucial to delivering a sustainably successful business.

It's important to prove to your team that you care. Take the example of Timpson, the shoe repair and key-cutting business. They give staff who have been with them for at least a year £250 towards driving lessons (Mason, 2019). Home Depot in North America pay for staff who want to have further education. They also help staff when they're in financial difficulty (Charan, 2019).

The points below should give you a good overview of how to become an employee-first business:

- Empower your employees to make decisions without the need to go up the chain of command. Home Depot's store colleagues can give customers a $50 discount in store (Dindar, 2016).
- Empower your contact centre team to make service and customer satisfaction decisions without having to get approval from a manager.
- All employees should have the opportunity to learn new skills through a learning and development programme tailored to them.

- Career progression – if I work hard, I can see there will be opportunities for me to progress within the business.
- Never penalize failure.
- Always celebrate success and never take it for granted.
- Reward ideas that make a difference.
- Encourage and enable employees to support their community.
- Encourage and enable employees to embrace additional education and skills.

Is there value in doing this? It should be a no-brainer. But if you need proof, look at businesses such as Home Depot, which tick all of these boxes and whose value and success over many years have increased year on year. Home Depot's share price increased by over 130 per cent between 2015 and 2020 (Financhill, 2020). Much of their success has to do with the environment they've created for employees and the fact that they employ people who genuinely want to help other people in the first place.

Understand customers and their wants and needs (turn data into insight)

Every business I know has more data than they know what to do with. Data comes from multiple sources – from online orders, to in-store purchases, from Google Analytics and other analytical software, to consumer responses to marketing activity and customer issues at the contact centre. The problem is you can count on a few fingers the businesses that have a single customer view (SCV).

By having all this data in one place, data scientists can analyse it, interpret it and surface insight that can be used to ensure we deliver increasingly relevant experiences for our customers.

Even without a SCV, there is much we can do to surface insight that can help us to improve how we serve and engage with customers. Here are just a few of the ways to achieve this:

- What are the barriers on the customer's path to purchase? There is always a load of low-hanging fruit to get after. When was the last time you conducted mystery shopping? When you walked in the customers' shoes and made a purchase online and offline and went through all of the different scenarios? Or called the contact centre with an issue? Or tried to return your order?

- When was the last time you mystery-shopped competitors to see how effective they are at the end-to-end customer journey? What might they be doing better than you?
- When was the last time you got in touch with lapsed customers and asked them why they don't want to engage with you anymore? There is so much insight you generate by doing this.
- When you identify the more profitable cohorts of customers, go and find others like them. It's a great driver for your acquisition activity.
- Adopt an approach for maximizing customer lifetime value. You must play the long game if you want to stay in the game. Some examples of how to achieve this include:
  - encouraging repeat purchases with a simple discount code off of a second purchase;
  - offering a tiered loyalty programme with increased incentives as the customer's value increases;
  - random acts of kindness such as unexpected gifts with purchase are great ways of making customers feel wanted.
- Walk the floor. When was the last time you talked to your customers? There is no better way to generate insight than to ask them what they like and what they don't like. The founder of Walmart, Sam Walton, visited most, if not all, of the 2,000 or so Walmart stores before he died. The first thing he did when he got there was to get on the tannoy, introduce himself as Sam, and say that he would love to talk to customers for the next half hour (Encyclopedia, 2020). You can imagine how much insight he generated as a result.
- The same applies to talking to your staff on the front line. They'll tell you what's working and what isn't. Listening to your staff is every bit as important as listening to your customers.

Technology that empowers consumers

I'm a fairly practical person. As such, I struggle with some of the parlance and terminology that does the rounds in our industry. Take 'digital transformation'. As lovely as it sounds, if I asked 100 people in 100 different businesses what it means, I'm confident I'd get 10,000 different answers!

Therefore, how helpful is that as a framework for transitioning your business or doing a better job of engaging customers if everyone has a different understanding of what digital transformation actually means?

At the end of the day, technology is an enabler. It is not the end in itself. It can help to deliver the experience customers seek. But if you start with the technology and build something just because you can, it may lead you down a rabbit hole from which there is no return.

We've all done it. We've all chased the silver bullet, the next new great technological solution that is going to revolutionize our business and our sales performance. Take the implementation of 'the endless aisle', usually unmanned kiosks that were intended to offer customers more choice of products than were available in store. The problem is that customers don't interact with these. They only ever work when they are staff assisted. It's what we call 'assisted sales'. Yes, they can play a part in driving sales, particularly if you have a broader range of stock available online. But they aren't a magical technological solution in and of themselves.

As outlined in Chapter 10, if you look at the disruptors, from Airbnb to Uber, from Deliveroo to Monzo Bank, they all have one thing in common: they identified a consumer problem, all of which centred around lack of empowerment, and they were able to leverage technology to solve this.

No one size fits all. Take Generation Z and Millennials. They do not want to use credit cards. They prefer to pay then or to have the flexibility of a buy now pay later solution such as Clearpay (Afterpay in the US and Australia). Therefore, you need to ensure you're able to meet the needs of different customer cohorts and understand what their drivers are across the whole customer journey.

There is always a balance to be achieved. When customers tell you what they want, there is often a gap between what they say and what they end up doing or how they behave. Nonetheless, it's good practice to get a sense-check of how they might respond to new technology you have planned to implement.

There are elements of the customer journey that technology can improve which you would class as a no-brainer, because it's delivering significant sales and engagement. Omnichannel is one of them, which can be defined as a 'customer experience is made up of individual customer touch points, over a variety of channels that seamlessly connect, allowing customers to pick up where they left off on one channel and continue the experience on another' (Bare, 2020). On this basis, it has much to offer customers and therefore should be a key focus for technology that can empower consumers.

Another is click and collect, as it empowers customers to get their order when and where they want it rather than wondering when it might be delivered and what might happen if they're not in when the courier attempts delivery.

Given most brands now generate more sales and traffic through mobile than they do through a desktop website experience, it is vital that mobile versions of the site are fully optimized, be that responsive and/or adaptive design.

Until recently, I'd have considered it highly questionable whether or not your customers will have the same appetite for an app. After all, how many apps can we realistically be expected to engage with? However, some brands are going down the progressive web app (PWA) path as they recognize the consumer-driven need for faster-loading content, ecommerce and better overall experiences.

To a large extent your decision will be led by the engagement frequency. If the frequency of purchase is there, an app can really build consumer engagement. If on the other hand it's infrequent, don't waste your time or money going down the app path.

A short checklist for you when considering new technology:

- Does it solve a tangible customer problem?
- Does it empower customers?
- Is it likely to increase engagement?
- Have we sense-checked it with key customers?

Be where your customers are

This might sound obvious, but many businesses are not doing this. For a retailer or a consumer product brand, this might mean being on Amazon. While some brands have a reticence to do so, you need to remember that these days, more consumers search for products on Amazon (63 per cent) than they do on Google (48 per cent across all search engines) (Statista, 2020). If you're not there, you won't be found, and competitors' products will.

For other brands, being where your customers are, or where they want to be, means offering click and collect.

For car dealers it means offering a virtual test drive or sending me videos of the car I'm interested in.

For banks it means offering the full suite of in-branch financial services online.

Due to the Covid-19 pandemic and the increase in working from home (WFH), customers are now staying locally and shopping locally. Will national retailers see the opportunity to tap into this with smaller-format stores in more local areas? Why not? Independents are doing well and will continue to do so. Why can't national chains?

Social media is an increasingly important route to market. You only have to consider how much time is spent on social media channels by most age groups, even more so Generation Z, to know that this is arguably the best way to engage with customers and potential customers of your brand.

Gen Z spends two to three times more shopping on social channels than the average consumer. Platform wise, Instagram (Insta) and Snapchat (Snap) are the core channels, while older consumers such as Generation X prefer shopping on Facebook.

Channels of distribution have become increasingly fragmented. This is a real challenge for brand owners. At the end of the day, you don't have to be everywhere. But you do need to be where your most important customers are.

My top tips are:

- No one size fits all. Work out what the most relevant channels to market are for your most important customer segments.
- Social commerce is an opportunity to pursue.
- Consider how consumer behaviour has changed due to the pandemic (such as WFH) and what this means for your business and how you need to adapt your operating model.
- Find out what channel experiences your most important customers are looking for, eg click and collect, kerbside pick-up, subscriptions, etc.

Purpose, values and social responsibility

The first thing to look at when it comes to purpose, values and sustainability is to consider whether or not the business is treating this like a 'tick box' exercise, doing the minimum to demonstrate to shareholders that it's taking action, which includes 'kicking the can down the road' by declaring a date long in the future when it will become purposeful, sustainable or socially responsible. Or, whether it's taking all of these hugely important elements seriously through its actions and ongoing commitment to its ethics, supply chain and all.

You might define brand purpose as having a bigger reason to exist – a higher purpose. In the absence of this, brands should not jump on the purpose bandwagon, as it's highly likely to backfire. But if you thought of it as having a 'societal commitment' and think about the approach of numerous brands during the Covid-19 pandemic, there are so many examples of those that have demonstrated this and that have subsequently continued with an obvious commitment to society.

Never put profit before purpose. If you lead with purpose, you will become a more profitable business. Brands with a clear sense of purpose have enjoyed a 175 per cent increase in their brand valuation over a 12-year period, whereby those without had a 70 per cent increase (Kantar, 2020).

As I discussed in Chapter 8 with the example of CVS stopping selling cigarettes, role-modelling is an effective approach to demonstrating brand purpose, values and societal commitment (Cohen, 2017).

Another good example of a socially responsible brand is Hotel Chocolat, which have a planet pledge to have fully compostable packaging by 2021 (lilpackaging, 2019). None of this 'kicking the can down the road' for them.

Kathmandu, the New Zealand outdoor retailer whose share price rose by 85 per cent from 2015 to 2019 (NZX, 2019), is a certified B Corp. They are a brand that strives to be customer-centric in all they do, including being one of the most sustainable retailers on the planet.

The rapid increase in our awareness of our own carbon footprint is the main driver for the change in our values and our behaviour. You might call it 'the shift from value to values'. As consumers we will increasingly look to engage with brands that have a purpose that centres around the environment and social responsibility – a business that puts its people first, a brand that is authentic and transparent in all that it does and that demonstrates values that are aligned with our own.

Prior to the pandemic, consumer behaviour had already begun to shift more towards experiences and away from buying stuff. The pandemic has accelerated this.

So, does all this mean that it's the end for retail, for automotive and other consumer sectors? Of course not. But it's a time for course correction for the majority of brands. Customers will still buy stuff, albeit less frequently. But they'll increasingly want to buy products that are recyclable, derive from recycled or environmentally friendly materials. They'll increasingly purchase electric cars. They'll also increasingly look to rent cars rather than own. We're moving rapidly into the circular economy.

The points below should help you on this path:

- If you treat any of this as a tick-box exercise, customers will see through it.
- Put purpose before profit and profit will follow.
- Think about your values even more than how you deliver value.
- Don't kick social responsibility and sustainability into the long grass. You need to embrace it now and make the necessary changes.

Diversity and inclusion

The Black Lives Matter movement has of course addressed an extremely serious issue of racial profiling and the mistreatment of people who are from ethnic minorities, sometimes referred to as BAME (black, Asian and minority ethnic) communities. It has also been interesting to see how businesses have responded to this. There is clearly a disconnect between what some global brands have said about Black Lives Matter and the lack of diversity within their own business, particularly at board level.

Diversity and the inclusion of diverse groups of customers means meeting the needs of many different consumers. This includes: ethnicity and religion, age, gender, sexuality, demographics, disability and hidden disabilities.

If you don't have a diverse and inclusive business, from the shop floor to the board, can you really expect to serve the needs of your customers to the best effect?

I also firmly believe that consumers will increasingly look to engage with brands whose organizational structures are more representative of them and their needs. Even if they don't, surely having a board that is more representative of the customer base has to be the way to go? Otherwise, how can any brand that targets consumers expect to provide the right products, services and experience for its core customers if it doesn't truly understand them?

As outlined in Chapter 9, diversity is a big issue. Nearly 20 per cent of the UK population is from an ethnic minority (gov.uk, 2011), yet 37 per cent of the FTSE 100 boards are all white (Kinder, 2020). Women drive 70–80 per cent of all purchase decisions (Bloomberg, 2019), yet in the FTSE 350 there are approximately 12–14 female CEOs (30percentclub.org, 2019), which is a decrease from 18 in 2016! This has to change.

These are my tips for getting this right:

- From the shop floor to the boardroom, ensure you have a level of diversity that is representative of your customer base.
- Have processes, procedures and experiences in place that enable all customers to engage with your brand. It is entirely unacceptable (and illegal) that today some stores still turn away customers with visual impairment who have guide dogs. Or that we don't know how to meet the needs of customers who are in wheelchairs, have hearing impairments, Crohn's disease or other hidden disabilities.

Personalization – a customer is for life (not just for Christmas)

How many brands that you engage with make any real attempt to build a relationship with you? We've been talking about CRM (customer relationship management) for 20 years. Yet you can count on one hand the brands that provide personalized experiences today. This is where I believe the national chains have really been caught out. You could argue that you get a much more personal experience going into any of your local retailers as they know you by name, often know your family and have good recall of what you like to buy.

Retailers are not alone when it comes to delivering lack of personalized experiences. Why is it that most of us take out two-, three- or four-year contracts for our cars, either personal contract purchase (PCP) or hire purchase (HP), yet outside of servicing the car, the car dealer communicates with us maybe once or twice over that period? There is no attempt made to build a relationship, no attempt made to find out who else is in my life, in my ecosystem that they might also sell a car to.

Why is there almost no communication that is truly tailored to what we like, what we don't like, what we bought, what else we might like, the content we engage with and so on? Personalization doesn't need to be complicated. It would help to start by capturing a customer's preferences up front about what they want to hear about and how often. It would also help to let them know what's in it for them if they do look to engage with your brand now and in the future.

I've heard industry luminaries say that loyalty is dead. Loyalty is not dead. In most cases, it never really existed. If customers were loyal in the past, it's because they had limited choice. The proliferation of choice has changed that. But customer loyalty still represents a big opportunity. However, it has to be earned. It cannot be achieved simply by giving someone a loyalty card and a few points every time they make a purchase. Loyalty is achieved by being a truly customer-centric business and delivering all the elements of this framework.

Hotel Chocolat, whose share price increased 140 per cent from 2015 to 2019 (London Stock Exchange, 2020), is an example of a customer-centric brand. Born out of a direct mail catalogue and now with a full multichannel business, Hotel Chocolat has a truly personalized approach to marketing. You don't just receive a bog-standard email; moreover, the messaging and incentives are related to you, what you've purchased previously, who you are, what you like and what you don't like.

There are also lots of small, relatively inexpensive things you can do to build engagement and loyalty. I recently purchased a pair of Levi's and when my jeans arrived, there was a really nice message about a gift with purchase, or in this case what I'd call 'a random act of kindness'. It was a very nicely designed face mask – a small gesture that really resonated with me, and one that I amplified through social media.

Finally, outsourcing your customer service to another country where the labour cost is cheaper and the levels of local language are different is not going to engender a sense that you really care about your customers. It more often than not leads to a deeply frustrating experience for consumers who are hoping for a resolution to their issues with your brand.

Here are some tips around personalization:

- As the old adage goes, 'if you've got nothing nice to say, say nothing at all.' Is sending customers generic emails going to drive them to purchase or to churn? It's not difficult to at least tie email communication back to what's been purchased and therefore send something that's more behavioural in nature.
- Random acts of kindness go a long way. What might you do on someone's first purchase to secure their future loyalty?
- Even just writing my name on a pre-printed card offering me a discount off a second order is a good start.
- Capturing preferences up front should help you to send more relevant communication to customers.
- Personalization can also relate to customization. Enabling customization of products even just by adding a name to them can make the whole experience so much more engaging.

Hyper-localization

Much can be lost in translation. And if we really expect customers in international markets such as Spain, France or Germany to buy from us, we must give them a localized experience. Of course, that means more than just language. From the checkout and payment methods available to delivery and returns, customers must feel as though they are engaging with a local brand.

Even when brands go after local-language countries, they can easily get it wrong. There are many factors that are different from one country to the next. Some of this includes:

- Sizing and size guides are different.
- Terminology is different.
- Marketing channels behave differently.
- Payment methods are different.

To help, you might want to work with a cross-border platform such as ESW (eshopworld), which can help provide all the levels of localization required.

Of course, localization and hyper-localization are not merely relevant for brands that are going international. It's just as relevant for consumer businesses to be as local as they can be within their domestic market.

Independent retailers that can offer the consumer a differentiated proposition from the national chains, which consumers perceive to have too much homogeneity, are winning because their propositions are more targeted to the needs of local customers.

For the national chains, they need to behave like independents and empower their store managers to define and execute range, marketing, visual merchandising and service on a more localized basis. They need to see customer service as a profit centre as opposed to a cost centre. Hyper-localization and relentless focus on customer service can help the national chains to deliver more relevant, personalized local customer experiences.

Aligning everyone with the direction of travel

You will never successfully transform your business unless everyone is pointing in the same direction. That most definitely cannot be achieved with the traditional silos that many businesses work in. Having those responsible for product, technology, the physical environment, the digital channels and customer service all working separately with limited interaction and collaboration is not only counterintuitive, but it is completely at odds with delivering the joined-up experience the customer expects.

The more enlightened businesses will create the role of chief customer officer or customer director. This is a good start, but on its own will never be enough to deliver the change and transformation required. The reason is that in most businesses today, the different business units have conflicting KPIs and objectives.

Imagine you run customer service and the contact centre, and your business unit is seen as a cost centre. One of your main KPIs for your team is likely to be to answer all calls within two minutes and end them within five minutes. However, owing to the focus on your function being a cost centre, what they're not being measured on is the percentage of customer calls and issues that are resolved first time. You're essentially being measured on quantity as opposed to quality.

Another example might be with logistics, where the distribution centre is being measured on how many orders were shipped within 24 hours. While timing is obviously important to customers, so is receiving the right product, packed in the right way with all the components included. A focus on speed could negatively impact this.

My tips for ensuring everyone is aligned to the direction of travel are:

- Underpinning the successful transformation is to have a cross-functional team, normally the heads of the different business units (stores, online, logistics, technology, buying and merchandising, marketing, supply chain, etc), steering the successful transformation of the business.
- Everyone should be working with shared objectives and KPIs that are aligned around driving customer-centricity or, at the very least, non-conflicting and synergistic KPIs.
- Last but most definitely not least, the business needs a leader who understands the value in being customer-centric, as they are the most important agent of change and the one to facilitate and empower colleagues to transform the business. Customer-centricity is also driven by the culture of the business and culture comes from the top.

Measure what really matters

I've been involved in hundreds of trading meetings over the years where we reported on the performance of our area of the business. I always felt a strong sense of 'so what?' So what if our average order values are up or down by 10 per cent? So what if our conversion rate was down 20 per cent? So what if our ROAS (return on advertising spend) was up 25 per cent? What was always more interesting was to understand why we were up or down. The KPIs were simply a statement of performance, not a view of what was really working and why and what wasn't working and why.

At the end of the day, to improve performance we need to know what's working well and why, so that we can do more of the same, and the reverse is true for what's not working and why, that needs to be stopped. Wherever possible, we want to understand how customer behaviour is impacting all of these commercial metrics.

There are of course many factors that can determine how we perform, not least product. If that doesn't sell, our average order values (AOVs) go down, conversion goes down, units per transaction (UPTs) go down and of course sales and profitability go down. If a competitor is running a sales promotion and we're not, that's also going to affect our performance.

When it comes to what we measure, if we focus on customers and their drivers, we have a far better chance of understanding what's going on with our business and what we need to do to maximize sales and profitability.

Two common measures of customer satisfaction are net promoter score (NPS) and customer satisfaction (CSAT). Both have merit in being measured and monitored but both do different jobs. While CSAT measures a customer's satisfaction with a product or service, NPS measures customer loyalty.

CSAT's focus on customer satisfaction is normally answered by providing the customer with a number of statements for them to agree or disagree with, such as 'Overall, I was satisfied with your product or service.' NPS is determined by asking a single question based on a customer's overall interaction with a company, ie 'How likely are you to recommend our company/product/service to your family, friends and colleagues?'

If our objective is to be truly customer-centric, we need to measure both. If customers are not satisfied with products or services we have sold to them, that will obviously have an impact upon how they feel about our brand.

Both NPS and CSAT have the 'so what?' factor. What we need to understand is why customers feel the way that they do. That is best measured by some form of qualitative research so that we can understand what the issues are that are driving a decline in either CSAT or NPS and do something about it. This insight can be generated through interviews, focus groups and user testing, in order to really understand the reasons behind the numbers and to ensure we have actionable outcomes to address any issues uncovered.

To follow are just a few of the measures that can help us to understand why customers feel the way they do and therefore how this might be impacting our commercial performance:

- Availability – there's nothing more frustrating than wanting to make a purchase and not being able to do so because they are out of stock on the website. We live in a multichannel world and customers often research online then buy in store. If we don't showcase our range in store, we will lose demand offline.
- The percentage of first-time resolution of customer service issues will be a key driver as to whether or not customers buy from us again. The more effective this is, the less amplification there will be on social media of customer dissatisfaction. This has benefits both in relation to brand integrity and reduction in the churn of customers who have been influenced by detractors.
- The percentage of returns that were due to incorrect products being picked and delivered will give us an indication of potential customer frustration. If we really want to understand the impact, we can trace these returns to individual customers and see whether or not they purchase again!
- If our search function on the website doesn't deliver relevant returns, we will lose demand. We may also discover that customers are searching for products we could be selling that aren't currently available. This will affect our conversion rates and site abandonment rates.
- Consumers often complain that there is not enough staff in store to serve them. If you see conversion rates going down in your stores, this is probably a major factor for this.
- It's also important to look closely at customer churn – and alongside that, the recency, frequency and value of different customer cohorts. I'd want to understand why different types of customer were behaving the way they were.

This is a small representation of the types of insight that really matter as they have a direct impact upon sales and customer satisfaction and will determine whether or not customers buy in the future.

While not specifically addressed in my framework, at the heart of being a customer-centric business is to some extent a shift in mindset from one of 'we sell stuff' to 'we provide a service'.

Just selling stuff isn't enough. Consumers expect all consumer-facing brands to be service providers: 'I don't just want to buy wallpaper; I want you to hang it for me.' 'Yes, I'll buy a new car from you, but please will you pick it up from me when it needs a service?'

While IKEA's traditional model is you buy it and you build it yourself, they have recognized the need to offer a different proposition to consumers who don't do DIY and would prefer a 'do it for me' model, or 'DIFM'. To this end, they acquired TaskRabbit, a platform that marries up local skilled workers with consumer demand, which in turn has enabled them to broaden their service proposition and, at the same time, strengthen relationships with consumers. Where is IKEA on the list of most valuable brands? At the time of writing this book, number 76 in the top 100 globally (Brandz, 2020).

Are you seeing a pattern yet?

John Lewis, one of the UK's leading department store chains, has added a plethora of services to their proposition. From fitting kitchens and bathrooms to interior design services to styling services for men's and women's fashion, they have understood the requirement to build long-term relationships with customers and the opportunity provided to do so by becoming more service-oriented.

While they have had a tough time, as almost anyone has in the retail sector, I believe their focus on improving customer service, as mentioned in the Introduction, and seeing themselves as more of a service provider than just a retailer, is what has helped to sustain the business (Bedoya, 2020).

Doing the right thing doesn't have to be rocket science!

In April 2020, my team and I at Customer Service Action launched a survey to determine what consumer behaviour looked like before, during and after lockdown. More than 70 per cent said they would boycott a brand that demonstrated bad behaviour during Covid-19 – be that to their staff, customers or the environment. This is not to say they'll all follow through, but we can safely estimate that at least 25–30 per cent will (Newman, 2020). That would have quite an impact when it comes to sales and customer retention, don't you think?

Of course, bad behaviour on the part of a brand is never something to be welcomed. The following are just a few examples of brands that were clearly doing the right thing before, during and after Covid-19, and in the process, demonstrating their purpose and their focus on customer-centricity.

Asda and the flu jab drive-through

I don't know about you, but I've met a few people feeling insecure about going to their GP during the pandemic. In fact, most practices would not allow people to come in unless absolutely necessary and would take consultations over the phone.

So, what does Asda do? They think about their customers' safety and put a drive-through system in place to greet vulnerable people (the elderly and pregnant women) and give them a flu jab for free. It's not just about feeding the nation anymore; it's about helping it stay safe and healthy (BBC, 2020).

Patagonia – self-taxing

I've highlighted Patagonia already in the book as a socially responsible brand. Another example of this is where Patagonia is self-taxing and makes a contribution of 1 per cent of profits to environmental non-profit organizations (Patagonia, 2020).

This very much plays to their very genuine and authentic focus on sustainability and social responsibility. What might the impact be upon climate change if every brand followed their example?

Ella's Kitchen and Green Friday

Green is the new black for food brand Ella's Kitchen, whereby they donate all of their profits from Black Friday to Tree For Life. I've talked a lot about conscious consumption; this is more a case of conscious and responsible retailing (Briggs, 2020).

Lush and washing your hands for free

At the beginning of the pandemic, it was not surprising to see Lush stores encouraging their customers to come in and wash their hands for free. If you think of busy city centres (and let's not forget the biggest Lush shop is on Oxford Street in London, one of the busiest streets in the world), this initiative was more than welcome! If you have the means and opportunity, sometimes it's all it takes to be remembered by your customers (Wood, 2020).

I can hear you say: 'How is it better than just putting hand sanitizers at the entrance of your shop like everybody else?'

Well, sometimes, some people can be allergic to the gel in hand sanitizers. The fact they are also so heavy in alcohol dries your hands very quickly, making you prone to eczema and other issues. Being a cosmetic brand, Lush knows this – and thus proves they take extra good care of their customers.

Co-op and its determination to make shoppers' lives better

Back in 2019, Co-op had already partnered with Deliveroo for rapid delivery in London. They are now opening up their partnership to 400 stores. One can say Co-op has always been quite innovative, and this didn't start with Covid-19 (Farrell, 2020).

Moreover, this year, as mentioned in Chapter 13, Co-op became very aware of the strain that restrictions around funerals were having on families who had lost a loved one. So what did they do? They put a brand-new system in place so that mourners could still pay their respects (Mathers, 2020).

You don't need to be a big brand to make a big difference: in 2020, I came across a small independent coffee shop called Crushed Bean in Croydon, which were offering free school breakfasts and NHS discounts. It proves that you don't need big promotions (and the big advertising budget that goes with it) to make an impact on your community. Sometimes, it just comes from the heart, and I can guarantee that anyone passing by, being a customer or not, remembers their gesture – I certainly do!

The traditional return to shareholder focus is a broken model

Too many CEOs are, for all intents and purposes, being handcuffed by shareholders. They are essentially being disincentivized to focus on anything other than the short-term performance of the business.

After all, if your remuneration including your bonus depends upon what you achieve in the next 12 months, you're highly unlikely to invest in technology or anything else that might improve customer experience if it will have a medium- to long-term payback. Anything that risks the 12-month EBITDA (earnings before income tax, depreciation and amortization) will be put on the back burner. That is a conflict of interest. It has to change.

The issue lies not with the CEO themselves; it is the responsibility of the shareholders to ensure that the CEO is empowered to make longer-term decisions and not be penalized for doing so. It should really be the opposite, where they're encouraged to meet both short-term and longer-term objectives, as the former is necessary to ensure the business is a going concern and the latter will determine the viability and success of the business in the longer term.

The board needs a makeover

Look at the board of most businesses and you'll see the same challenges – not enough diversity, be that from gender, ethnicity, sexuality, demographics or disability perspectives.

I'm a firm believer in having the right person for the right job. However, this scenario must be improved. It's not only the right thing to do to have a diverse board and leadership team; it's also a commercial imperative. If a board is not representative of its customer base, how can it be expected to make all the right strategic decisions about how best to serve customers?

At least 10 years ago, Aurora/Mosaic fashions implemented a shadow board (Faulkner, 2012) – a board made up of younger people in the business who could advise the board on changes to technology and behaviour among younger customers and what the business should do to maintain its relevance. This was and still remains a highly innovative move. In the previous chapter, I described how the CEO of Gucci has done the same thing to great effect.

I'd like to suggest that we go even further now and that boards not only address the diversity issues above, but also the lack of connection and understanding of the two most important customer segments to most consumer-facing businesses: Millennials and Gen Z – those born between 1981 and 1995, and 1996 and 2015, respectively. The best way to achieve this? Appoint a Millennial and Gen Z to the full board. Yes, have two people who represent the interests of consumers their age. But I'd go even further. I'd appoint a customer advisory board – a small collection of real-life consumers who are customers of the brand. Imagine the insight this would generate! Too many business decisions are taken without any conversation or consultation with staff on the front line or with customers. Both of these groups will tell you exactly where you're going wrong.

Conclusion

There is irrefutable proof, as I've laid out throughout this book, that being customer-centric is the only relevant strategy that can guarantee sustainable commercial success over the short, medium and long term.

It is also crystal clear that the brands that don't adopt this as their core strategy will ultimately go out of business. The only question is whether that happens quickly or slowly over a number of years.

The last word

Thank you for reading the book. I sincerely hope that it provides you with the insight, framework and practical actions you can take to drive your business to a new and more successful place.

Good luck on your journey towards true customer-centricity! I urge you to adopt my framework and share it with your colleagues. That way you can get everyone working together and pulling in the same direction to drive better levels of service and experience for consumers and in turn help to secure the future for your business.

References

30percentclub.org (2019) [accessed 13 April 2020] FTSE 350 hits 30% women on boards for the first time in 450 years, *30% Club* [Online] https://30percentclub.org/press-releases/view/ftse-350-hits-30-women-on-boards-for-the-first-time-in-450-years (archived at https://perma.cc/6B3T-DGMH)

Bare (2020) [accessed 27 November 2020] The advancement of omni-channel customer experience, *BARE International India* [Online] https://www.bareinternational.in/the-advancement-of-omni-channel-customer-experience/ (archived at https://perma.cc/EZ2U-PBVF)

BBC (2020) [accessed 27 November 2020] Asda launches 'first of its kind' flu jab service, *BBC News* [Online] https://www.bbc.co.uk/news/business-54462626 (archived at https://perma.cc/HME2-C68E)

Bedoya, D (2020) [accessed 9 April 2020] John Lewis says all 50 of its stores will close on Monday night due to coronavirus, *Infosurhoy.com* [Online] https://infosurhoy.com (archived at https://perma.cc/BG79-A7B2)

Bloomberg (2019) [accessed 9 April 2020] Are you a robot?, *Bloomberg* [Online] https://www.bloomberg.com/company/stories/top-10-things-everyone-know-women-consumers/ (archived at https://perma.cc/YM42-KZDD)

Brandz (2020) [accessed 9 April 2020] Brandz, *Brandz.com* [Online] https://www.brandz.com/Global (archived at https://perma.cc/562Z-SQ98)

Briggs, F (2020) [accessed 27 November 2020] Ella's Kitchen to donate all profits from online sales from Black Friday to Cyber Monday to Trees For Life, *Retail Times* [Online] https://www.retailtimes.co.uk/ellas-kitchen-to-donate-all-profits-from-online-sales-from-black-friday-to-cyber-monday-to-trees-for-life/ (archived at https://perma.cc/64H2-YWTN)

Charan, R (2019) [accessed 25 October 2020] Home Depot's blueprint for culture change, *Harvard Business Review* [Online] https://hbr.org/2006/04/home-depots-blueprint-for-culture-change (archived at https://perma.cc/KV4X-CBMY)

Cohen, R (2017) [accessed 20 July 2020] When CVS stopped selling cigarettes, some customers quit smoking, *Reuters* [Online] https://uk.reuters.com/article/us-health-pharmacies-cigarettes/when-cvs-stopped-selling-cigarettes-some-customers-quit-smoking-idUKKBN16R2HY (archived at https://perma.cc/T4KB-LGZ7)

Dindar, S (2016) [accessed 24 November 2020] Home Depot gives 50 dollar discounts to customers: Here's how and why, *QuickTapSurvey* [Online] https://www.quicktapsurvey.com (archived at https://perma.cc/L3NF-7QLF)

Encyclopedia (2020) [accessed 24 November 2020] Sam Walton, *Encyclopedia.com* [Online] https://www.encyclopedia.com/people/social-sciences-and-law/business-leaders/sam-walton (archived at https://perma.cc/4QR9-F646)

Farrell, S (2020) [accessed 27 November 2020] Co-op partners with Deliveroo for rapid delivery in London, *The Grocer* [Online] https://www.thegrocer.co.uk/online/co-op-partners-with-deliveroo-for-rapid-delivery-in-london/576377.article (archived at https://perma.cc/D73Q-KTDV)

Faulkner, R (2012) [accessed 24 November 2020] Stepping out from the shadows, *Drapers* [Online] https://www.drapersonline.com/people/the-drapers-interview/stepping-out-from-the-shadows (archived at https://perma.cc/7TKX-L9RR)

Financhill (2020) [accessed 24 November 2020] Why is Home Depot stock so high?, *Financhill* [Online] https://financhill.com/blog/investing/why-is-home-depot-stock-so-high (archived at https://perma.cc/R787-7XQL)

Gov.uk (2011) [accessed 27 November 2020] UK population by ethnicity, *Gov.uk* [Online] https://www.ethnicity-facts-figures.service.gov.uk/uk-population-by-ethnicity (archived at https://perma.cc/GXH3-3H53)

Kantar (2020) [accessed 20 July 2020] Purpose 2020: Purpose-led growth, *Kantar* [Online] https://consulting.kantar.com/wp-content/uploads/2019/06/Purpose-2020-PDF-Presentation.pdf (archived at https://perma.cc/C2R9-FFFC)

Kinder, T (2020) [accessed 13 April 2020] A third of FTSE 100 companies set to miss ethnic diversity targets, *Financial Times* [Online] https://www.ft.com/content/945ce30e-4762-11ea-aeb3-955839e06441 (archived at https://perma.cc/ZC5W-CQW6)

lilpackaging (2019) [accessed 24 November 2020] How can we celebrate World Environment Day 2020?, *Hotelchocolat.com* [Online] https://www.hotelchocolat.com/uk/blog/environmentandamp%3Bethics/how-can-we-celebrate-world-environment-day-2020-2.html (archived at https://perma.cc/94XW-6EYB)

London Stock Exchange (2020) [accessed 18 January 2021] HOTEL CHOC Share Price (HOTC), *London Stock Exchange* [Online] https://www.londonstockexchange.com/stock/HOTC/hotel-chocolat-group-plc/company-page?lang=en (archived at https://perma.cc/MGH7-YVB9)

Mason, V (2019) [accessed 25 October 2020] Timpson owner speaks of his successful, yet unusual, business method at Skipton event, *Craven Herald* [Online] https://www.cravenherald.co.uk/news/17987495.timpson-owner-speaks-successful-yet-unusual-business-method-skipton-event/ (archived at https://perma.cc/5BBX-THTS)

Mathers, M (2020) [accessed 25 October 2020] Co-op introduces new services to help mourners unable to attend funerals, *Independent* [Online] https://www.independent.co.uk/life-style/coronavirus-funeral-service-co-op-lockdown-a9504231.html (archived at https://perma.cc/N56Y-XBQP)

Newman, M (2020) [accessed 21 July 2020] CSA consumer survey 2020, *Customerserviceaction.com* [Online] https://customerserviceaction.com/read-our-consumer-survey-insights (archived at https://perma.cc/5GSM-KYGW)

NZX (2019) [accessed 9 April 2020] KMD Kathmandu Holdings Limited Ordinary Shares – NZX, *Nzx.com* [Online] https://www.nzx.com/instruments/KMD (archived at https://perma.cc/F6JL-9GJG)

Patagonia (2020) [accessed 27 November 2020] Environmental activism, *Patagonia.com* [Online] https://www.patagonia.com/activism/ (archived at https://perma.cc/BRM2-XLHE)

Reichheld, F and Schefter, P (2020) [accessed 24 October 2020] The economics of e-loyalty, *HBS Working Knowledge* [Online] https://hbswk.hbs.edu/archive/the-economics-of-e-loyalty (archived at https://perma.cc/58LN-FLZ5)

Statista (2020) [accessed 24 November 2020] Online sources for product searches worldwide 2020, *Statista* [Online] https://www.statista.com/statistics/1034209/global-product-search-online-sources/ (archived at https://perma.cc/3KB5-JY2H)

Wood, Z (2020) [accessed 25 October 2020] Lush offers public free hand washes to halt coronavirus spread, *Guardian* [Online] https://www.theguardian.com/world/2020/feb/27/lush-offers-public-free-hand-washes-to-halt-coronavirus-spread#:~:text=Cosmetics%20chain%20Lush%20is%20opening,says%20is%20a%20public%20service (archived at https://perma.cc/7BS5-SBQN)

INDEX

Note: Numbers are filed as spelled; 'Mc' and acronyms are filed as presented; '#' is ignored for filing purposes. Page locators in *italics* denote information within a figure or table.

Ace & Tate 146
Action Works 121
adaptation 11, 44, 53, 63, 74, 148, 164
adhocracy-oriented culture 97
advertising (ads) 73, 84, 113, 124, 193, 203, 206–07, 213, 217
advocacy 33, 101, 194
Afterpay 150
agility 9, 32, 42, 53, 72, 97, 100
agriculture 121, 122
Ahrendts, Angela 58–59
AI (artificial intelligence) 12, 15, 51, 52, 74
Airbnb 49, 85, 145, 222
airline sector 12–13, 29, 49, 51, 59–60, 74–75, 173–76, 181, 190
    see also Delta Air Lines; easyJet; JetBlue; KLM
Alaska Airlines 12–13
Alexa 149
algorithms 175–76
Alibaba 8, 9
alignment 10, 13, 20, 191–92, 204, 210, 225, 229–30
allyship 138
Amazon 3–4, 8, 9, 30, 44, 48, 84, 106–07, 223
    see also Alexa; Amazon Go; Prime
Amazon Go 4, 160
America *see* US (United States)
Andrew, Trevor 73
Apple 8, 9, 56, 57–58, 61
Apple Pay 172
apprenticeship levy 46
apps 14–15, 72, 102, 149, 162, 194, 223
Arcadia 43
Arsenal Football Club 75
ArtLab 72
Asda 48, 234
ASOS 9, 42
assisted sales 15, 222
ASX companies 17
Aurora/Mosaic fashions 236
Australia 17, 30, 133, 222

authenticity 9, 10, 67–68, 113, 120, 192, 193, 197, 205–08, 234
automotive sector 27, 143, 148–49, 177, 178–79
    see also BMW; car dealers (industry); Rolls-Royce; Tesla
average order values 88, 89, 90, 231

B Corp companies 12, 121, 225
baby boomers 202, 203
Bailey, Christopher 58–59
BAME (ethnic minority) community 11, 137, 139, 226
banking sector 2, 15, 69–70, 170–72, 173, 224
    see also Monzo Bank
Barratt 158
Barre 17
Battersea housing development 158
beauty brands 92, 187–88
Bella Italia 46
best employer list (*Forbes*) 105
bets, placing 42, 43
Big Knit campaign 122
Bizzarri, Marco 204
Black Badge 71–72
Black Lives Matter movement 226
Blockbuster Video 42, 43, 44–45, 62, 143
BMW 70–71, 76, 78
board representation 11, 17, 134–35, 137, 226, 227, 236
    see also CEOs
Boo.com 42
Boohoo Group (Boohoo) 9, 194
Booking.com 49, 145
Borders 43, 44
bots *see* chat bots; Insomnobot-3000
Boxpark 159, 161
Boy Brow 187
brand reputation 134
branding 50, 73, 78, 134–35, 195, 197
    see also heritage brands; standalone brands

Bravo, Rosemary 58–59
brick-and-mortar (high street) stores 3, 30–32, 68–69, 145, *155*, 156–61, 166, 190
Burberry 58–59, 113
business rates 46, 157
business-to-business sector 19
buy-back services 118
buy now pay later 150, 172–73, 203, 222
buyerarchy of needs 165
By Rotation 208
Byron Burger 84

cabin crew 174
camaraderie 115
car dealers (industry) 11, 15, 27, 46–47, 148, 176–79, 223, 227
  see also automotive sector; BMW; electric cars; Rockar; Rolls-Royce; Tesla
carbon dioxide emissions 29
carbon footprint 10, 26, 29, 120, 165, 203, 225
carbon neutral policies 29, 120
career progression 104, 108, 116, 138, 220
caring 116, 134, 178, 186
Carl, Fred 37
Carluccio's 46, 84
cash flow 43
Casper 32–33
CDLP 185
celebrations 115
  see also success sharing
celebrities 46, 63, 203, 211
CEOs 11, 17, 52–53, 54, 117, 134, 144, 180, 226, 236
challenger banks 170–72
  see also Monzo Bank
channel shift (migration) 157, 163
chat bots 51, 181
China 30, 32, 73
choice 145, 154, *155*, 175, 176
churn
  customer 51, 82, 92, 180, 232
  employee 43, 98, 113, 134, 178
circular economy 11, 160, 164, 203, 208, 226
Citizen's Bank 70
clan-oriented culture 97
clarity 76, 151, 211
Clearpay 172–73
click and collect 15, 85, 89, 158, 223, 224
Clintons Cards 43
Co-op 186, 235
Coal Drops Yard 158

Coca-Cola 9, 122
coffee shops 36
  see also Starbucks
collaboration 86, 97, 136, 154
communication 89, 92, 115, 116, 178, 211, 228
  see also customer feedback; emails; language; personalization; sign language; social media; word of mouth
community 14, 101, 116, 160, 203, 220, 235
company voluntary administration 43, 157
competitive margin metrics 74
competitors 53, *86*, 97, 190, 221, 231
configurators 71
Confucius 42–43
'connected experience imperative' 2–3
connection 33, 34, 68, 99, 117, 181, 236
conscious consumption 10, 25–40, 158–59, 164–65, 209, 234
considered consumption 27
consistency 46, 62, 76, 89, 117, 174
consumer choice 145, 154, *155*, 175, 176
consumer promiscuity 46
consumerism 10
contact centres 51, 81, 180, 188, 230
content (posts) 193–94, 195, 197
content clips 74
contests (competitions) 192–93
convenience 30, 149, 150, 159–60
core values 101, 106, 115, 118–21
Cornerhouse cinema 35
cost management 50, 54, 82, 124
courier services 161, 166
Covid-19 10–11, 16, 26, 206, 224
  and brand response 113, 124–25, 163, 173, 186–87, 233–35
creativity 69, 99, 104, 133, 209
credit cards 172–73, 203, 222
cross-functional teams 230
Crushed Bean 235
culture, organizational *42*, 43, 97–98, 114–21, 125–26, 230
customer advocacy 33, 101, 194
customer churn 51, 82, 92, 180, 232
customer empowerment 15, 143, 148–49, 162, 163, 172, 173, 179, 180–81, 189
customer feedback 94, 102, 117, 162, 185, 187
customer journey mapping 70
customer lifetime value 82, 84, 92, 99, 119, 175, 180, 218, 221
customer loyalty 33, 85, 90, 101, 170, 177–78, 187, 197, 227–28, 231

customer loyalty programmes 15, 46, 51, 175, 221
customer needs and wants 14–15, 64, 67, 220–21
customer personas 70
customer ratings (reviews) 70, 108, 162, 192, 194, 211
customer relationship management 18–19, 20, 106, 138, 178, 189–90, 227, 233
customer responses 190–92, 196
customer satisfaction 82, 85, 93, 94, 177–78, 231
customer service 51–52, 81–82, 89, 94, 154–55, 173–76, 178, 180, 232–33
    Dyson 77
    Emirates 74–75
    Hunkemöller 102–03
    social media 192, 196
customization 71, 228
CVS 113, 225

Dao, David 175
Darbyshire, Toby 146–47
Day One Thinking 107
Debenhams 43, 153
decision-making 105, 133
Deliveroo 42, 46, 85, 149, 186, 235
delivery services 15, 30–31, 46, 69, 89, 149, 161–62
Delta Air Lines 59–60, 64, 174
demand vs supply 41, 42
democratic design concept 118
democratization of retail 2, 9, 52, 118
department stores 20, 153–54
    see also John Lewis & Partners; Selfridges
Depop 195, 208
Diageo 136–37
Dick's Sporting Goods 114
diet 28–29, 123, 160
differentiation 44, 57, 69, 76, 84, 101, 159, 229
digitalization 15, 31–32, 58–59, 61, 64, 72–74, 146–48, 156, 164
    see also challenger banks
direct messaging 189
direct to consumer 143, 144, 145, 154, 188, 197
disabilities 11, 18, 88, 131–33, 137, 139, 226, 227, 236
Disability Confident scheme 137
discounts 37, 63, 119, 162, 210, 219, 221, 228, 235
Disney 9
disruptors 42, 44, 46, 142–52
    see also Airbnb; Amazon; Deliveroo; Just Eat; Monzo Bank; Uber
distinctiveness 73, 76
distribution centres 59, 106, 230
diversity 11, 17–18, 91, 130–41, 226–27
    see also BAME (ethnic minority) community; LGBT community
Diversity University 136
Dixons 44
Dom 15
Domino's Pizza 15
DownYourHighStreet.com 156
DPD (DPD Design Space) 161–62
Dreamery 33
Dreams 117
Dyson, James 77
Dyson 77

Early Learning Centre 48
easyJet 29, 49, 144–45
eBay 9, 30
EBITDA 235
ecommerce 9, 44, 145, 155, 157–58, 164
    see also Amazon; ASOS; Boo.com; Boohoo Group (Boohoo); Burberry; Domino's Pizza; eBay; Etsy; Neiman Marcus; online shopping; Pattern
Ego Barbers 185, 193
electric cars 11, 27, 47, 71, 178
electric-powered aircraft 29–30
Ella's Kitchen 234
Elvis see Presley, Elvis
emails 12, 20, 51, 185, 228
Emirates 74–75, 174
empathy 33, 104, 203, 207
employee benefits 103
employee churn 43, 98, 113, 134, 178
employee empowerment 76, 90, 94, 97–98, 104, 154, 192
    Gucci 205
    Home Depot 219
    John Lewis 105–06
    Pret A Manger 101
    Timpson 86, 100
employee-first culture 13–14, 44, 57, 60, 64, 96–111, 206, 218–20, 221
employer brand 134–35, 197
    see also best employer list (*Forbes*)
empowerment see customer empowerment; employee empowerment
endless aisle concept 15, 222
entrepreneurialism 41, 86, 97, 142, 144

environmental impact 9–10, 26, 27–28, 93, 121, 205–06, 234
escalation procedures 192
ESW (eshopworld) 229
ethical products 17, 122, 210
ethnic minority (BAME) community 11, 137, 139, 226
Etihad 174
Etsy 9, 83–84
evolution vs revolution 50
Expedia 49, 145
experience economy 26
experiential retail 69, 154
Extinction Rebellion 10, 26
eyewear 145–46

Facebook 9, 26, 193, 194, 224
fail fast 13, 54
fashion sector 10, 27–28, 50, 124, 160, 164, 206, 208
    see also ASOS; Aurora/Mosaic fashions; Boo.com; Boohoo Group (Boohoo); Burberry; By Rotation; Gucci; Nudie Jeans
fast fashion 10, 27–28, 50, 160, 208
feedback 94, 102, 117, 162, 185, 187
financial management 43
financial services sector 3
    see also banking sector
fintech 172–73
First Direct 170
first-time resolution 192, 232
fitness sector 16, 148
flexitarianism 29, 50
flight overbookings 175–76
food industry 28–29, 135, 160
    see also veganism; vegetarianism ('veggie')
Forbes 105
Ford, Tom 73
Ford 83, 177
Forever 21 43
Fortune 500 companies 17
founder syndrome 97
four Ps (marketing mix) 211–12
frugality 107
FTSE 100 boards 11, 134, 137, 226
FTSE 350 boards 11, 17, 226

Gant 164
GBK 84
gender diversity 134–36, 137
Generation X 173, 224
Generation Z 9, 31, 36, 171–72, 187, 195, 201–16, 224, 236
    employment patterns 13, 116

gesture-based marketing 16, 86–87, 101, 228, 235
    acts of kindness 221
Get the Balance Right campaign 120
Gett 2
GG logo 73
Global Education Leave programme 103
Glossier 187–88
GMC 47
goods era 85–86
Google 9, 103–04, 112, 223
Google Alerts 190
Google Analytics 220
Google Pay 172
Great Places to Work 136
Green Friday 234
greenwashing 123–25, 126
Greggs 62–63, 64
Greggs Breakfast Club 63
Greta see Thunberg, Greta
grocery retail sector 37, 107–08, 113, 160, 186
    see also Co-op
Gucci 72–73, 204–05
gym sector 16, 143, 147–48

Hamleys 45
happiness 98, 105–06, 203
Hard Rock Hotel 33–34
Hard Rock International 105
Hard Rock Palms Spring 34
Harley-Davidson 68
Harley Owners Group 68
hashtags 190, 192
hearing impairments 132–33, 227
Heist 146–47
heritage brands 58–59, 67–80
hidden disabilities 18, 88, 139, 227
hidden trade-offs 124
hierarchy orientation 97–98
high street (brick-and-mortar) stores 3, 30–32, 68–69, 145, *155*, 156–61, 166, 190
High Street Taskforce 166
hiring (recruitment) 94, 99, 102, 105, 121, 134, 137, 218
Home 35
Home Depot 9, 116, 219, 220
Honda 68, 148
honesty 106, 207, 211
hospitality sector 16, 35, 160–61, 202
    see also restaurant sector
Hotel Chocolat 12, 225, 228
hotel sector 3, 19–20, 33–34, 136
House of Fraser 153

House of VANS, The 35
household good sector 92
housing developments 158
Hoxton Hotel Group 19–20
HRC Corporate Equality Index 136
HSBC 69, 170
Hubbell & Hudson 37
Hummer 47
Hunkemöller 102–03
hybrid cars 27
hybrid gym membership 148
hyper-localization 19–20, 54, 159, 229

IBM Watson 74
Iceland 92–93
ideas generation 99–100, 108, 162, 204
IKEA 118–19, 233
iMac 58
incentives 12, 192, 209–10
inclusion 17–18, 19–20, 88, 91, 130–41, 226–27
    see also BAME (ethnic minority) community; LGBT community
independent retail 154, 156, 159, 160, 161, 165, 229, 235
influencers 33, 121, 190, 195, 207
Ingka 118
Innocent Drinks 121–22
Innocent Foundation 122
innovation 68, 71, 75, 133, 147, 194
innovation labs 15, 151
Insomnobot-3000 33
Instagram 20, 184, 187, 188, 193, 195, 211, 224
integrity 106, 209, 211
Intel 101
interactive experiences 31–32
internet 2, 9, 47–48, 84
    see also ecommerce; online shopping
iPod 58
issue resolution 92, 192, 232
Ive, Jony 58

Jack Wills 43
Jaguar Land Rover 148, 177
Jamie's Italian 45–46, 84
JC Penney 43
JD 209
JD Sports 12
JetBlue 87
Jobs, Steve 57
John Lewis & Partners (The John Lewis Partnership) 2, 105–06, 153, 157, 163, 233
Johnson & Johnson 135–36

Just Capital 100–01
Just Eat 42, 46, 85

Kathmandu 12, 17, 225
Kawasaki 68
King's Cross housing development 158
KLM 188–89
Knudstorp, Jorgen Vig 60
KPIs 20, 82, 94, 103, 230, 231

Lab Series 86
Lab 12 147
labelling 123, 124
Land Rover 37, 148, 177
language 171, 191, 228
lapsed customers 193, 221
last mile logistics 161–62, 166
lastminute.com 49, 145
leadership 42–43, 44, 64, 67, 68, 76, 133, 230
    see also board representation; CEOs
Leadership Principles (Amazon) 107
learning and development 44, 102, 104, 108, 116, 219
    see also training
LEGO® 60–61
LEGO® Friends 61
LEGO® Movie 60
Leon 122–23
Levi's 86, 228
LG 75
LGBT community 136, 137, 139
Library Theatre Company 35
Lidl 157
lingerie sector 102–03, 146–47
Links of London 43
live chat 51, 171
Lizee 164
local authorities 158, 160, 166
localization 16, 19–20, 59, 159, 224, 229
logistics functions 161–62, 166, 230
Logue, Mike 117
long queues 30–31
Louis Vuitton 9
LoveFilm 44
loyalty programmes 15, 46, 51, 175, 221
Lush 234–35
Lyft 2

Marcario, Rose 16
market-oriented culture 97
marketing mix 211–12
Marks & Spencer (M&S) 28, 49–50, 153
Marriott 136

Mastercard 9, 171
McDonald's 9
measurement 21, 85–87, 230–33
    see also average order values; competitive margin metrics; KPIs; net promoter score
merchandising 18, 31, 50, 56, 69, 132, 229
Michele, Alessandro 73
micro-influencers 207
micromanagement 98
Microsoft 9, 58, 101
Miele (Miele Experience Centre) 37
Millennials 31, 36, 72, 172–73, 187, 188, 206–07, 210, 211
    employment patterns 13, 104, 116
    engagement with 204, 205, 236
    social responsibility 9, 16, 201–02
misleading marketing (labelling) 124
mobile 33, 74, 119, 149, 170, 172, 223
mobile apps 14–15, 72, 102, 149, 162, 194, 223
Monzo Bank 2, 42, 143, 171–72, 222
Morrisons 186
Mothercare 43, 47–48, 51
Mr Selfridge 69
multi-sensory shopping 30–32
multichannel propositions 44, 59, 105, 158, 177, 228, 232
multiple store strategy 153–54
music 30, 31, 34, 36
My Starbucks Barista 149
mystery shopping 220–21

Nando's 46
nap rooms (Casper) 33
National Electric Vehicle Sweden 47
National Living Wage 46
Neiman Marcus 20
net promoter score 18, 82, 231
Netbase 190
Netflix 45, 61–62, 64, 143
Newton MessagePad 57
Next 157
Nike 9, 112
'noodle lab' 85
Nudie Jeans 119–20

Ocado 12, 30, 50, 85
Oliver, Jamie 45–46
omnichannel 155, 222
online sales taxes 158
online shopping 2, 30, 44–45, 49–50, 88, 145–46, 154, 157–58, 161
    see also ecommerce

'open house' cultures 19
order fulfilment 89–90
organizational culture 19, 42, 43, 97–98, 114–21, 125–26, 230
organizational history 117–18
organizational silos 20, 64, 154, 229–30
outsourcing 86, 164, 228
overbookings 175–76
overexpansion 157

packaging 12, 93, 123, 209, 211–12, 225
paid ads 193
Palm Springs (Hard Rock) 34
participation 211, 212
Patagonia 16, 120–21, 234
Patagonia Provisions 121
Pattern 117
pay (remuneration) 44, 63, 104, 107, 174, 235
Pay Point 171
peer-to-peer 145, 211, 214
Peloton 143
Pepsi 113
personal (real) stories 191, 207–08
personalization 18–19, 54, 89, 156, 159, 193, 203, 227–28
    BMW 71
    Burberry 59
    CDLP 185
    Hotel Chocolat 12
    Leon 123
Pinterest 26, 197
pivoting 64, 77, 163
place ('where your customers are') 15–16, 212, 223–24
placing bets 42, 43
Plant Kitchen (M&S) 28, 50
pop-ups 35, 50, 69, 161, 188
posts (content) 193–94, 195, 197
Presley, Elvis 34
Pret A Manger 101–02
Prezzo 84
pricing 145, 177, 208–09, 212
Primark 161
Prime 69, 78
problem-solving 133
product (product proposition) 50, 51, 175, 212
product development 57, 61, 68, 75, 77–78, 99–100, 187
product tips/tricks 193
profit, before purpose 124–25
progressive web app 223
promotion (product search) 212, 232

promotional offers 33, 185
Psycle 16
pureplays 47–48, 145
purpose 14, 16–17, 76, 112–29, 212, 224–26
    and Covid-19 113, 124-25, 163, 173, 186–87, 233–35
    purpose washing ('purpose bandwagon') 113, 126

Qantas 174
queues 30–31

#RaceTogether 113
Ragyard 209
random acts of kindness 86, 101, 221, 228
Range, The 125
ratings (reviews) 70, 108, 162, 192, 194, 211
re-commerce 164
Real Madrid 75
real (personal) stories 191, 207–08
recruitment (hiring) 94, 99, 102, 105, 121, 134, 137, 218
recycling 11, 17, 119, 120, 122, 124, 147, 209, 225
Reddit 190
regenerative agriculture 121
reinvention 50, 76, 77
    see also Emirates; Gucci; LEGO®; LG; Rolls-Royce
relationship management 18–19, 20, 106, 138, 178, 189–90, 227, 233
remuneration (pay) 44, 63, 104, 107, 174, 235
renewable energy 29, 118, 209
rental economy 11, 44–45, 61–62, 143, 164, 178–79, 208
repair services 77, 83, 119, 120
    see also Timpson
resale consignment model 208, 210
resources 67
restaurant sector 84–85, 122–23, 149
    see also Carluccio's; Jamie's Italian
retail sector 3, 18, 30–32, 35, 69, 131–33, 145–46, 153–68
    democratization of 2, 9, 52, 118
    independent 229, 235
    see also Asda; brick-and-mortar (high street) stores; Burberry; department stores; Dick's Sporting Goods; ecommerce; grocery retail sector; Home Depot; Hunkemöller; Iceland; IKEA; JD; JD Sports; Lush; Marks & Spencer (M&S); Morrisons; Mothercare; online shopping; Range, The; Rêve En Vert; Sports Direct; Toys R Us; Walmart
retail sector (1994 vs 2020s) 155
return on advertising spend (ROAS) 217, 231
returns 89, 229, 232
Rêve En Vert 210
reviews (ratings) 70, 108, 162, 192, 194, 211
Revolut 170, 171
revolution vs evolution 50
Robert Wood Johnson Foundation 101
Rockar 85, 143, 148, 177
role-modelling 113–14, 225
Rolls-Royce 71–72, 76, 78
Royal Thai 174
Ryanair 49

SAAB 47
sabbaticals 103
Salesforce 101
salespeople 143, 177, 178
screen grabs 193
seamless experience 146, 154, 164, 222
self-service technology 88
Selfridge, Harry 69, 76
Selfridges 68–69, 76, 153
Selfridges Plus 69
Seminole Tribe 34
sentiment analysis 8, 82
service development 57, 68, 77–78, 89, 166, 188–91
    see also customer service
service era 85–86
serviced offices 20
shadow boards (committees) 204–05, 236
shareholders 100, 224, 235–36
short-termism 52–53, 124–25, 175, 236
sight loss (visual impairment) 18, 131–32, 227
sign language 132
sign offs 191
silos 20, 64, 154, 229–30
Singapore Airlines 174
single customer view 155, 220
Skills for Employment programmes 118
Snag Tights 147
Snapchat 195, 224
sneaker stores 36
social brands 186–87
social listening 189–91, 197

social media 32, 83, 183–200, 207–08, 224, 232
  see also Facebook; Instagram; Twitter
social media guidelines 191–92
social media monitoring 190
social media operating model 184
social responsibility (societal commitment) 10–11, 16–17, 63, 90–91, 113, 205–06, 225, 234
social shopping 155, 184, 194–95, 197
Sodexo 135
Spirit of Ecstasy 72
sponsorships
  commercial 68, 75
  employee 138
Sports Direct 125
staff see employee benefits; employee churn; employee empowerment; employee-first culture; pay (remuneration); staff assistance
staff assistance 31, 87–88, 232
standalone brands 37, 50
Starbucks 9, 36, 113, 149
Starling Bank 2, 170, 171, 172
start-ups 41, 42, 107, 120, 150
stock availability 59, 89, 222, 232
store leases 161, 166
Storr 211
storytelling 72–73, 194, 207–08
Strada 84
sub-brands 50
success sharing 105, 115, 117, 220
succession planning 44, 104
Sunday Times (100 best companies) 105
Super Bowl 73
supply vs demand 41, 42
sustainability 29, 50, 118–24, 147, 203, 206, 208–09, 224–26, 234

TaskRabbit 233
technology 15, 88, 91, 159, 221–23
  see also AI (artificial intelligence); apps; digitalization; fintech; iMac; internet; iPod; mobile
telecoms sector 149
  see also mobile
Temkin customer experience ratings 70, 108
10Cs of company culture 114–21
terms and conditions 171
Tesla 83, 148, 178
third-party logistics 15, 161, 166
Thomas Cook 43, 48–49, 51
ThreadUp 210
Thunberg, Greta 9, 10, 26

Timpson 86, 100, 219
Toms Shoes 186–87
Tottenham Hotspur 125
Toys R Us 43, 45
trackers 15
training 60, 85, 102–03, 104, 131, 163, 185
transparency 10, 177, 190, 211
travel sector 3, 29–30, 144–45
  see also Booking.com; Expedia; lastminute.com; Thomas Cook
Trump, President Donald 16
trust 178, 190, 191, 197, 203, 207, 211
Twitter 26, 87, 190, 193

Uber 2, 42, 85, 143, 150
Uber Eats 46, 149
UK (United Kingdom) 27, 29, 30–31, 37, 45–46, 116, 158, 208, 226
  disabilities provision 18
  and diversity 11, 134, 226
  failed brands 43, 44
understanding see empathy
Unilever 137
United Airlines Flight 3411 175
units per transaction 231
upcycling 209–10
US (United States) 17, 30, 37, 100, 116, 134, 158, 211
  banking sector 69–70
  failed brands 43, 44

value propositions 77, 145, 151, 170–72
values 10, 16–17, 224–26
  see also core values
VANS 35–36
Veg-NonVeg 36
vegan make-up 208
veganism 28–29, 46, 50, 208
vegetarianism ('veggie') 28, 29, 50, 102
Veggie Pret 102
Veterans Magazine ('Best of the Best'award) 136
Viking Range (Cooking Schools) 37
Virgin Atlantic 74, 174
visual impairment (sight loss) 18, 131–32, 227
voice ordering technology 15
Volkswagen emissions scandal 124

Wagamama 84–85
Waitrose & Partners 105, 106, 163
Walker, Richard 93
walking the floor 94, 117, 221
Walmart 112, 221

Walton, Sam 221
waste management 209–10
Weatherspoons 125
web *see* internet
Wegmans 107–08
Well Made Clothes 210
WestJet 174
'where your customers are' (place) 15–16, 212, 223–24
White Stuff 105
Wimbledon 73–74

women workers 11, 17, 134–36, 137, 144, 226
word of mouth 82, 83, 84, 87, 101
Worn Wear 120
Wright, Dave 117

Yoga 16

ZeroLight platform 148–49
Zipcar 179
Zizzi 46